Charles Spurgeon once
belongs to someone who isn't. In *Musings That Matter*,
Philip masterfully coupled scripture with his theologically sound,
inspiring, and illuminating reflections on various biblical topics with
powerful life applications. This book is insightful, encouraging, and
a great blessing from beginning to end.

**Louis Guiliano**
Pastor/Hospice Chaplain
Jackson, New Jersey

Today, many believers are numbed, vacant, floundering, anxious,
depressed, and neutralized in the face of intensifying spiritual
warfare in the ever-deepening darkness of the surrounding world
system. In *Musings That Matter*, Dr. Philip draws our attention to
divine truths worthy of our reflection for deepening our prayer
relationship, life-giving ministry to one another, and effectual public
witness. He points out that our last freedom is our will to act
according to God's revealed eternal, convicting, and comforting
truths. The church urgently needs to muse on these matters.

**Pamela Peterson, Ph.D.**
Former Dean of Women's Studies
Trinity Theological Seminary
Newburgh, Indiana

Biblical, bold, and concise, these *Musings That Matter* are just that—
musings that matter. Dr. Abraham Philip addresses key issues with
biblical truth, practical application, and personal challenge.
Thoughtfully and helpfully arranged, these expositions are rich in
thought though brief in length. As such, this volume will be a
blessing to read and an added blessing to share with someone else.

**David L. Olford, Ph.D.**
Chairman of the Board and President
Olford Ministries International
Memphis, Tennessee

Often a person's musings never see the light of day in a written form. In his book *Musings That Matter*, Dr. Abraham Philip shares rich, thoughtful, and encouraging musings that deal with theological, devotional, behavioral, and societal matters from a biblical perspective. His insightful musings on these themes flow out of his intimacy with God and leave the reader with a fresh challenge to think about God for spiritual enrichment. This book is a must-read for those who desire to know God better.

**Daniel E. Lewis, D. Min.**
Executive Director, International Association of Grace Ministries
Associate Pastor, Grace Connection Church
Saint Petersburg, Florida


We live in a time when the information age has segued into the propaganda news and social media era. Our minds, and thus our thoughts, are constantly bombarded by distracting stimuli that are often damaging and destructive to our overall well-being. In *Musings That Matter*, Dr. Philip has masterfully woven together an excellent remedy for us to be transformed by renewing our minds (Rom. 12:2) in the key areas that matter as they make up the essential parts of our spiritual lives.

**Robert Tucker**
Senior Pastor, Five Rivers Church
Elkton, Maryland


Dr. Abraham Phillip has done what most of us wish we had: jot down the various aspects of our life's journey and draw biblical truths God wants to teach us. You will find his theological musings sound, devotional musings profound, behavioral musings practical, and societal musings insightful. This book is easy to read, full of "nuggets of gold" for life and living!

**Paul Harper**
Ministry Outreach Foundation
Cordova, Tennessee

*Musings That Matter* by Dr. Abraham Philip inspires the reader toward a deeper and more authentic experience of Christianity at the intellectual, emotional, and behavioral levels. I consider this book a timely and spiritual resource guide relevant for anyone seeking an insightful understanding of the Christian faith to renew their heart and relate with their fellow beings with respect and dignity.

**Thomas Idiculla, Ph.D.**
Agape Partners International
Boston, Massachusetts

## OTHER BOOKS AND BOOKLETS
## BY ABRAHAM PHILIP

Thrown Overboard: A reluctant prophet's encounter with a gracious God (Paperback & Kindle)

Strength to Strength: Christ-Centered Devotionals for Growing in Faith (Paperback & Kindle)

Basic Statistics in Quantitative Research: A Primer for Seminary Students (Paperback)

Divorce and Remarriage: A Biblical Perspective (Paperback)

Leadership in the Conceptual Age (Kindle)

Let Us Reason Together: A Philosophical Inquiry into the Origin of the Universe (Kindle)

Generational Curse Demystified: A Biblical Perspective (Kindle)

The United States Presidential Election: Some Biblical Guidelines for Evaluating Presidential Candidates (Kindle)

# Musings
# That
# Matter

*Reflections on Christian Faith
and Practice*

ABRAHAM PHILIP

While every effort was made to provide accurate Internet addresses at the time of publication, the author assumes no responsibility for errors or for changes that occur after the publication.

In the following pages, the forms LORD and GOD, in quotations from the Bible, represent the Hebrew *Yahweh*, while Lord and God represent *Adonai*, in accordance with the Bible version used.

ISBN: 9798839764040
Imprint: Independently Published

# DEDICATION

## To Larry Small

A friend more loyal than a brother;
A faithful disciple chosen by the Lord.

# CONTENTS

## *SOCIETAL /293*

# Preface

A few years ago, my seminary professor, Dr. Edgar Elliott, and I went to the Philippines to hold a workshop on expository preaching for pastors. One evening, as we were relaxing in our hotel room, Dr. Elliott made an insightful observation that I have never forgotten. He said, "Abraham, we are getting old and don't have the same energy we had to travel around the globe to train pastors. It is time to write our knowledge and understanding of God's Word (the Bible) and share them with all involved in Christian service." What he said struck a responsive chord with me and put me on a trajectory to write Christian literature. Since then, I have published four books and four Kindle booklets.

This book is a compilation of blogs and short articles I published over the past six or seven years on Facebook and in my ministry newsletter. These musings on various topics are culled from my publications in hopes that you, the reader, will find something of value to enrich your life in some small measure.

My experience has taught me that contemplation, introspection, meditation, and reflection are indispensable for our spiritual formation. The Bible encourages us to meditate and ponder on truths revealed in His Word. The psalmist wrote, "I waken through the night to muse upon thy word" (Ps. 119:148 MNT). Admittedly, it was customary for the psalmist to stay up long hours in the night and meditate on God and His word (Pss. 16:7; 63:6; 77:6; 143:5). The silence and serenity of the night watches are conducive to musings and reflections.

A variety of circumstances can trigger musings; at least, that has been my experience. It may be a piece of troubling national news, a crisis somewhere in the world, the freshness of the air one breathes while walking through the woods, or a gentle whisper of the Lord during quiet time with His Word (the Bible) in hand. Some time ago, I read the story about a veteran who returned home after serving in Afghanistan with severe post-traumatic stress disorder (PSD). He became an alcoholic, got into many alcohol-related infractions, and was sentenced to spend a night in jail on one occasion. Because the offender suffered from chronic panic attacks and phobia, the judge decided to allay his fears by spending the night in jail with him. That heart-warming story caused me to muse how our Lord and Savior Jesus Christ put aside His judicial robe or His robe of glory and entered our experience to suffer pain and alienation. He did so to rescue us from divine condemnation and the wages of sin, which is death.

One day, during my morning quiet time, the Lord spoke to me from Isaiah 45:18 ESV, where we read: "For thus says the Lord who created the heavens (he is God), who formed the earth and made it (he established it; he did not create it empty, he formed it to be inhabited!)." I spent the rest of the day musing about the beautiful truth that God made the universe to make it suitable for life. As I pondered, I realized that long before modern science discovered the "anthropic principle," God had revealed it in His word.

The anthropic principle says that from the moment of the Big Bang, all the physical constants were fine-tuned to have precise values to make life possible on earth. Any infinitesimal change in one of the physical constants would have made life impossible. I was overwhelmed by the thought that God had me in His mind when He brought forth the universe out of nothing (*ex nihilo*). I burst into praise: "Oh, the depth of the riches and wisdom and knowledge of God! How unsearchable are his judgments and how inscrutable his ways!" (Rom. 11:33 ESV).

The musings presented in this book touch on various theological, devotional, behavioral, and societal aspects of the Christian life. They are meant neither to be comprehensive nor extensive; the goal is to encourage you to cultivate the discipline of thinking deeper and musing on spiritual things that matter. Each musing is tied to some aspect of the person, work, and teaching of Jesus Christ, making it thoroughly Christ-centered and distinctive. They aim to show that the core of the Christian faith and practice is Jesus and Him crucified (1 Cor. 1:23; 2:2).

You may choose to read these musings consecutively or selectively depending on the need, available time, and occasion. I hope that this book will motivate you, to borrow a line from the prayer of Richard, the Anglican bishop of Chichester (1197–1253), "to know God more clearly, love Him more dearly, and follow Him more nearly."[1]

By definition, musings are personal reflections that capture one's thoughts at a given moment in time. But thoughts have a way of straying into uncharted terrain, which may require theological and historical steering to keep them on course. So, I am deeply indebted to the Bible commentators and historians I consulted on occasion during this project to ensure the clarity, accuracy, and reasonableness of the facts and biblical views expressed. I am profoundly grateful to my editor, William Collins, for his exceptional editing and guidance in making this book meet its intended objective. His knowledge of the English writers and other historical events helped me keep my facts straight.

---

1. Richard, Bishop of Chichester, "See Clearly, Love Dearly, Follow Nearly," Episcopal Day School, accessed May 17, 2022, https://www.edsaugusta.com/religious-life/see-clearly-love-dearly-follow-nearly/.

I am thankful to my wife, Annie, for her prayers on my behalf and her behind-the-scenes encouragement and support. Most of all, I thank my Lord and Savior, Jesus Christ, for strengthening me to write the blogs over the years and for helping to bring this book to fruition. I owe my utmost to Him, who called me into His marvelous light out of the darkness. He is my constant companion, my shelter, and my shield. His unfailing love is my succor. To Him belong glory and majesty forever and ever.

Abraham Philip
Newark, Delaware

# Introduction

What matters in life? It depends on whom you ask. What matters to people varies based on where they are in life. What matters to a newborn baby? It is feeding on time and sleeping. To a toddler, it is playing with toys; to a teenager, perhaps it is driving a car; to a college student, it is passing exams and graduating with a degree, getting a job, and maybe getting married. To a family man or woman, what matters may be making that doctor's appointment, cutting the grass, trimming the shrubs, checking the mail, cleaning the house, shopping for groceries, paying the bills, and taking care of the children. To the unemployed, getting a job might matter the most. Things that matter in our lives depend on our age, gender, vocation, educational background, and station in life.

To muse about things that matter is part of the human experience. Of all the things we may muse about, what topics or themes should occupy our minds? James Allen (1864–1912) compares our mind to a garden that requires attention and careful management. If we don't cultivate a garden properly or neglect it, weeds will soon take over the garden. He notes: "Just as a gardener cultivates his plot, keeping it free from weeds, and growing the flowers and fruits which he requires, so may a man tend the garden of his mind, weeding out all the wrong, useless, and impure thoughts, and cultivating toward perfection the flowers and fruits of right, useful, and pure thoughts."[2]

---

2. James Allen, *As a Man Thinketh*, (New York: Publisher unknown, n.d.), 16, Kindle.

Meditation, musing, and reflection are means of cultivating the "garden" of our minds. The Hebrew words *haga* and *shea* in the Old Testament mean to "ponder," "contemplate over a matter," "mourn," "imagine," "mutter," "and "sweep away in thought."[3] In the New Testament, the Greek word *meletao* conveys a similar meaning of muttering and pondering. Musing is analogous to a cow chewing its cud and enjoying every bite. In the chewing of the cud, the cow gets the most out of the grass it has eaten. Similarly, musing on matters of importance is good for nourishing the soul.

From an eternal perspective, what matters are worthy of our musing? The psalmist answers this question by saying, "Oh, the joys of those who do not follow the advice of the wicked, or stand around with sinners, or join in with mockers. But they delight in the law of the LORD, meditating on it day and night" (Ps. 1:1–2 NLT). With profound satisfaction, he points out: "My eyes are awake through the night watches, that I may meditate on Your word" (Ps. 119:148). Meditating on God's word helps us know the divine precepts to live by and gain the wisdom to navigate the vicissitudes of life.

The late Elizabeth Elliott, the wife of Jim Elliott, who suffered martyrdom at the hands of Auca Indians in Ecuador, was no stranger to musing about God. When faced with a crisis on one occasion, she recalled, "I lay awake in the wee hours, repeating Scripture about God's faithfulness, trusting, casting all cares, waiting. I had to keep offering up my worries and my impatience. At four, I was up reading the story of Abraham and Isaac. Abraham called the place where he had offered up Isaac 'The Lord Will Provide.' I took that as the Lord's word to me that morning."[4] Musing on God's promises gave Elizabeth Elliott strength for the day.

---

3. Jeff A. Benner, *Ancient Hebrew Lexicon of the Bible*, (College Station: Virtualbookworm.com Publishing, 2005), 101.

4. Elizabeth Elliott, *Keep a Quiet Heart* (Grand Rapids: Revell, 1995), 134.

A Christian can think no greater thoughts than about God and His wondrous works. When Daniel was in captivity in Babylon, he faced the challenge of interpreting the dream of king Nebuchadnezzar. A failure to accurately interpret the dream would have resulted in his execution. So, Daniel asked the king to give him some time to tell the king what the dream meant. The Bible says Daniel went to his friends and urged them to pray that God would reveal the meaning of the king's dream. In his prayer, Daniel recalled and thought of the sovereignty of God, His mercy, wisdom, power, and providence (Dan. 2:20–23). On another occasion, during his prayer, Daniel thought of God's faithfulness in keeping His covenant with Israel, His mercy, forgiveness, justice, and judgment (Dan. 9:4–19). Musing on the attributes of God is a "measure of how much, or how little, we know God."[5]

The apostle Paul understood well that knowing God experientially and thinking of Him are most significant compared to anything we can do or believe about our earthly life. After meeting Jesus on the road to Damascus, his life changed radically, and he became a zealous herald of the gospel to the Gentiles. Paul wrote to the church at Philippi that what things were gainful to him before his conversion—his education, pedigree, status in the Jewish community, and pharisaical zeal—became rubbish compared to the high honor of knowing and gaining Christ (Phil. 3:7–9). For Paul, musing about Christ mattered most, to the point that he asked Timothy to bring him the Torah parchments and the books while languishing in a Roman prison, waiting to be executed.

Musings that matter should center on the triune God (Trinity) and His dealings with His creation, including His church. To the churches at Colossae and the Lycus Valley, the apostle Paul wrote these encouraging words: "If then you were raised with Christ, seek those things which are above, where

---

5. J. I. Packer, *Knowing God* (Downers Grove: InterVarsity Press, 1973), 25.

Christ is sitting at the right hand of God. Set your mind on things above, not on things on the earth." (Col. 3:1–2). Paul gave the Christians at Philippi this exhortation: "Finally, brethren, whatever things are true, whatever things are noble, whatever things are just, whatever things are pure, whatever things are lovely, whatever things are of good report, if there is any virtue and if there is anything praiseworthy—meditate on these things" (Phil. 4:8).

When we are preoccupied with the thoughts of God, we become more pliable for His transformative work in our lives (Rom. 12:2). The apostle Paul encouraged Timothy, saying, "Till I come, give attention to reading, to exhortation, to doctrine.... Meditate on these things; give yourself entirely to them, that your progress may be evident to all" (1 Tim. 4:13, 15). The transformative effect of divine musing empowers us to impact others positively. C. S. Lewis eloquently captures the influence of heavenly-minded people on society:

> If you read history, you will find that the Christians who did the most for the present world were just those who thought most of the next. The apostles themselves, who set on foot the conversion of the Roman Empire, the great men who built up the Middle Ages, the English Evangelicals who abolished Slave Trade, all left their mark on earth, precisely because their minds were occupied with Heaven. It is since Christians have largely ceased to think of the other world that they have become so ineffective in this. Aim at Heaven and you will get earth "thrown in": aim at earth and you will get neither.[6]

My prayer is that you will receive this book as an invitation to engage in musings that matter for your spiritual growth and intimacy with God. May your musings lead you to the thrill of knowing God in ways you have never known Him before.

---

6. C. S. Lewis, *Mere Christianity* (New York: Macmillan Publishing Company, 1952), 118.

# THEOLOGICAL

But as for you, speak the things which are proper for sound doctrine.

—Titus 2:1

Peace, if possible, truth at all cost.

—Martin Luther

# The Ultimate Sacrifice

I am the good shepherd. The good shepherd gives His life for the sheep. My Father loves Me, because I lay down My life that I may take it again. No one takes it from Me, but I lay it down of Myself. I have power to lay it down, and I have power to take it again.

—John 10:11, 17–18

Memorial Day is a revered day on our national calendar. It is a day in which we take time to honor the soldiers who paid the ultimate price of their lives to preserve our freedom. As a citizen of East Indian descent, I am proud to be an American, and I am honored to call America my home. It's been 55 years, as of the year 2022, since I stepped on the golden shores of this majestic land, which Francis Scott Keys termed "the land of the free and the home of the brave." During this time, I have had the privilege of enjoying the freedom, generosity, and opportunities no other country on earth would have accorded me. Yes, I have had my share of struggles and pain living in America. Still, despite the foibles and checkered past of this great land, America stands unique in my experience. As history bears witness, it remains the beacon of hope, attracting what Emma Lazarus called the "tired, the poor, and the huddled masses yearning to breathe free."[7]

---

7. "The New Colossus," Britannica, accessed March 30, 2022, https://www.britannica.com/topic/The-New-Colossus.

As I pay my respects to the soldiers who gave their lives in the line of duty defending our nation at home and abroad, I cannot help but remember the One who gave His life for me to live beyond the grave. The Bible calls it eternal life. My life on earth and the freedoms I enjoy are not permanent; they will end one day. But the life that Jesus gave me will continue forever. Jesus said, "I am the resurrection and the life. He who believes in Me, though he may die, he shall live" (John 11:25).

Jesus' death was unique in all history. In John 10, Jesus describes His death as follows: "I am the good shepherd. The good shepherd gives His life for the sheep. My Father loves Me, because I lay down My life that I may take it again. No one takes it from Me, but I lay it down of Myself. I have power to lay it down, and I have power to take it again" (John 10:11, 17–18). From these verses, we can learn three truths.

First, Jesus died vicariously. Jesus said, "I am the good shepherd. The good shepherd gives His life for the sheep." Jesus died in your place and mine. He did not die for Himself; He died for us.

Consider the example of a Polish Franciscan priest named Maximilian Kolbe.[8] On February 17, 1941, Kolbe was arrested by the Nazi Gestapo and eventually imprisoned in the Auschwitz concentration camp, where he was constantly harassed and sometimes beaten. In July of that year, a prisoner escaped from the camp, which prompted the prison commander, Karl Fritzsch, to randomly pick ten men and subject them to starvation until death as a deterrent. One of these men, Franciszek Gajowniczek, cried out, "My wife, My children." When Kolbe heard his cry, he stepped forward and volunteered to take his place. Kolbe and the other nine men were denied food and water. After two weeks, all but Kolbe had died. The guards wanted the bunker to be emptied, so they

---

8. "St. Maksymilian Maria Kolbe," Britannica, accessed March 31, 2022, https://www.britannica.com/biography/Saint-Maksymilian-Maria-Kolbe.

gave Kolbe a lethal injection of carbolic acid. He died on August 14, 1941. Maximilian Kolbe died vicariously for Franciszek Gajowniczek because he wanted Gajowniczek to return to his family.

The apostle Paul puts the matter into perspective: "For scarcely for a righteous man will one die; yet perhaps for a good man someone would even dare to die. But God demonstrates His own love toward us, in that while we were still sinners, Christ died for us" (Rom. 5:7–8). Jesus said, "The Son of Man did not come to be served, but to serve, and to give His life a ransom for many" (Matt. 10:45). Jesus died in our place when we were undeserving, sinners condemned before a holy God.

Second, Jesus died voluntarily. He said, "I lay down My life. No one takes it from Me, but I lay it down of Myself. I have power to lay it down, and I have power to take it again." Maximilian Kolbe also died willingly. But in his case, the circumstances were different. He was a helpless prisoner. He had no family to go to, and he was dying of tuberculosis. But in the case of Jesus, it was different.

When Judas and a great multitude of people came with swords and clubs to Gethsemane to take Jesus, He could have decimated them in a second. Jesus said, "Do you think that I cannot now pray to My Father, and He will provide Me with more than twelve legions of angels?" (Matt. 26:53). In other words, 72,000 angels were ready with their swords drawn to descend upon them instantly at the command of Christ. But Jesus refused to use His power. Instead, He was willing to go to the cross to die for His sheep.

Third, Jesus died victoriously. He said, "I lay down My life that I may take it again. I have power to lay it down, and I have power to take it again." He died knowing that He would rise again. On the day of Pentecost, Peter preached about the resurrection of Jesus Christ and told his listeners that the grave could not hold Jesus' body, nor did His body see corruption. Peter said, "This Jesus God has raised up, of which we are all witnesses. Therefore being exalted to the right hand of God, and having received from the Father the promise of the Holy Spirit, He poured out this which you now see and hear" (Acts 2:33).

Friend, when you celebrate Memorial Day, I pray that the Holy Spirit will draw your attention to the great sacrifice that God in Christ has made for you. Jesus was put to death because of our sins and was raised from the grave "because of our justification" (Rom. 4:25). The most God-pleasing response you can give is to offer yourself to Christ and receive Him as your Lord and Savior. Make every Memorial Day a day to remember what Christ has done for you and anticipate the glorious day when you will sit at the banquet table with Him.

# Filling up What is Lacking in the Sufferings of Christ

I now rejoice in my sufferings for you, and fill up in my flesh what is lacking in the afflictions of Christ, for the sake of His body, which is the church.

—Colossians 1:24

In Colossians 1:24, the apostle Paul makes a statement regarding Christ's suffering that is somewhat confusing and troubling to me. He wrote, "I now rejoice in my sufferings for you, and fill up in my flesh what is lacking in the afflictions of Christ, for the sake of His body, which is the church."

The plain reading of most English translations of the Greek text suggests that there must have been a lack in Christ's sufferings for His church, which Paul was eager to fill through his sufferings on behalf of the churches he established in his ministry. This notion of a "lack in Christ's suffering" does not comport with Christ's verdict about His suffering for the church. After going through the most excruciating pain and torture on the cross, He said, "It is finished." In other words, the sufferings that Jesus had to go through as payment for the penalty of our sins were complete; there was no lack in His suffering for our redemption and expiation of our sins.

What then did Paul mean when he said that he was filling up what was lacking in the sufferings of Christ? We know that Christ is not physically present in our midst today to suffer for the church. Nevertheless, because He is the head of the church

(His "body"), He does suffer when the members of His body (you and me) suffer. This is what Paul meant, for instance, when he wrote about "sharing in the sufferings of Christ" (Phil. 3:10). Just as the Father allotted Christ the cup of suffering from which He drank in complete obedience to the Father's will, there is a cup of suffering assigned to the church, the body of Christ. Each of us fills that cup with the sufferings we bear for Christ. The "lack" Paul was talking about is not any deficiency in Christ's suffering for our redemption; rather, it refers to the suffering allotted to the church that remains yet to be fulfilled. Paul was eager to contribute his share and more.

When the church suffers, Christ suffers because we are His body. It is worth noting that just as those who suffer for Christ at the hands of unbelievers fill up the cup of suffering allotted to the church, those who persecute Christians "fill up the measure of their sins." (1 Thess. 2:14–16). God said to Abraham that his descendants would not enter the Promised Land for four hundred years because "the iniquity of the Amorites is not yet complete" (Gen. 15:16). God shows His forbearance toward unbelievers to allow them to repent and turn to God. When His forbearance runs its course and the unrepentant people "fill up the measure of their sins," the judgment of God is unleashed in justice and truth.

A Christian's suffering is not wasted. The Bible says that Christ gave Himself for us, "an offering and a sacrifice to God for a sweet-smelling aroma" (Eph. 5:2). It thus stands to reason that our suffering on behalf of the church, the body of Christ, is a sweet-smelling aroma to God.

# Living the Easter Life

> And if Christ is not risen, your faith is futile; you are still
> in your sins! Then also those who have fallen asleep in
> Christ have perished.
>
> —1 Corinthians 15:17–18

Christians worldwide celebrate the resurrection of Jesus Christ,
known as Easter. We cannot overstate the significance of
Christ's resurrection from the grave. The apostle Paul argued
that Christianity stands or falls with the resurrection of Christ.
"And if Christ is not risen, your faith is futile; you are still in
your sins! Then also those who have fallen asleep in Christ
have perished" (1 Cor. 15:17–18). The resurrection of Christ is
indispensable to the veracity of the Christian faith.

The resurrection of Christ is a historical fact attested by
biblical and empirical data, skepticism of agnostics and atheists
notwithstanding. But more importantly, Christ's resurrection
is an existential force for Christians, empowering them to live
a quality of life not possible otherwise. That's why Paul's
singular ambition in life was to "know Christ and the power of
His resurrection, and the fellowship of His sufferings"
(Phil. 3:10).

Paul never doubted for a moment his physical resurrection
from the grave at the appearance (*parousia*) of Christ (Rom. 6:5;
1 Cor. 15:12–13; 2 Tim. 4:6–8). But Paul's certainty of his
future resurrection did not subvert his longing to experience
Christ's resurrection power here and now. He added, "If, by
any means, I may attain to the resurrection from the dead"

(Phil. 3:11). Paul used the Greek word *ex-anastasis* for "resurrection" in Phil. 3:11, which appears only here, not anywhere else in the entire Bible. It literally means "out-resurrection," or that which is produced by the resurrection.

While Paul awaited his future resurrection from the dead, he longed to live the kind of Christian life granted only by the resurrected Christ. What was this quality of life? It was to be "perfected" or become more and more like Christ (Phil. 3:12). However, he realized that though he had not attained that lofty aim, he resolved to press toward that "goal for the prize of the upward call of God in Christ" (Phil. 3:14).

Easter is more than a historical fact; it is a force for transformed living. Because Jesus rose from the dead, we can lay hold of His resurrection power here and now through the "living Christ" who dwells in us. Do you know this living Christ? I pray that Jesus Christ will lay hold of you on Easter and usher you into a new dimension of living.

# Love and Suffering

In this you greatly rejoice, though now for a little while, if need be, you have been grieved by various trials, that the genuineness of your faith, *being* much more precious than gold that perishes, though it is tested by fire, may be found to praise, honor, and glory at the revelation of Jesus Christ.

—1 Peter 1:6–7

Walk in love, as Christ also has loved us and given Himself for us, an offering and a sacrifice to God for a sweet-smelling aroma.

—Ephesians 5:2

Egyptian actor Omar Sharif, who became famous for his roles in *Lawrence of Arabia* and *Doctor Zhivago*, was interviewed by the Canadian television talk show host Dini Petty. Mr. Sharif had been married to an Egyptian actress, and at the time of the interview, he was divorced from his wife for nearly twenty-eight years. Ms. Petty asked Mr. Sharif if he ever found another woman to love. He replied: "I thought I did…you know, many times I thought I was in love, but I never suffered, so I guess I wasn't because I always associated love and suffering." He asked: "How can you love someone if you never suffered?" Dini Petty humorously challenged Sharif: "So you want to suffer! We can go on, and I can make you suffer." Without missing a beat, Sharif responded: "But I have to love you first."[9]

Born into a Roman Catholic family but later converted to Islam, Omar Sharif learned a profound truth from his life experience: love and suffering go together. The supreme and unparalleled attestation of this eternal principle was given by our Lord and Savior Jesus Christ. "For God so loved the world that He gave His only begotten Son that whosoever believes in Him should not perish but have everlasting life" (John 3:16). Jesus came down from heaven to suffer and die because He loved us (Rom. 5:8). So, if we say that we love God, we ought to be willing to suffer for Him when necessary. The apostle Peter reminds us that the genuineness of our faith and love for God are tested in the crucible of suffering (1 Peter 1:3–9).

The suffering motif also undergirds our love for one another. The Bible says, "Love suffers long" (1 Cor. 13:4). The apostle Paul wrote, "Walk in love, as Christ also has loved us and given Himself for us, an offering and a sacrifice to God for a sweet-smelling aroma" (Eph. 5:2). In a marriage relationship, husbands are exhorted to love their wives, just as Christ loved the church and gave Himself for her (Eph. 5:25). We who are enlightened by the gospel should be prepared and ready to embrace suffering as a testament of our devotion to God and love for one another.

---

9. From Dini Petty's interview of Omar Sharif posted on YouTube. See https://www.youtube.com/watch?v=FJZ9rloTHJQ.

# The Splendor of God's Grace

> So he called the name of the place Massah and Meribah,
> because of the contention of the children of Israel, and
> because they tempted the LORD, saying, "Is the
> LORD among us or not?"
>
> —Exodus 17:7

In Exodus 17:1–7, we read about the Israelites quarreling with Moses at Rephidim in the wilderness of Sin because there was no water to drink. Two terms are used in this text to describe their actions. First is the word Meribah. The verb *rib* (from which we get Meribah*)*, translated "contend," in this passage means to bring a lawsuit or sue someone for wrongdoing. In essence, the Israelites accused God of breaking the covenant, saying, "Is the LORD among us or not?" (Ex. 17:7). Since they could not bring a lawsuit against God, they directed their revolt against Moses, His representative, and were ready to stone him (Ex. 17:4). Stoning an offender to death after due process was an accepted legal remedy. Edmund Clowney notes: "Stoning is not mob violence but judicial execution by the community, with witnesses throwing the first stones."[10]

The second word used in this passage is Massah. The verb *nasa*, from which the term "Massah" is derived, means testing

---

10. Edmund P. Clowney, *Preaching Christ in All Scripture* (Wheaton: Crossway, 2003), 28.

or putting someone on trial. In the context of this passage, the Israelites charged God with breaking a covenant and put Him on trial. But in so doing, they stood guilty of condemnation before a Holy God.

How was this legal tension resolved? God told Moses to take the rod with which he judged Egypt, gather the elders of Israel, and go before the people to the "rock in Horeb." God told Moses that He would stand before him there on the rock, and He instructed Moses to strike the rock with his rod of judgment. Paul later identified the rock as Jesus Christ (1 Cor. 10:4). Though the Israelites were guilty of contending with God and justly deserved punishment, God took the penalty and executed justice. The Lord was not guilty, yet He bore the judgment to meet the legal requirement and resolve the tension.

In this event at Horeb, we see the enactment of God's covenant grace. In the words of the hymn writer Julia Johnston, what was shown there was, "Grace, grace, God's grace, grace that will pardon and cleanse within; grace, grace, God's grace, grace that is greater than all our sin."[11] This adjudication resulted not in death in the wilderness from thirst but life through drinking the living water.

Friend, have you tasted Jesus Christ, the living water? If not, won't you respond to His invitation? "Anyone who is thirsty may come to me! Anyone who believes in me may come and drink! For the Scriptures declare, 'Rivers of living water will flow from his heart'" (John 7:38–39 NLT).

---

11. Julia H. Johnston, "Grace Greater than Our Sin," *Hymns of Glorious Praise* (Springfield: Gospel Publishing House, 1969), 200.

# Divine Appointments

Now the LORD had prepared a great fish to swallow Jonah. And Jonah was in the belly of the fish three days and three nights.

—Jonah 1:17

And the LORD God prepared a plant and made it come up over Jonah, that it might be shade for his head to deliver him from his misery. So Jonah was very grateful for the plant.

—Jonah 4:6

I am convinced that nothing happens in our lives by chance. If God is sovereign over His creation, we must conclude that whatever happens to us is by divine appointment. This is not to say that we have no responsibility for what happens to us. God uses our choices and actions—good and bad—to fulfill His sovereign will.

A case in point is Jonah. God explicitly told Jonah to preach to the people of Nineveh about His impending judgment. But he chose to go against God's will and headed to Tarshish. The subsequent chain of events recorded in the book of Jonah ensued from the choice Jonah made. Nonetheless, God was actively involved in what happened to him.

The Lord hurled a great wind to stop Jonah from sailing to Tarshish. Knowing that Jonah would be thrown into the sea, the Lord "appointed" in advance a great fish to rescue him from the watery grave. Jonah preached to the people of

Nineveh and waited outside the city to see what would happen to it. The Lord "appointed" a plant to give him shade and to relieve his discomfort. The next day, the Lord "appointed" a worm to wither the plant. When the sun rose, the Lord "appointed" a scorching east wind, and the sun beat down on Jonah's head. In this narrative, we find five events in the life of Jonah by divine appointment that involved an action he took and the sovereignty of God. To ignore this dynamic tension between man's responsibility and God's sovereignty is to grope in darkness.

From the book of Jonah, we learn that God has appointed our seasons of deliverance, comfort, and trials. We can take solace because we are not alone when we go through these seasons of life. The Lord of hosts is with us (Ps. 46:7).

In the Gospels, we learn of a more significant prophet than Jonah: Jesus Christ, the Son of God (Matt. 12:41). His incarnation, suffering, death on the cross, and resurrection from the grave took place by divine appointment (Acts 2:23; Gal. 4:4). In contrast to Jonah, however, Jesus rose from the grave as the first fruit of our resurrection (1 Cor. 15:20) and never will die again. In Jesus, who grew up like a young plant out of the dry ground (Isa. 53:2), we find rest for our souls from the withering winds of life (Matt. 11:29). In Christ, we see the One who endured hostility despite His obedience to God's will so we may not grow weary or fainthearted (Heb. 12:3). Our seasons of deliverance and comfort and endurance in trials find their ultimate meaning and fulfillment in Jesus Christ. Do you know this Jesus as your deliverer, comforter, and strengthener?

# The Meaning of Being Present in Spirit

> For I indeed, as absent in body but present in spirit, have already judged (as though I were present) him who has so done this deed.
>
> —1 Corinthians 5:3

Imagine a pastor calling his congregation for a special meeting, but one member after another says to him, "Pastor, I would like to attend, but I can't because of a conflict. But I'll be there in spirit." I don't think the pastor likes the idea of speaking to an empty auditorium with a bunch of "spirits" in it. He would like to see people present in the body, not in the spirit. The Bible says, "Present your bodies a living sacrifice" (Rom. 12:1).

The notion of being present in spirit is not a cliché or a fancy modern expression; in a technical sense, it is biblical. In 1 Corinthians 5, the apostle Paul instructed the church at Corinth on what to do with a man living in an incestuous relationship with his father's wife. In his instruction to the church, he said that he would be present with them in spirit while carrying out the disciplinary action of removing the man living in the incestuous relationship (1 Cor. 5:3). Elsewhere, Paul wrote: "For though I am absent in the flesh, yet I am with you in spirit, rejoicing to see your good order and steadfastness of your faith in Christ" (Col. 2:5).

How are we to understand Paul's presence in spirit with the church at Corinth? Did Paul mean that his unseen ghost would be hovering over them as they conducted their deliberations? I believe the context of 1 Corinthians 5:3 and the verse following gives us some insight. The context is church discipline, and in 1 Corinthians 5:4, Paul wrote, "In the name of our Lord Jesus Christ, when you are gathered together, along with my spirit, with the power of our Lord Jesus Christ...." Paul meant that when they gathered in the name of Christ, Christ was with them (Matt. 18:20). And if Christ was with them, Paul was also with them because of his union with Christ and Corinthian Christians through the Holy Spirit. The Bible says, "For by one Spirit we were all baptized into one body—whether Jews or Greeks, whether slaves or free—and have all been made to drink into one Spirit" (1 Cor. 12:13).

Another way of looking at Paul's "presence in spirit" in this context is to view it as Paul approving the discipline administered by the church at Corinth. Paul had already judged the guilty man (as though he were present in person), and now he was saying to the elders, "think of me as though I am present with you to give my apostolic stamp of approval to excommunicate the guilty person."

I hasten to add that 1 Corinthians 5:3 and the related Colossians 2:5 are difficult passages to interpret and are subject to debate among scholars. One thing for sure is that it is not a license for skipping church services or the assembling of God's people (Heb. 10:25).

# The Intercession
# of the Spirit

Likewise the Spirit also helps in our weaknesses. For we do not know what we should pray for as we ought, but the Spirit Himself makes intercession for us with groanings which cannot be uttered.

—Romans 8:26

Do you feel at a loss when you go to the Lord in prayer? Does the sorrow and pain you bear make you utterly incapable of verbalizing your petition to the Lord? Or is it possible that you do not know what to pray for as you ought? Perhaps you are frustrated that you are not sure if what you are praying for is in the will of God. If any of these situations sound familiar to you and hinder you from approaching God boldly in prayer, don't be disheartened or lose hope. Help is available!

God fully understands our weakness and inability to make our requests known to Him as we ought. Often, we do not know how to pray according to the will of God. God knows that we would run into difficulties in our prayer life, so He made a gracious provision to aid us in praying. He sent His Spirit—the third person of the Trinity—to help us in our prayer. Notice what the Bible says: "Likewise the Spirit also helps in our weaknesses. For we do not know what we should pray for as we ought, but the Spirit Himself makes intercession for us with groanings which cannot be uttered" (Rom. 8:26). The Greek word translated "helps" conveys the imagery of a massive log being carried by two people, one at each end. The Holy Spirit comes to our side and aids us to pray as we ought. How? By making intercession for us "with groanings which cannot be uttered." The Holy Spirit intercedes for us with inexpressible groanings. Does it mean that the Holy Spirit makes groaning sounds, which we can distinguish from our own? No, not at all! It means that the Holy Spirit takes the sighs and groaning that rise from the depth of our hearts and relays them to God, the Father, who searches our hearts and responds to what the Holy Spirit conveys from our groanings because He knows the Spirit intercedes for the saints according to His will.

The great American missionary to India, John Nelson Hyde, affectionately called the "praying Hyde," spent countless nights lying on the cold bare floor, saying, "Oh God, Oh God." His prayer amounted to making groanings and sighs for the souls of India.[12] You can approach the throne of grace with your deep sighs and groanings. The Holy Spirit is the divine interpreter. He will interpret your groanings to the Father in heaven, who searches our hearts and knows "what the mind of the Spirit is, because He makes intercession for the saints according to the will of God" (Rom. 8:27).

So, don't let your weaknesses keep you from approaching the throne of grace boldly. He is waiting for you, and the Holy Spirit is ready to take your groaning and intercede for you. Make your move and experience God!

---

12. Colin Whittaker, *Seven Guides To Effective Prayer* (Minneapolis: Bethany House Publishers, 1987), 173.

# The Intercession
# of the Son

Who *is* he who condemns? *It is* Christ who died, and furthermore is also risen, who is even at the right hand of God, who also makes intercession for us.

—Romans 8:34

We learned that the Holy Spirit's function is to intercede on our behalf and facilitate our communication with our Father in heaven. We need the aid of the Holy Spirit to pray as we ought according to the will of God. The Spirit helps in our weakness by taking our groanings and making intercession for us, communicating our deepest needs to the Father in heaven.

The problem in our relationship with God is not limited to our inability to pray as we ought. There is a deeper problem that is pernicious and often paralyzing: the problem of condemnation. One of the most potent weapons in the armory of the devil is the weapon of condemnation. He uses it to keep God's people under oppression and defeat. No wonder the Bible calls the devil "the accuser of our brethren" (Rev. 12:10). His mission is to accuse us day and night before God and tell Him how unworthy and hopeless we are. The devil is also called the father of lies (John 8:44). He lies to keep us under condemnation and in defeat.

Left to our own resources, we are no match for the devil in neutralizing the onslaught of condemnation hurled at us. We need someone to speak for us and defend us. Hundreds of years before Christ, Job voiced the cry of every person: "Nor is there any mediator between us [God and man], who may lay his hand on us both" (Job 9:33). Yes, there is! God made the provision for freeing us from the devil's condemnation through the mediation (1 Tim. 1:5) and intercession of Jesus Christ. The Bible says, "Who is he who condemns? It is Christ who died, and is also risen, who is even at the right hand of God, who also makes intercession for us" (Rom. 8:34). Christ's intercession is aimed at freeing us from the condemnation of the devil.

In Zechariah 3, we read about Zechariah's vision in which he saw Joshua, the high priest, standing before the Angel of the Lord. Joshua was dressed in dirty clothes, and Satan, who stood at Angel's right hand, began to accuse him. The Lord rebuked Satan and said of Joshua, "Is this not a brand plucked from the fire?" He then spoke to those standing all around: "Take away the filthy garments from him." He said to Joshua, "See, I have removed your iniquity from you, and I will clothe you with rich robes." He also had them put a turban on Joshua's head.

The atoning work of Christ on the cross is the basis of His intercession for us. Having reconciled us to the Father, He has clothed us with His righteousness. When the devil accuses us before the Father, Christ reminds the Father that we stand before Him in Christ's righteousness. Hence, the Father sees us not condemned but justified. Is it any wonder that the apostle Paul asks, "Who shall separate us from the love of Christ?" He then asks if any of these circumstances separate us: tribulation, distress, persecution, famine, nakedness, peril, sword, death, life, angels, principalities, powers, things present, things to come, height, depth, or any other created thing.

I recall hearing a sermon preached by Dr. Thomas Long, who was a professor of preaching at Princeton Theological Seminary at that time. He told the story about a Sunday School annual function in which a group of young children, accompanied by their teacher, came to the platform to recite Romans 8:34–39. Each child bravely recited the six verses flawlessly and received applause of commendation from the audience. Then it was little Susie's turn to recite the verses. She had Down syndrome. Her teacher asked: "Susie, who shall separate us from the love of Christ?" The teacher continued, "Honey, you can do it. Don't be afraid." The audience was on the edge of their seats. They didn't know if Susie could remember all the verses. The teacher asked again: "Susie, who shall separate us from the love of Christ?" Susie looked at the audience and confidently blurted: "NOTHING!" The audience gave her a standing ovation!

NOTHING can bring us under condemnation or separate us from the love of Christ. "There is therefore now no condemnation to those who are in Christ Jesus, who do not walk according to the flesh, but according to the Spirit" (Rom. 8:1).

Let us thank God for the intercession by the Holy Spirit and Jesus Christ.

# The Suffering Church

Yet indeed I also count all things loss for the excellence
of the knowledge of Christ Jesus my Lord, for whom I
have suffered the loss of all things, and count them as
rubbish, that I may gain Christ and be found in Him, not
having my own righteousness, which *is* from the law, but
that which *is* through faith in Christ, the righteousness
which is from God by faith; that I may know Him and
the power of His resurrection, and the fellowship of His
sufferings, being conformed to His death.

—Philippians 3:8–10

Beloved, do not think it strange concerning the fiery trial
which is to try you, as though some strange thing
happened to you; but rejoice to the extent that you
partake of Christ's sufferings, that when His glory is
revealed, you may also be glad with exceeding joy. If you
are reproached for the name of Christ, blessed *are
you*, for the Spirit of glory and of God rests upon
you. On their part He is blasphemed, but on your part
He is glorified.

—1 Peter 4:12–14

Recently, I came across a moving story that was published in
*Repent America* online magazine. It's the story of a German
Christian who grew up in Nazi Germany, as told to Penny Lea,
a pro-life activist. As a young boy, he and his family attended
church every Sunday. There was a railroad track behind their

small church, and at a particular time during the service, they would hear the whistle of a train passing by the church. One Sunday, as the train passed by, they heard cries coming from the train. They realized it was the cry for help from the Jews being taken to the gas chambers.

As the train passed, the Jews would cry out for help week after week, but the church folk did nothing to help those "poor miserable people." "Yet their screams tormented us," said the man. He continued, "We knew exactly at what time that whistle would blow, and we decided the only way to keep from being so disturbed by the cries was to start singing our hymns. By the time that train came rumbling past the churchyard, we were singing at the top of our voices...Years have passed, and no one talks about it much anymore, but I still hear that train whistle in my sleep. I can still hear them crying out for help. God forgive all of us who called ourselves Christians yet did nothing to intervene."[13]

Isn't this precisely what is happening to us in America today? We gather week after week in our comfortable churches for fellowship and sing our favorite choruses louder and louder, blasting the latest sound systems and amusing ourselves with our slick audiovisuals, all the while drowning the cry of the suffering church. The voices of Christians being taken to their execution in Syria, Iraq, Afghanistan, India, and Pakistan, just to name a few, are being blocked from reaching our ears by our "loud singing." You know what I mean!

To be sure, if we try to respond to the cry of our suffering brothers and sisters and stand up for the truth, we will suffer persecution (2 Tim. 3:12; Phil: 1:29). It is already happening in America. The apostle Paul understood this inevitable reality of Christian life. When he had an encounter with Christ, he set as

---

13. "Sing a Little Louder," Repent America, accessed May 29, 2021, http://www.repentamerica.com/singalittlelouder.html?searchText=sing+l ounder.

his highest priority to know Him in the "power of His resurrection and the fellowship of His suffering" (Phil. 3:10).

We give a resounding "Amen" for knowing Christ in the "power of His resurrection." That resounding "Amen" soon subsides into a deafening silence when we are challenged to know Christ in the "fellowship of His suffering." When the body of Christ suffers, Christ suffers. And when we suffer for Christ, we participate in His suffering (1 Peter 4:12–14) and fill the measure of affliction allotted to us (Col. 1:24).

Where do we begin? First, let's start on our knees. Let's commit to praying daily for the suffering Christians around the world. Second, financially help ministries equipped to assist those who are hurting, especially in hard-to-reach places. Third, let us resolve to stand for the truth, even if it means facing hardship and suffering. If we suffer with Christ, we will reign with Him (Rom. 8:17; 2 Tim. 2:12). That's a promise!!

# The Night Is Coming

Jesus answered, "Neither this man nor his parents sinned, but that the works of God should be revealed in him. I must work the works of Him who sent Me while it is day; *the* night is coming when no one can work. As long as I am in the world, I am the light of the world."

—John 9:3–5


In John 9:1-41, we read that Jesus healed a man who was born blind. The story is a fascinating one. It exposes the anatomy of disbelief of the Pharisees who were determined to reject the messianic mission of Christ despite all the evidence to the contrary. But, at least for me, the most gripping detail in the story is what Jesus said before He healed the blind man: "I must work the works of Him who sent Me while it is day; the night is coming when no one can work."

"I must work while it is day...the night is coming" was the motto engraved on the heart of Jesus. It drove Him to manage His time well and keep Himself busy doing the work the Father in heaven gave Him to do. The night descended upon Jesus when He went to the cross at Golgotha. But before the sunlight of the day gave way to the darkness of the night, Jesus prayed to the Father, saying, "I glorified you on earth, having accomplished the work that you gave me to do" (John 17:4 ESV).

Can you say that about yourself? Perhaps you are in the sunshine of the morning. Or you may be in the brightness of the noonday light. Don't forget that the day will not last forever. The night is coming. The only way to prepare for the night is to use wisely the time of your life. Keep busy during the day, doing what your hand finds to do with all diligence, passion, and strength (Eccl. 9:10).

The average Christian in the United States, who lives to the age of seventy-five, spends 23 years sleeping, 19 years working, nine years watching TV or other amusements, 7.5 years in dressing and personal care, 6 years eating, 6 years traveling, and 0.7 years worshipping.[14] Did you notice that only 0.7% of their life is spent worshipping God or engaging in that which is of eternal significance? It is a sobering statistic, indeed! It is said that Sir Walter Scott (1771–1832) went down in history as one of the most prodigious poets and authors because he was driven by the words of Jesus recorded in John 9:4. He had a sundial in his garden on which was engraved three Greek words, translated "The night cometh." He applied the words of Jesus to regulate his life's productivity.

So, pick up that book and read what you have been putting off. Visit that friend who needs to know that you care. Write that book that is bursting to come out of you. Read that Bible that's been collecting dust while it is still day. Get on your knees and pour your heart out to God while you have the strength to do so. Do what you need to do now, for the night is coming. The daily ration of time (1,440 minutes) given to you is the same for the richest and the poorest man on earth. You cannot carry it over for tomorrow. What you don't use today, you lose forever.

Of all the activities you can do now, the most urgent is securing your soul by believing in the Lord Jesus Christ (Matt. 16:26). The Bible says, "Behold, now is the accepted time; behold, now is the day of salvation" (2 Cor. 6:2). Don't put it off for another day. "The night is coming." And it will come to you! Are you ready?

---

14. Mark Porter, *The Time of Your Life* (Wheaton: Victor Books, 1984), 16.

# The Pandemic of Sin

Therefore, just as through one man sin entered the world, and death through sin, and thus death spread to all men, because all sinned.

—Romans 5:12

If we say that we have no sin, we deceive ourselves, and the truth is not in us. If we confess our sins, He is faithful and just to forgive us *our* sins and to cleanse us from all unrighteousness. If we say that we have not sinned, we make Him a liar, and His word is not in us.

—1 John 1:8–10

The Coronavirus crisis has popularized the adjective "pandemic," a word that is derived from Latin (pan, "all," demos, "people"). It refers to anything that affects a large proportion of people in a wide geographic area. As I reflected on the pandemic of Coronavirus and its epidemiology, I saw three parallels between it and the pandemic of sin.

First, the spread of the Coronavirus infection had to have begun with one person infected with this virus in a particular place and at a specific time. According to the "South Morning China Post," a 55-year-old individual from Hubei province in China may have been the first person to have contracted COVID-19, which then began to spread rapidly in China and across the globe. That case dates to November 17, 2019, almost a month before doctors started to see patients with this infection in Wuhan, China.[15] The problem of sin has a similar history. The Bible teaches that "through one man sin entered the world, and death through sin, and thus death spread to all men because all sinned" (Rom. 5:12). In other words, when Adam sinned, we sinned due to our shared humanity with him. The epidemiology of sin involves a person (Adam) and a specific location (garden of Eden).

Second, we note that though the Coronavirus can infect any human being, the most susceptible people are those whose immune system is compromised due to age or other underlying diseases. Similarly, sin affects all because all are compromised from a relationship with God. It is worth noting that sin is not a "thing" or some "force" but a relational construct, a falling away from a good relationship that once existed at the fundamental level. Nearly all biblical words (Hebrew and Greek) referring to sin point to this idea: *pasha* (transgression), *chata* (to miss the mark), *shagah* (to go astray), *hamartia* (shortcoming), and *paraptoma* (offense). This falling away from a relationship with God is called alienation, which results from not conforming to the "law of God in act, habit, attitude, outlook, disposition, motivation, and mode of existence."[16] The Bible says, "All we like sheep have gone astray" (Isa. 56:6). We are all sinners by nature, choice, and divine verdict.

Third, we are told that presently there are no antiviral agents available for treating Coronavirus. Until a vaccine is developed to keep people from being infected with this virus, the quickest way to treat an infected patient is to use antibodies from a patient recovered from COVID-19 infection, otherwise called serum therapy. This approach dates to 1891 when it was first used to treat a child with diphtheria. What about the problem

---

15. As of June 2021, mounting evidence began to accumulate that the virus may have originated from the Wuhan Virology Laboratory.

16. J. I. Packer, *Concise Theology: A Guide to Historic Christian Beliefs* (Carol Stream: Tyndale House Publishers, Inc., 1993), 82.

of sin? There is no known human therapy for the problem of sin. The only successful treatment is the blood of Jesus, who conquered sin on the cross of Calvary. By His stripes, we are made whole from the sickness of sin. The apostle Peter wrote, "He [Jesus] himself bore our sins in his body on the tree, that we might die to sin and live to righteousness. By his wounds you have been healed" (1 Peter 2:24 ESV).

Just as the serum of a person recovered from the COVID-19 infection is the most effective and immediate treatment, the only effective and permanent therapy for sin's problem is the blood of Jesus. He bore in His body our sins and conquered death. And the only way to appropriate the blood of Christ for the remission of our sins is to confess our sins and believe in the Lord Jesus Christ. "If we confess our sins, He [Jesus] is faithful and just to forgive us our sins and to cleanse us from all unrighteousness" (1 John 1:9).

If you are under the dominion of sin, I plead with you by the mercies of God to believe in the Lord Jesus Christ and be made whole.

# Once to Be Born
# and Once to Die

My days are swifter than a weaver's shuttle, and are spent without hope.

—Job 7:6

Whereas you do not know what *will happen* tomorrow. For what *is* your life? It is even a vapor that appears for a little time and then vanishes away.

—James 4:14

Some time ago, I attended two funerals in one week. The first one was that of an 82-year-old man of deep faith and piety, who faithfully served the Lord and the church all his life. The second funeral was that of a 31-year-old woman, the daughter of a dear friend. Death took her when she was at the height of her chosen profession. These funerals brought to the fore the indisputable reality that death is the great equalizer that strikes us all at God's appointed time, irrespective of our gender, race, ethnicity, age, or station in life. George Bernard Shaw wrote, "Life's ultimate statistic is the same for all people; one-out-of-one dies."[17] The psalmist exclaimed, "What man can live and not see death? Can he deliver his life from the power of the grave?" (Ps. 89:48).

---

17. "Death," World Wit & Wisdom, accessed April 8, 2022, https://worldwitandwisdom.com/topic/death/page/3/.

As I sat through these funerals, I could not help but ponder on the brevity of life and the fact that I, too, will pass by the same road someday. Job, said, "My days are swifter than a weaver's shuttle, and are spent without hope" (Job. 7:6). The apostle James wrote, "For what *is* your life? It is even a vapor that appears for a little time and then vanishes away" (James 4:14). The Greek poet Homer called a man "a leaf, the smallest and weakest piece of a short-lived, unsteady plant."[18] Yet, we labor, toil, sweat, and shed many a tear for that which is here today and gone tomorrow, all the while neglecting our soul's condition. Jesus said, "For what profit is it to a man if he gains the whole world, and loses his own soul? Or what will a man give in exchange for his soul?" (Matt. 16:26).

The Bible says, "And as it is appointed for men to die once, but after this the judgment" (Heb. 9:27). Given the certainty of death and future judgment of God, how should we live here and now? Thomas à Kempis, the fourteenth-century Dutch monk, answers: "Happy is the man who hath the hour of his death always before his eyes, and daily prepareth himself to die."[19] We are to prepare daily for death, which the Bible calls the enemy of the soul. How do we do that? We do it by surrendering our lives to Jesus Christ, who conquered the last enemy of the soul, death, by His resurrection from the grave (1 Cor. 15:55). So then, those in Christ are truly prepared for what Jeremy Taylor (1613–1667), the English theologian, called "holy dying."

For me, the highlight of that week of death was the opportunity to spend a few minutes with an 82-year-old stalwart of faith. He was on the threshold of heaven, waiting eagerly to be with His Lord. As he lay on his bed, unable to

---

18. Quoted in Jeremy Taylor, *Holy Living And Holy Dying: With Prayers Containing the Whole Duty of a Christian* (New York: Cosimo, 2007), 300.

19. Thomas à Kempis, *The Imitation of Christ* (Uhrichsville, Ohio: Barbour and Company, 1984), Book 1, XXIII (1).

move or feed for himself, he radiated such a glorious and blessed hope of seeing his maker soon. As I stood by his bed with my Bible opened, he whispered to me: "Sing 'What a Friend We Have in Jesus.'" I sang this beloved hymn of the church, and I could see a glow on his face. He served the Lord faithfully for over sixty years and touched hundreds of lives through his ministry as a pastor. The only thing that mattered to him at the moment of his death was the "upward call of God in Christ Jesus" (Phil. 3:14).

# We No Longer Know Christ in the Flesh

> Therefore, from now on, we regard no one according to the flesh. Even though we have known Christ according to the flesh, yet now we know *Him thus* no longer.
>
> —2 Corinthians 5:16

In his letter to the church at Corinth, the apostle Paul categorically affirmed that the historicity and the resurrection of Christ are the indispensable pillars of the Christian faith (1 Cor. 15:13–14, 17–19). If Christ had not risen, our preaching is useless, our faith is in vain, and we have no forgiveness of sin.

But what does Easter mean to us in our daily lives? One Easter weekend, I had the opportunity to watch on the Trinity Broadcasting Network (TBN) the spectacular play, "Jesus." It was Sight and Sound's original stage production filmed in front of a live audience. As I watched the awe-inspiring story of Jesus masterfully brought to life on the screen, I could not help but think how wonderful it would be if I could only go back in time and spend a moment walking with Jesus on the dusty roads of ancient Israel. When the queen of Sheba saw for herself Solomon's wisdom, she exclaimed: "Happy are your men and happy are these your servants, who stand continually before you and hear your wisdom" (1 Kings 10:8). I, too, wondered how fortunate the disciples of Jesus were to walk with Him and know Him in the flesh.

Then suddenly, the Holy Spirit gently whispered into my ears 2 Corinthians 5:16: "Even though we have known Christ according to the flesh, yet now we know Him thus no longer." It was great that the disciples of Christ knew Him in person, but we who live in the twenty-first century no longer know Him that way. We have a more excellent and intimate way of knowing Christ because of His resurrection from the grave. The Holy Spirit, who dwells in us, helps us to understand Him intimately. That's why the apostle John wrote, "But you have an anointing from the Holy One, and you know all things" (1 John 2:20).

The apostle Paul's greatest aspiration was not to have known Jesus in the flesh, but to know Him and the power of His resurrection. He wrote, "If, by any means, I may attain to the resurrection from the dead" (Phil. 3:11). He used the Greek word *exanastasis* ("out resurrection"), which appears only here in the New Testament. Paul was not referring to his future resurrection from the grave at the return of Christ. Nor was he expressing any doubt about partaking in that resurrection. By "out resurrection," Paul meant the power of the risen Savior that can be experienced here and now. He was referring to a quality of life that is only possible by the power of the risen Christ working in us. It's a standard of living that distinguishes us from among the spiritually dead around us. This resurrection power is communicated to us by the Holy Spirit, who dwells in us (Rom. 8:11).

I challenge you to go beyond the historical and theological significance of Christ's resurrection. Focus on its existential importance and ask whether you are living in the resurrection power of Christ. Are you growing in the knowledge of Christ in ways not possible if you had only physically walked with Him? Are you living according to the flesh or according to the Spirit? I pray that you will make it your aim to know Jesus in the power of His resurrection.

# We Preach Christ Crucified

> But we preach Christ crucified, to the Jews a stumbling
> block and to the Greeks foolishness.
>
> —1 Corinthians 1:23

In *The Cross and Christian Ministry*, New Testament scholar
D. A. Carson notes the appalling image of crucifixion in the
first century.

> Crucifixion was reserved for slaves, aliens, barbarians.
> Many thought it was not something to be talked about
> in polite company. Quite apart from the wretched
> torture inflicted on those who were executed by hanging
> from a cross, the cultural associations conjured up
> images of evil, corruption, abysmal rejection. Yet today,
> crosses adorn our buildings and letterheads., grace our
> bishops, shine from lapels, and dangle from our ears—
> and no one is scandalized.[20]

Nevertheless, in His wisdom and providence, God chose to
save those whom He called, both Jews and Gentiles, through
the message of the cross. The message of the cross is primarily
regarded as foolishness by those who are perishing, but for
those who are being saved, it is the power of salvation through
God (1 Cor. 1:18). The Bible says, "It pleased God through the
folly of what we preach to save those who believe" (1 Cor. 1:21

---

20. D. A. Carson, *The Cross And Christian Ministry: Leadership Lessons From 1
Corinthians* (Grand Rapids: Baker Books, 2018), 13.

ESV). Therefore, the divine line of separation runs not between rich and poor, educated and uneducated, male and female, or Jew and Gentile, but rather between those who are perishing and those who are saved. The apostle Paul maintained that humanity could not be saved through human philosophy nor by man's appetite for the miraculous, but only by the power and wisdom of God contained in the message of the cross.

The message of the cross is foolishness to many people because the central figure of the message is One who died an ignominious death on the cross. The apostle Paul wrote: "For Jews demand signs and Greeks seek wisdom, but we preach Christ crucified, a stumbling block to Jews and folly to Gentiles, but to those who are called, both Jews and Greeks, Christ the power of God and the wisdom of God" (1 Cor. 1:22–24 ESV). The cross is an offense to those who want God to show His miraculous power at their beck and call. For them, the cross represents scandalous defeat, weakness, and shame, not a display of power and greatness. On the other hand, the atheistic academics and scholars of our day consider the message of the cross a folly because it does not fit the framework of their worldview regarding life and how one should make sense of reality.

But the apostle Paul said, "We preach Christ crucified." The rugged cross of Christ, disdained by unbelievers, stands towering over the wrecks of time as a symbol of the "power of God and the wisdom of God." It demonstrates that the "foolishness" of God is wiser than men, and the "weakness" of God is stronger than men (1 Cor. 1:25). Think about it for a moment. The crucifixion of Christ, the God-man, was the greatest evil ever committed in human history. Yet out of this "grotesque and abhorrent" act came the greatest blessing, the redemption of millions who put their trust in Christ. In the cross, we see a staggering reversal of man's wisdom and strength so that one who boasts should boast only in Christ.

Let us not shirk from preaching Christ crucified to bring hope to perishing humanity. Jesus said, "And I, when I am lifted up from the earth, will draw all people to myself" (John 12:32 ESV). From the blood-stained cross streams the glistening radiance of the redeeming love of the Son of God, beckoning all who are perishing to find refuge in Him. Let all who are redeemed by the grace of God glory in the cross of Christ by which the world has been "crucified to [them] and [they] to the world" (Gal. 6:14). That is, the world holds no attraction to a follower of Christ, for they are dead to the enticements of the world.

# Why Does the Universe Exist?

For by Him all things were created that are in heaven and that are on earth, visible and invisible, whether thrones or dominions or principalities or powers. All things were created through Him and for Him.

—Colossians 1:16

The world mourned the death of Stephen Hawking, considered the most brilliant theoretical physicist since Einstein. He was known for his seminal work in cosmology, but outside the academic world, he was popularized by his bestselling book *A Brief History of Time*. I read his book, but I must admit that there are concepts in it that are beyond my comprehension. What struck me the most, though, was how he ended his book. He wrote, "Up to now, most scientists have been too occupied with the development of new theories that describe what the universe is to ask the question why . . . we and the universe exist. If we find the answer to that, it would be the ultimate triumph of human reason—for then we would know the mind of God."[21]

No wonder Hawking devoted his life to trying to discover why the universe exists. When he was asked what his goal in life was, he said, "My goal is simple. It is a complete

---

21. Stephen Hawking, *A Brief History Of Time: From The Big Bang To Black Holes* (New York: Bantam Books, 1990), 174–175.

understanding of the universe, why it is as it is, and why it exists at all." Sadly, Hawking, who sought to know the "mind of God," rejected God's existence *a priori* and died without finding the answer to his question. Or perhaps he died refusing to accept the explanation that God revealed in creation (Rom. 2:19–21).

So why does the universe exist in the first place? The answer to this question has eluded many brilliant minds, but it is given to us in God's Holy Writ. The Bible says, "For by Him [Jesus Christ] all things were created that are in heaven and that on earth, visible and invisible, whether thrones or dominions or principalities or powers. All things were created through Him and for Him. And He is before all things, and in Him all things consist" (Col. 1:16–17). From this text, we learn that Christ has been in existence before the creation of time, space, and matter. Second, we learn that God in Christ created all things, both visible and invisible. Third, God in Christ created this vast and incomprehensible universe for Himself.

Our universe exists for the pleasure and glory of God. The Bible says: "The Lord has made all [things] for Himself, yes even the wicked for the day of doom" (Prov. 16:4). "This people I have formed for Myself; they shall declare My praise" (Isa. 43:21). "For of Him and through Him and to Him are all things, to whom be glory forever. Amen" (Rom. 11:36). This universe exists for God's glory—nothing more, nothing less.

But how God glorifies Himself in creation is beyond our comprehension or reasoning. The great mathematician and philosopher Blaise Pascal noted: "The supreme achievement of reason is to bring us to see that that there is a limit to reason."[22] Our reasoning will only take us so far and no further. To leap over the chasm, we must turn to God in faith. When

---

22. "Blaise Pascal Quotes," AZ Quotes, accessed June 3, 2021, https://www.azquotes.com/author/11361-Blaise_Pascal.

we do, He will meet us graciously in revelation, which He has made in nature, Scripture, and ultimately in Jesus Christ.

Do you know this Jesus Christ in whom dwells the fullness of the Godhead bodily and in whom are hidden all the treasures of wisdom and knowledge?

# Books versus Book: Is There a Difference?

And I saw the dead, small and great, standing before God, and books were opened. And another book was opened, which is *the Book* of Life. And the dead were judged according to their works, by the things which were written in the books.

—Revelation 20:12

W. H. Auden, the British-American poet, said, "A real book is not one that we read, but one that reads us."[23] Reflect on that for a moment. In my view, there is only one book on earth that meets this criterion in the truest sense; it is the Bible, the written Word of God. The writer of Hebrews says, "For the word of God is living and powerful, and is sharper than any two-edged sword, piercing even to the division of soul and spirit, and of joints and marrow, and is a discerner of the thoughts and intents of the heart" (Heb. 4:12).

God, who gave us His written word for regulating our lives on earth, also has two sets of books in His dwelling place. These are called Books and Book. They are meant to read us when we stand before Him to give an account of our lives. In Revelation 20:12–15, the apostle John wrote, "And I saw the

23. "W. H. Auden," Goodreads, accessed April 16, 2022, https://www.goodreads.com/quotes/11899-a-real-book-is-not-one-that-we-read-but.

dead, small and great, standing before God, and books were opened. And another book was opened, which is *the Book* of Life. And the dead were judged according to their works by the things which were written in the books. And anyone not found written in the Book of Life was cast into the lake of fire." From this text, we learn three important truths concerning God's sets of books.

First, the books (plural) represent divine retribution. Interestingly, opening the books is mentioned in two places in the Bible—Daniel 7 and Revelation 12. And in both these instances, they are mentioned in connection with divine retribution. The fact that more than one book is used to record people's names destined for divine retribution suggests many more names in the "books" than in the "book." Jesus said, "Wide is the gate and broad is the way that leads to destruction, and there are many who go in by it." The books contain the record of all the actions, thoughts, and words of the wicked during their life on earth. Notice, God does not take an egalitarian approach in administering His retribution. He punishes them according to their works. The severity and scope of His retribution are determined by the works recorded in the books. In Revelation 13:8, we read that this list also contains the names of those who have worshipped the beast or the anti-Christ.

Second, the book (singular) represents divine redemption. John saw another book opened, which is the Book of Life. This is also called the book of the living and the righteous (Ps. 69:28). The Bible calls this book the Book of the Life of the Lamb slain from the foundation of the world (Rev. 13:8). The names in this book are of those given the Lamb's life, which is Jesus Christ. And their names are written with the Lamb's blood. The apostle Paul calls these people chosen in Christ before the foundation of the world (Eph. 1:4). These are the ones redeemed by the blood of Jesus Christ.

Third, the book (singular) represents divine recognition. In Malachi 3:16, it is referred to as the book of remembrance. "So a book of remembrance was written before Him for those who fear the Lord and who meditate on His name." This book is also a record of the tears shed by the righteous when in pain and sorrow. David said, "You number my wanderings; put my tears into Your bottle; are they not in Your book?" (Ps. 56:8). A record of our tears and good works are maintained not because God is forgetful, but to demonstrate His justice and recognition of our good works and suffering.

Just as God is not egalitarian in His retribution, He is also not egalitarian in His recognition of our works. Jesus said, "And behold, I am coming quickly, and My reward is with Me, to give to every one according to his work" (Rev. 22:12). God will reward us according to our works. For instance, in Revelation 2:10 and in James 1:12, we read that those who are faithful until the end and suffer tribulation for Christ will receive a special reward called the crown of life.

I have many books in my library. But there are a few that I have not opened since I bought them. This is not the case with God's books representing divine retribution, divine redemption, and divine recognition. They will be opened for sure. The most important question is: in which book is your name written? If your name is in the books, you are bound for destruction. If it is in the Book of Life, you are destined for eternal life. Jesus said to His disciples: "Do not rejoice in this, that the spirits are subject to you, but rather rejoice because your names are written in heaven" (Luke 10:20)—that is, written in the Book of Life.

If you are not in Christ, your name is not in the Book of Life. If that's the case, repent of your sins and believe in the Lord Jesus Christ. I pray that you will make peace with God today and have your name written in the Book of Life.

# Can a Person Be Justified Before God?

Truly I know *it is* so, but how can a man be righteous before God? If one wished to contend with Him, he could not answer Him one time out of a thousand.

—Job 9:2–3

In 1981, Rabbi Harold Kushner wrote a book titled *When Bad Things Happen to Good People*, which became a *New York Times* bestseller. He was prompted to write the book because of his son's death at age 17 due to a degenerative genetic disease. Kushner's central thesis was that God is good, but He is limited by what He can do. Often, He is unable to stop the misfortunes that happen to us. In Kushner's view, bad things that happen to us have no meaning in themselves, but we can redeem these unfortunate events from their meaninglessness by ascribing meaning to them on our own.

If there ever was a person who legitimately struggled with the suffering of the innocent, it was Job. Notice what God said about Job: "My servant Job, there is none like him on the earth, a blameless and upright man, one who fears God and shuns evil" (Job 1:8). Yet this human paragon of virtue lost everything he had in one day and was struck with oozing sores all over his body. In the book of Job, we read about how he struggled to find why he, an innocent man, was suffering. The book opens with a scene in heaven where God had a conversation with Satan about Job and the wager regarding

Job's integrity. In chapter 3, we read about the testing of Job. In chapters 38 to 42, we read about God talking to Job. The story ends with Job getting a glimpse of God's majesty, wisdom, and power. And when that happened, Job acknowledged his utter unworthiness, and he was no longer interested in finding out why the innocent suffer.

I want to draw your attention to chapter 9, where Job asks a very profound question: "How can a man be righteous before God?" In chapter 8, his friend Bildad foolishly attributed Job's suffering to his sins and the sins of his children and suggested that, if Job were pure, upright, and blameless, these calamities would not have happened. Job wanted to know how a person can be righteous before God. This chapter teaches us three reasons we cannot earn our righteousness before God based on our merit.

First, God is unchallengeable. In verses 1–12, Job tells us that if one were to challenge God in any way, he would not be able to answer God even one time out of a thousand questions. God is unchallengeable in His wisdom. He does great things beyond our understanding. God is unchallengeable in His power. He is the Creator and Sustainer of the universe. He does wonders without number. God is unchallengeable in His freedom. He is free to do as He pleases. Job says, "If God takes away, who can hinder Him? Who can say to Him, 'What are you doing?'" Do you have such a high view of God's sovereignty, wisdom, and power? Or is your God a powerless cosmic being?

Second, God is unarguable. In verses 13–24, Job tells us that man is utterly incapable of winning an argument with God. He says, "How then can I answer Him and choose my words to reason with Him?" Job says, even if I am innocent, I could not answer God. I can only plead for His mercy. If I prayed to Him, and He responded to my payer, I could scarcely believe that He answered my prayer. Who am I that He should be listening to my request? Even if I am innocent, the moment I begin to argue with God, my mouth will condemn me and declare me perverse. If it's a question of justice, who can accuse God? In short, Job said, I cannot win an argument with God without incriminating myself.

Third, we cannot earn our righteousness because God is unequalable. In verses 25–35, Job comes to this inescapable conclusion about God: "For He is not a man, as I am, that I may answer Him." In essence, Job said, "I am not God's equal to demand that He declare me righteous." Job understood that he could not try to convince God of his innocence without being condemned by the holiness of God. Job says, "Even if I wash myself with soap and clean my hands with lye, you would plunge me into a muddy ditch, and my filthy clothing would hate me." Job realized that trying to earn his righteousness before God was in vain. Why? Because God is infinite, transcendent, immortal, and holy. In contrast, people are finite, earthly, mortal, and sinful.

Job concluded that he needed a mediator between himself and God, one who could bring them together and free him from the terror and judgment of God. The desperate cry of humanity since the time of the Fall has been for a mediator. And God answered this cry when He sent His Son Jesus to reconcile us to God. The Bible says, "For *there is* one God and one Mediator between God and men, *the* Man Christ Jesus" (1 Tim. 2:5). It is fascinating to note that in chapter 40, God asked Job: "Would you indeed annul My judgment? Would you condemn Me that you may be justified?" Unbeknown to Job, God had already planned to condemn His Son, Jesus Christ, on the cross for our justification. Two thousand years ago, Jesus was condemned on the cross because of our sins, and He was raised from the grave because of our justification (Rom. 4:25).

So, what does it mean to have Christ as our Mediator? It means that all who believe in the Lord Jesus Christ can stand righteous before God. We stand blameless before God not because we have become righteous, but because the righteousness of Christ is imputed to us. In justifying us based on the life, death, and resurrection of Jesus Christ, God demonstrates that He is both just and the justifier of anyone who believes in Jesus Christ (Rom. 3:21–26).

What does the mediation of Christ mean to us in our suffering? It means that we have a Mediator who understands our pain and can see us through what we are experiencing in this age and in the age to come, freeing us from pain, sorrow, sickness, and death. Though Job did not commit any sin deserving punishment, God permitted Satan to afflict him for a purpose. Job didn't know what that purpose was at the time of his suffering, but he knew that when his testing was over, he would come forth as gold (Job 23:10).

Friend, are you going through a tough time in your life right now? Remember, suffering is not meaningless. Unlike Rabbi Kushner's God, who is impotent to prevent bad things from happening to us, the God of Job is good, mighty, and wise. In His infinite wisdom, He permitted evil to enter the human experience. Suffering can be a means of divine discipline, correction, punishment, or spiritual formation. When we go through the dark night of our soul, let us trust God for who He is, ask what He is trying to do in us, examine ourselves, and seek God's direction.

# Does the Resurrection of Christ Matter?

And if Christ is not risen, then our preaching *is* empty
and your faith *is* also empty.

—1 Corinthians 15:14

In 1960, the famous Protestant theologian Paul Tillich visited
Japan to meet with some Buddhist scholars. During a
conversation with them, he asked them if Gautama, the
founder of Buddhism, had never actually existed, what would
be the consequence for Buddhism? The Buddhist scholars told
Tillich that it did not matter if Gautama (the Buddha) had lived
or not. They said they had the traditions and speeches
attributed to the Buddha and that the doctrine of Buddhism
was eternal; therefore, Buddhism did not depend on the
historicity of Gautama.[24] In essence, they said that the
teachings ascribed to the Buddha stand on their own even if
the Buddha had never lived or taught.

Can we say that about Christianity? Absolutely not! The
apostle Paul said that Christianity's edifice stands or falls with
the personage of Jesus Christ and His resurrection. No wonder
the apostles preached the resurrection of Jesus Christ

---

24. Tripp Fuller, "Paul Tillich on Christ & Buddha as Historical Figures,"
accessed June 3, 2021, https://trippfuller.com/2010/08/20/paul-tillich-
on-christ-buddha-as-historical-figures/.

everywhere they went. The centrality of the apostolic proclamation was the resurrection of Jesus Christ.

Does the resurrection of Christ matter? Absolutely. In 1 Corinthians 15:12–28, the apostle Paul lays out the implications of the resurrection of Christ for our faith and practice. He gives us three reasons why the resurrection of Christ matters.

First, the resurrection of Christ authenticates our proclamation. Paul wrote, "If Christ is not risen, then our preaching *is* empty and your faith *is* also empty" (1 Cor. 15:14). The content of our preaching is not some abstract ideas and concepts, but the person of Jesus Christ. That's why Paul said, "We preach Christ crucified" (1 Cor. 1:23). But the crucified Christ without the resurrection is a dead Christ, no different than the Buddha or Mohammad. What gives meaning to the cross is the resurrection. Our faith is not vacuous but rooted in the living Christ. The resurrection provides credulity to our message. It authenticates our proclamation.

Because Jesus rose from the dead, we can proclaim the gospel boldly, knowing that it is the power of God unto salvation for those who believe. When the crucified and risen Christ is lifted, He will draw all people unto Himself.

Second, the resurrection of Christ attests to our justification. Paul wrote, "And if Christ is not risen, your faith *is* futile; you are still in your sins" (1 Cor. 15:17). Paul uses the term "justification" in a legal sense and God declares us righteous in a legal sense. In Romans 4:24, we read that Jesus Christ was delivered up because of our offenses and was raised because of our justification. Jesus bore our sins in His body to satisfy the just demands of a holy God so that He might be just and the justifier of the one who has faith in Jesus (Rom. 3:26).

The resurrection of Jesus makes our justification or salvation effective. We can live in confidence that we can have victory over the power of sin and live a life pleasing to God by the power of the crucified and risen Jesus working in us through the agency of the Holy Spirit.

Third, the resurrection of Christ assures our resurrection. In verses 13, 17, and 18, Paul argues that if there is no resurrection of the dead, then Christ has not risen. If Christ has not risen, our faith is futile, and those who are dead in Christ have perished. If that's the case, we are, of all people, most pitiable. The resurrection of Christ assures that there is life beyond the grave. Long before Christ, Job said, "For I know that my Redeemer lives, and He shall stand at last on the earth; and after my skin is destroyed, this I know, that in my flesh I shall see God" (Job 19:25–26).

Jesus said, "Do not marvel at this; for the hour is coming in which all who are in the graves will hear His voice and come forth—those who have done good, to the resurrection of life, and those who have done evil, to the resurrection of condemnation" (John 5:28–29). What this means is that Jesus' resurrection assures us that there is a day of reckoning beyond grace. We will be raised from the dead to face that day of accounting. Are you prepared to meet your Creator? I pray that you will be drawn to Christ.

Yes, the resurrection of Christ matters. It authenticates our proclamation; therefore, we can preach the gospel with power and conviction. It attests to our justification; therefore, we can live in victory over sin and live righteously. The resurrection of Christ assures our resurrection; therefore, we who are in Christ will reign with Him. Indeed, Christ is risen, and we serve a living Savior!

# The Day After Pentecost

Then Peter said, "Silver and gold I do not have, but what
I do have I give you: In the name of Jesus Christ of
Nazareth, rise up and walk."

—Acts 3:6

Each year, we celebrate the historic Pentecost on the seventh
Sunday after Easter or fifty days after Passover. It signifies the
Holy Spirit's descent to the disciples of Christ and the birth of
the church. As we celebrate this historic event, we should ask:
What difference should Pentecost make in our lives? What
does it mean to live the meaning of Pentecost the day after the
sights and sounds of a mighty outpouring of the Holy Spirit
have subsided into silence?

In Acts 3:1–11, we have the first recorded miracle after
Pentecost. We read about Peter and John exercising the power
of Pentecost to heal a 40-year-old lame man. From this
narrative of the lame man's healing at the gate of the temple
called "Beautiful," we learn what Pentecost means to us the
day after.

First, Pentecost means radical engagement. "Now Peter and
John went up together to the temple at the hour of prayer, the
ninth hour." Around three in the afternoon, Peter and John
went to the temple to pray. They were doing what every devout
Jew did in the first century—pray at least three times a day. As
they engaged in their routine activity, they seized an
opportunity to exercise the power of Pentecost and boldly
witness for Christ. There were no tongues of fire resting on

their heads. There was no sound of a mighty rushing wind to draw the people. They were simply walking in the temple. But because they were full of the Holy Spirit, they seized an opportunity when it was presented to them and witnessed for Christ with spiritual power. Jesus said, "Go therefore and make disciples of all the nations" (Matt. 28:19). In Greek, it says, "Going therefore disciple all the nations." In other words, in our meandering, as we go about our daily life, we must seize the opportunities to make disciples. We must engage with our world for Christ.

Notice that Peter and John fixed their eyes on this lame man, something they had not done before. The lame man was a regular fixture at the temple. Peter and John had seen this fellow many times before. Under ordinary circumstances, it would have been so easy to ignore this crippled man, for, after all, they were on their way to the temple. They could have said, "Look, fellow, we'd like to help you, but we are already late for church. We must get going." No! Instead, they stopped and fastened their eyes on the lame man. They saw his impotence, impoverishment, and isolation.

Pentecost helps us see the people around us as Christ sees—weary, exhausted, and needing restoration—and respond to their needs. Think of the people that you see day in and day out who are lost without Christ. Have they become invisible to you? If your eyesight has become blurred, ask the Holy Spirit to adjust your spiritual lenses so you can see their actual condition and minister to them.

Second, Pentecost means radical empowerment. The lame man asked Peter and John for alms. He expected to receive one or two coins from them. But Peter and John had something more valuable to give. It was not silver and gold because silver and gold would not have satisfied his most profound need. He needed to be healed from his infirmity, which Jesus alone could do. Peter said, "Silver and gold I don't have, but what I have, I give unto you. In the name of Jesus of Nazareth, rise up and walk." The power to heal this lame man was the power of Christ through the Holy Spirit resident in Peter and John. The release of the risen Savior's power by invoking His name, coupled with their faith through Jesus Christ, brought about the healing. The man stood up and entered the temple, leaping and praising God. His life was changed forever.

Paul wrote, "But we have this treasure in earthen vessels, that the excellence of the power may be of God and not of us" (2 Cor. 4:7). The treasure deposited in us—weak and brittle as we are, like a vessel of clay—is the surpassing power of the risen Christ. And this power is dispensed through the proclamation of the gospel, which is "the light of the knowledge of the glory of God in the face of Jesus Christ" (2 Cor. 4:6).

Sadly, the church today has lots of silver and gold but lacks the transformative power of Christ. It is said that the great thirteenth-century theologian Thomas Aquinas went to the city of Rome to see the Pope. During his visit, the Pope proudly showed all the ornate appointments of the Papal palace and took him to the treasury to show him all the gold and silver received from all over the world. The Pope proudly said, "You see brother Thomas, we can no longer say, as did the first Pope, 'Silver and gold have I none.'" Thomas Aquinas looked into the eyes of the Pope and said, "No, neither can you say, in the name of Jesus Christ of Nazareth rise up and walk."[25] Radical Empowerment by the Holy Spirit to preach Christ is the theme of the book of Acts. We are encouraged to say, "Silver and gold I do not have, but what I do have, I give you."

Third, Pentecost means radical enlargement. The significance of this miracle is not that a lame man was healed but that this miracle opened the door for the proclamation of

25. "St. Thomas Aquinas meets Pope Innocent IV: Silver & gold," Something Latin, accessed May 28, 2022, https://somethinglatin.blogspot.com/2009/11/st-thomas-aquinas-meets-pope-innocent.html.

the gospel, leading to the conversion of two thousand souls. The church grew from 3,000 people to more than 5,000. When God's people live and witness Christ in the power of Pentecost, there will be a radical enlargement of the church as the Lord adds to the church those who are being saved each day.

This moment that we are living in right now is the "day after historic Pentecost." If the power of Pentecost is operative in us today, it should lead us to radical engagement, radical empowerment, and radical enlargement. I pray that the power of Pentecost will be a living reality in you today.

# Saving Faith

For by grace you have been saved through faith, and that
not of yourselves; *it is* the gift of God, not of works, lest
anyone should boast.

—Ephesians 2:8–9

The most crucial distinction between Christianity and every
other belief system is that in Christianity, we learn that
salvation is by grace through faith alone. While other religions
of the world require us to earn our salvation, in Christianity,
salvation is a gift of God received not by works but by faith.
The Bible says, "For by grace you have been saved through
faith, and that not of yourselves, *it is* the gift of God, not of
works, lest anyone should boast" (Eph. 2:8).

While faith in the Lord Jesus Christ is all that is required of
us to receive eternal life, in a real sense, our salvation is based
on works as well. How so? It is based on the works of Christ—
His sinless life, death on the cross for our sins, burial,
resurrection from the grave, and ascension. Therefore, the
Bible says, "Believe on the Lord Jesus Christ, and you will be
saved, you and your household" (Acts 16:31). Our salvation is
by grace alone, through faith alone, from Christ alone, and for
the glory of God alone.

The Reformers of the sixteenth century identified three
essential elements of saving faith mentioned in the New
Testament. In Latin, these are called *notitia*, *assensus*, and *fiducia*.
*Notitia* refers to knowing the content of the gospel. If we are
to believe in the Lord Jesus Christ, we need to know who He

is and what He has done to save us. The essence of the gospel is what God in Christ has done to lift us from the predicament of sin and despair and give us eternal life. Before we can believe in the Lord Jesus Christ, we must know about Christ, what He has done and continues to do for us.

*Assensus* refers to accepting a proposition to be true. Charles Hodge defined faith as "assent to the truth, or persuasion of the mind that a thing is true."[26] In other words, we must be persuaded of the truthfulness of the gospel and what Christ has done. It is not enough to know about Jesus Christ, but we must be convinced that the things we heard about Him are true. One can learn about Jesus Christ and not believe that it is true.

*Fiducia* refers to trusting. Saving faith leads us to put our trust in the Lord Jesus Christ as Savior and Lord. Theologian R. C. Sproul notes: "Knowing and believing the content of the Christian faith is not enough, for even demons can do that. Faith is effectual only if one personally trusts in Christ alone for salvation."[27]

In 1 Thessalonians 2:13, we see these three elements of saving faith converging magnificently. The apostle Paul wrote, "For this reason, we also thank God without ceasing because when you received the word of God (*notitia*), which you heard from us, you welcomed it not as the word of men, but as it is in truth (*assensus*), the word of God, which also effectively works in you who believe (*fiducia*)."

While saving faith or the inclination to believe in the Lord Jesus Christ is necessary for our salvation or justification, how does one get this saving faith? There is a fourth element that is

---

26. Charles Hodge, *Systematic Theology,* vol. 3, *Soteriology* (Peabody: Hendrickson Publishers, 2008), 42.

27. R. C. Sproul, *Everyone's a Theologian: An Introduction to Systematic Theology,* (Orlando: Ligonier Ministries, 2014), 229.

indispensable for the induction of such saving faith. That fourth element is *vivifying*.

Every person born into this world is a sinner by nature, choice, and divine verdict. The Bible calls this condition "dead in trespasses and sins" (Eph. 2:1). Theologians call it "radical depravity." This means that every aspect of our being is tainted by sin such that while we may have the natural ability to make choices, we lack the moral ability or disposition to seek God. Our natural inclination is to go our own way. In our depravity, we find sinning more desirable than seeking God (Rom. 3).

So, what needs to happen is for God to intervene graciously and make us alive from our spiritual deadness and impart the saving faith so we can respond to the gospel. The Bible says, "And you He made alive, who were dead in trespasses and sins" (Eph. 2:1). Just as a corpse cannot make itself alive, a spiritually dead person cannot turn to God of his own will, for his will is in the bondage of sin. God must first vivify or regenerate the person. The psalmist prayed, "Turn us again to yourself O God. Make your face shine down upon us. Only then will we be saved" (Ps. 80:3 NLT). God must turn us toward Himself. Bible says, "Everyone who believes that Jesus is the Christ has been born of God" (1 John 5:1 ESV). Being born of God or regenerated by the Holy Spirit precedes saving or justifying faith.

The Bible says, "Whoever calls on the name of the Lord shall be saved" (Rom. 10:13). Have you called on the name of Jesus for your salvation? If not, I pray that the Holy Spirit will vivify you from your spiritual deadness and give you the saving faith to believe in the Lord Jesus Christ for salvation.

# The Wonder of Christmas

> But when the fullness of the time had come, God sent
> forth His Son, born of a woman, born under the law, to
> redeem those who were under the law, that we might
> receive the adoption as sons.
>
> —Galatians 4:4–5

Albert Einstein once remarked: "I am a Jew, but the luminous
figure of the Nazarene enthralls me. . . No one can read the
Gospels without feeling the actual presence of Jesus. His
personality pulsates in every word. No myth is filled with such
life."[28]

Who was this luminous Nazarene who graced the landscape
of history two thousand years ago? The Bible teaches that He
was the eternal Word (*logos*) that became flesh and dwelt among
us, whose glory was as of the "only begotten of the Father, full
of grace and truth" (John 1:14). The Nazarene who walked the
dusty roads of ancient Palestine was none other than God in
the flesh—God incarnate. All too often, in the hustle and
bustle, glitter and glamor, lights and sounds of Christmas, this
truth is forgotten or missed.

In Galatians 4:4–5, we read, "When the fullness of time had
come, God sent forth His Son, born of a woman, born under
the law, to redeem those who were under the law, that we

---

28. Albert Einstein, "I Am Enthralled by the Luminous Figure of the
Nazarene," in *The Messiahship of Jesus*, ed. Arthur w. Kac (Grand Rapids:
Baker Book House, 1980), 36–37.

might receive the adoption as sons…Therefore you are no longer a slave but a son, and if a son, then an heir of God through Christ." The central message of Christmas is that when the commercial, geopolitical, cultural, and religious conditions were just right, the second person of the Trinity, the eternally begotten Son of God, took upon Himself human nature by being born to Mary through the Holy Spirit. In taking on human nature, the Son of God became the God-man, with two natures—divine and human—unified in one person "without any confusion, change, division, or separation."[29] Indeed, the story of the birth of Jesus is the story of divine condescension.

Historic Christianity affirms that when the second person of the Trinity took on human nature, He did not divest, subvert, deny, or impugn His deity in any way. He remained entirely God and fully man simultaneously, and when He ascended into heaven, He did not leave His human nature behind. It is forever a part of Him so that the Son of God who is presently seated at the Father's right hand is Jesus Christ, the God-man. No wonder the Bible says, "For *there is* one God and one Mediator between God and men, *the* Man Christ Jesus" (1 Tim. 2:5).

From our text in Galatians 4:4–5, we learn that the Christmas story proclaims to us three blessings we have in Christ. First, in Christ, we have the blessing of divine redemption. Our text says that Christ was born of a woman, born under the law, to redeem those under the law. In Galatians 3:13, we read, "Christ has redeemed us from the curse of the law, having become a curse for us." The Bible teaches that the law is holy, spiritual, just, and good, but because none could keep the Mosaic law, all are under the curse of the law, which is death. The law tells us what to do, but it

---

29. Justo L. González, *The Story of Christianity*, vol.1, *The Early Church to the Dawn of the Reformation* (Peabody: Prince Press, 20070, 257.

does not empower us to keep the law. It is intended to show our sinfulness and point us to Christ, who alone can redeem us.

The English word "redeem" is a composite translation of three Greek words—*agaradzo, exagaradzo,* and *lutrao.* Together, these words convey the idea of buying a slave in the slave market, removing the slave from the slave market, and setting him free. This is what Christ has done for us. He bought us with His precious blood (1 Peter 1:19), transferred us from the realm of darkness into the kingdom of Christ (Col. 1:13), and freed us from the dominion of sin (Gal. 5:3).

Second, in Christ, we have the blessing of divine adoption. Our text says that Christ came that we might receive the adoption as sons. The apostle Paul is the only one who used this concept of adoption in the New Testament, for a special reason. In the Greco-Roman culture in which Paul lived, a Roman father could disown his biological son for any physical deformities because he got a son with imperfections that he did not ask for. But in the case of adoption, a Roman father could not disown his adopted son because he adopted that child with full knowledge of the child's limitations and imperfections. Paul wanted to emphasize the fact that our adoption as sons is a permanent status. The apostle Paul asked, what shall separate us from the love of Christ? The answer is "nothing." In Christ, we have the authority—*exousia*—to become the offspring of God. Isn't that a matchless blessing— to be called the inseparable children of God?

Third, in Christ, we have the blessing of divine promotion. Our text says that someone in Christ is no longer a slave but a son and an heir of God through Christ. In Christ, we are promoted from a slave of sin to a son and heir of God. When we enter into a covenant relationship with God through Christ, God says, "I am your God and you are My people" (Ex. 6:7). We become a chosen generation, a royal priesthood, a holy nation, and God's special people in our promoted status. We become joint heirs with Christ (1 Peter 2:9). We are made to "sit together in the heavenly places in Christ" (Eph. 2:6).

Friend, does Christmas herald for you the blessings of divine redemption, divine adoption, and divine promotion? If not, I pray that you will believe in the Lord Jesus Christ and receive the authority to become a son or daughter of God. May Jesus Christ, born in Bethlehem 2000 years ago, be born in your heart today and lead you to experience the wonder of Christmas.

# God's Covenantal
# Preservation of His People

On the same day the LORD made a covenant with
Abram, saying: "To your descendants I have given this
land, from the river of Egypt to the great river, the River
Euphrates—the Kenites, the Kenezzites, the
Kadmonites, the Hittites, the Perizzites, the Rephaim,
the Amorites, the Canaanites, the Girgashites, and the
Jebusites."

—Genesis 15:18–21

John Newton is a beloved personality in church history. He
was a slave trader who encountered the Lord amid a life-
threatening storm and came out of that experience a changed
man. He composed the well-known hymn, "Amazing Grace."
One of the stanzas in the song goes like this: "Through many
dangers and toils and snare, I have already come. It's grace that
brought me safe thus far, and grace will lead me home." In
these words, Newton invoked God's covenantal preservation
of His people.

In Genesis 12, 15, and 17, we read of the covenant God
made with Abraham. According to the ancient Near East
traditions, this was a covenant between two unequal parties,
known as the Suzerain/Vassal covenant. As in all the
covenants made in those days, Abrahamic covenant involved
promises, blessings, and obligations assigned to the parties
entering the covenant. The most crucial duty of Abraham was

to walk humbly before God and remain loyal to Him. God ratified His covenant with Abraham by what is known as a self-maledictory oath. Typically, in this ritual, some animals are cut into two halves and placed opposite each other. The parties entering into the covenant will walk between the pieces, saying, "If I don't keep my part of the responsibilities and obligations of this covenant, may I become like these dead animals." Hence it is said, "cutting a covenant."

In the case of Abraham, however, something unusual happened. Abraham fell into a deep sleep, so God, who initiated the covenant, walked alone between the pieces in the form of a flaming torch. In essence, God was promising to keep His end of the covenant and ensure that Abraham would be faithful to Him as well. Also, God was saying to Abraham, "If you or your descendants fail to keep my covenant, I will pay the price in blood." If you fast-forward to redemption history, God did pay the price in blood for the sins of Abraham, his descendants, and all the families of the world when Jesus Christ, the Son of God, was crucified on the cross.

What's most significant in the Abrahamic covenant is that God unilaterally promised that He would preserve Abraham so that the promises built into the covenant would be fulfilled. God ensured that Abraham would become a great nation and that all the nations of the earth would be blessed in him. Having been justified by faith, Abraham lived by faith, remained a friend of God, and looked forward to a city whose builder and maker is God. God inducted Abraham into the hall of faith.

As with all other covenants in the Bible, the Abrahamic covenant was a pointer to a better covenant with better promises cut by the blood of God's own Son, Jesus Christ. Under this new covenant, we are given every spiritual blessing in heavenly places in Christ. We can take comfort that He who has begun a good work in us will complete it until the day of Jesus Christ (Phil. 1:6). We learn about God preserving His people in several passages of the Scripture. For example, in Jude's benediction recorded in Jude 24, we read that God is the one who keeps us from falling and presents us faultless before God. The apostle Peter reminds us that the power of God keeps us through faith unto salvation (1 Peter 1:5). Writing to Timothy, the apostle Paul expressed his confidence that the Lord will deliver him from every evil work and preserve him for His heavenly kingdom (2 Tim. 4:18).

Jesus said, "He that endures to the end shall be saved" (Mark 13:13). And Jesus also said, "For without Me, you can do nothing" (John 15:5). Jesus prayed to the Father that He keep His disciples from being lost. Based on the certainty that He would keep them, Jesus said to the disciples, "I will not drink of this fruit of the vine until that day when I drink it new with you in My Father's kingdom" (Matt. 26:29).

It's a mistake to think that we can endure to the end in our own strength unaided by the Lord. The Bible says, "Therefore let him who thinks he stands to take heed lest he fall." (1 Cor. 10:12). Divine preservation does not mean that we will not falter or fail in our Christian life; it means that when we fall, we have the Holy Spirit in us to convict us of sin and cause us to repent and be restored to fellowship with the Father. Therefore, we can live in victory, knowing that if God is for us, who can be against us? Nothing in heaven or on earth can separate us from God's love, which is in Christ Jesus. This doctrine of divine preservation is liberating! At the end of our life's journey, we too can say with Newton, "it's grace that brought me safe thus far, and grace will lead me home."

# Who Is a Christian?

I thank my God always concerning you for the grace of God which was given to you by Christ Jesus, that you were enriched in everything by Him in all utterance and all knowledge, even as the testimony of Christ was confirmed in you, so that you come short in no gift, eagerly waiting for the revelation of our Lord Jesus Christ, who will also confirm you to the end, *that you may be* blameless in the day of our Lord Jesus Christ. God *is* faithful, by whom you were called into the fellowship of His Son, Jesus Christ our Lord.

—1 Corinthians 1:4–9

Many Christians in America and around the world were recently saddened and shocked to read in the news about two well-known Christians—pastor and author Josh Harris and Hillsong worship leader Marty Sampson—renouncing their Christian beliefs.[30] Presumably, they have disavowed their faith in Jesus Christ as Lord and Savior. The news of their departure from the faith they once held should cause us to pause and examine carefully how the Bible defines a faithful follower of Christ. Barna Research Group found that in 2020 only one in four Americans was a practicing Christian. Practicing Christians in this survey identified themselves as Christians,

---

30. "Another Pop-Culture Christian Loses His Faith," National Review, accessed April 28, 2022, https://www.nationalreview.com/2019/08/another-pop-culture-christian-loses-his-faith/.

agreed that faith is very important for their lives, and attended church at least once within the previous month. According to Barna, the percentage of practicing Christians has been steadily decreasing since 2000.[31] Data such as this compel us to search the Scripture to know what the Bible teaches about the characteristics of a follower of Christ.

The apostle Paul begins his first letter to the church at Corinth by defining a Christian. Paul had received reports that there was strife, divisiveness, and sexual immorality among some church members. Though the church at Corinth was gifted in many ways, it also struggled with many problems. Paul wrote this letter to address these issues. In chapter 1:1-9, he gives three salient characteristics of a follower of Christ.

First, we learn that a Christian or a follower of Christ is consecrated in Christ. In verse two, the apostle Paul called the believers in Corinth "sanctified in Christ Jesus, called to be saints." The word "sanctified" means consecrated or set apart for God. The same Greek word is also translated as "saints" or "holy." A Christian has been born of God and is separated by God to be holy and blameless (Eph. 1:4). Though the followers of Christ live in this fallen world, they are not of this world. They do not conform to the pattern or ways of this world. As theologian John Stott puts it well, they are holy, called out of the world to worship God, and at the same time apostolic, sent back into the world to witness and serve. Alec Vidler captures this double identity of a Christian by the phrase "holy worldliness."[32]

If you are a follower of Christ and are led by the Spirit of God, you will have no confusion about your identity in Christ. You are called by God and set apart for God and His purposes.

---

31. "Barna: State of the Church," Barna, accessed April 28, 2022, https://www.barna.com/research/changing-state-of-the-church/.

32. John Stott, *Contemporary Christian* (Downers Grove: InterVarsity Press, 1992), 243–244.

Christians stand in contradistinction to the decadence and perversion that surround them. Because God is holy, we must reflect His character in our behavior as children of God. In other words, to be holy means more than belonging or being dedicated to God; it means to be radically different from unbelievers in our conduct in every sphere of our lives.

Second, we learn that a Christian or a follower of Christ is one who is enriched in Christ. In verses 4 through 7, Paul commends Christians at Corinth for being enriched by divine word, divine wisdom, and divine work. Christians at Corinth were enriched by God's word: that is, to speak and witness for Christ. The gift of prophecy or exhortation was prominent in their midst. A Christian is empowered by Christ to speak for Him effectively. In the book of Acts, we read how the Holy Spirit emboldened the apostles to witness for Christ. Paul asked the church in Ephesus to pray that utterance would be given to him to boldly speak as he ought to speak and reveal the mystery of the gospel.

A follower of Christ is enriched by divine wisdom. Christians at Corinth increased in all utterance and all knowledge. The knowledge they possessed, most importantly, was the knowledge of the person and work of Christ. The Spirit gave them the word of wisdom and the word of knowledge. A Christian is progressively enriched with the knowledge of God's word in all wisdom and shares that knowledge with others for encouragement, exhortation, and edification. Paul prayed for the church at Colossae that they would be filled with the knowledge of God's will in all wisdom and spiritual understanding.

Divine works also enriched the church at Corinth. They were witnesses to the confirmation of the gospel through various spiritual gifts such as speaking in tongues, interpretation of tongues, healings, miracles, and discerning of spirits. Followers of Christ exercise the spiritual gifts God has given them for the profit of all and participate in the work of

God. At Corinth, the church's problem was not a lack of spiritual gifts, but the misuse of spiritual gifts resulting in strife and disunity. Just like the Christians at Corinth, many Christians today are guilty of misusing their gifts, making the gospel of Christ of no effect.

Third, we learn that a Christian or a follower of Christ is one who is preserved in Christ. In verses 7 through 9, Paul assured the Christians at Corinth that God is faithful to sustain them to the end to stand blameless before the Lord when He is revealed. The elect of God endure till the end because Christ, through His Spirit, preserves them. In His High Priestly prayer, Jesus prayed to the Father: "Those whom You gave Me I have kept; and none of them is lost except the son of perdition, that the Scripture might be fulfilled" (John 17:12). The Bible says, "He who has begun a good work in you will complete *it* until the day of Jesus Christ" (Phil. 1:6). The apostle Paul was confident of his perseverance in the faith: "I know whom I have believed and am persuaded that He is able to keep what I have committed to Him until that Day" (2 Tim. 1:12). Similarly, Jude concluded his letter: "Now to Him who is able to keep you from stumbling, and to present you faultless before the presence of His glory with exceeding joy...be glory and majesty" (Jude 24). Christ, through His Spirit, preserves to the end those whom He has saved.

This does not mean that born-again believers cannot backslide or fall into sin. But when they do, they are out of character and come under the conviction of the Holy Spirit. So, they repent and seek restoration. Therefore, when we hear about individuals who once professed their faith in Christ and later denied the Lord, it behooves us to ask if they were truly born of the Spirit of God in the first place. In 1 John 2, the apostle John mentions apostate Christians or antichrists who went out from them but were not of them. If they were of them, they would have continued with them. They went out because they were not part of the church of God. Not all who profess to be Christians are necessarily followers of Christ. Jesus said, "Not everyone who says to Me, 'Lord, Lord' shall enter the kingdom of heaven but he who does the will of My Father in heaven" (Matt. 7:21).

God knows His sheep, and His sheep hear His voice. Do you know Him as your Lord and Savior? If you profess to be a Christian, be even more diligent in making your call and election sure (2 Peter 1:10). May the Lord speak to you through His word and strengthen you in your walk with the Lord.

# Divine Colonialism

Therefore, if anyone *is* in Christ, *he is* a new creation; old things have passed away; behold, all things have become new.

—2 Corinthians 5:17

But God, who is rich in mercy, because of His great love with which He loved us, even when we were dead in trespasses, made us alive together with Christ (by grace you have been saved), and raised *us* up together, and made *us* sit together in the heavenly *places* in Christ Jesus, that in the ages to come He might show the exceeding riches of His grace in *His* kindness toward us in Christ Jesus.

—Ephesians 2:4–7

"Colonialism," wrote the late Alfred Moleah, professor of political science at Temple University and my neighbor in Wilmington, "was first and foremost an act of dispossession. It was also dispossession of life. Marauding European colonial invaders had a brutal sense of entitlement to whatever others possessed and owned. Wherever it occurred, central to colonialism was dispossession."[33]

There is a striking parallel between European colonialism and the divine invasion of our lives, with one major exception.

---

33. Alfred T. Moleah, *South Africa: Colonialism, Apartheid and African Dispossession* (Wilmington, Delaware: Disa Press, 1993), xi.

God invades our lives at our invitation and for our benefit. He does not intrude on our lives without our consent. And when there is a willingness for His intrusion, it is graciously granted to us by a Sovereign God.

When God invades us, He wants to transform us and make us new (2 Cor. 5:17), something we cannot do through our own strength. God does His transformative work to benefit us eternally and glorify Himself in the process. C. S. Lewis grasped the essence of this divine colonialism when he wrote: "Christ says 'Give me all. I don't want so much of your time and so much of your money and so much of your work: I want you. I have not come to torment your natural self but to kill it. No half-measures are any good. I don't want to cut off a branch here and a branch there; I want to have the whole tree down. I don't want to drill the tooth, or crown it, or stop it, but to have it out. Hand over the whole natural self, all the desires which you think innocent as well as the ones you think wicked—the whole outfit. I will give you a new self instead. In fact, I will give you Myself: my own will shall become yours.'"[34]

Divine colonialism leads to the dispossession of our old life and possession of God-life and all that God has in store for us. The apostle Paul understood this well. He wrote, "But God, who is rich in mercy, because of His great love with which He loved us, even when we were dead in trespasses, made us alive together with Christ (by grace you have been saved), and raised *us* up together, and made *us* sit together in the heavenly *places* in Christ Jesus, that in the ages to come He might show the exceeding riches of His grace in *His* kindness toward us in Christ Jesus" (Eph. 2:4–7). Divine colonialism is not something to be afraid of or despised; it should be welcomed by all who desire to have a radical change for the better.

---

34. C. S. Lewis, *Mere Christianity*, 167.

# Christian Fasting

Moreover, when you fast, do not be like the hypocrites, with a sad countenance. For they disfigure their faces that they may appear to men to be fasting. Assuredly, I say to you, they have their reward. But you, when you fast, anoint your head and wash your face, so that you do not appear to men to be fasting, but your Father who is in secret will reward you openly.

—Matthew 6:16–18

Fasting is a religious practice observed in many religions, including Christianity. In Matthew 6:16–18, Jesus briefly touched on this subject and gave three essential truths about fasting. First, we learn of the place of fasting. Jesus said, "When you fast." This suggests that fasting is a discipline that is not commanded but expected of us. In the Old Testament, we read about private and public fasting (Dan. 9:3; Neh. 9:1; Jonah 3:5), often with sackcloth and ashes to show one's grief, sorrow, repentance, and remorse (Ps. 35:13; Est. 4:3). But fasting took on a new meaning when Jesus came and inaugurated the kingdom of God. Piper writes, "The birthplace of Christian fasting is homesickness for God."[35]

In Matthew 9:15–17, the disciples of John the Baptist ask Jesus, "Why do we and the Pharisees fast often, but Your disciples do not fast?" Jesus told them His disciples had no reason to mourn and fast while He, the bridegroom, was with

---

35. John Piper, *A Hunger For God* (Wheaton: Crossway, 1997), 13.

them. Then Jesus said, "But the days will come when the bridegroom will be taken away from them, and then they will fast." That day has arrived—the time between Jesus' ascension to heaven and His return—when the followers of Christ will fast, yearning to be with Him even though His presence is with us through His indwelling Spirit. Yes, fasting has a place in our lives (Acts 13:3; 14:23; 2 Cor. 6:5; 11:27). But unlike old covenant fasting, new covenant fasting is motivated by a hunger for intimacy with God; it is not trying to manipulate God or twist His arm but to have more of Him. The aim of Christian fasting is to feast on God more than on earthly perishable food. It is a celebration of the dawning of the kingdom of God and our blessings in Christ resulting from His finished redemptive work.

Second, we learn of the practice of fasting. Jesus told His disciples not to display their fasting for people to see. The Pharisees loved to publicize their fast (Luke 18:12). Jesus says one's motivation for fasting determines whether one's fasting is pleasing to God. The admonition to fast in secret, not to be seen by men, also applies to charity and prayer (Matt. 6:1–7). We must guard against the temptation to brag about our fast or draw the public's attention when fasting. Our fast is seen as hypocritical when motivated by a desire for admiration rather than by love for God. What counts is that God sees our fast! If our lifestyle is displeasing to God, that would nullify our fast and its reward (Isa. 58: 3–9).

Third, we learn of the prize of fasting. What is the reward of Christian fasting? It is God Himself (Gen. 15:1)—His supremacy in every facet of our lives. Any other material or temporal blessing that may result from seeking God is secondary. Ironically, fasting for God done in secret is rewarded openly, for people will see for themselves God's power, purity, and presence in our conduct and disposition.

So, voluntarily denying an otherwise normal function for intimacy with God is a discipline well-pleasing to God.

# Pentecost: What Does It Mean?

But you shall receive power when the Holy Spirit has come upon you; and you shall be witnesses to Me in Jerusalem, and in all Judea and Samaria, and to the end of the earth.

—Acts 1:8

Each year, fifty days after Easter, the Christian church celebrates Pentecost, a remembrance of the descent of the Holy Spirit and the birth of the church in its fullness. Acts 2 gives us a detailed description of the events surrounding the manifest outpouring of the Holy Spirit upon those who waited for Him in one accord. This phenomenal and historic event in the church's history, which was foretold by the prophet Joel, perplexed the people who witnessed it so much that they asked: "What could this mean?"

As Christians, we should continually ask this question to remind ourselves of Pentecost's significance and transformative effect in our daily lives. From this chapter, I would like to draw your attention to three essential truths regarding the meaning and might of Pentecost.

First, Pentecost means the impartation of God, the Holy Spirit. The work of the Holy Spirit did not begin with Pentecost. The Holy Spirit has been at work in the universe since its creation. The Bible says, "In the beginning, God created the heavens and the earth. The earth was without form, and void; and darkness was on the face of the deep. And the Spirit of God was hovering over the face of the waters" (Gen. 1:1–2). The Holy Spirit moved the men of God in the history of Israel from time to time to accomplish the purposes of God (Ex. 11:24–25; Num. 11:26; 2 Peter 1:21). But what is significantly different about the Holy Spirit since Pentecost is the democratization of the Holy Spirit. God, the Holy Spirit, came down to dwell permanently in all who believe in the Lord Jesus Christ.

Interestingly, on the first Easter Sunday evening, Jesus appeared to His disciples and blessed them, saying, "Peace be with you." He said, "As the Father has sent Me, I also send you." Then Jesus breathed on them and said to them, "Receive the Holy Spirit" (John 20:22). A few days later, just before He ascended into heaven, Jesus said, "But you shall receive power when the Holy Spirit has come upon you, and you shall be witnesses to Me in Jerusalem, and in all Judea and Samaria, and to the end of the earth" (Acts 1:8). When Jesus breathed on them and said, "Receive the Holy Spirit," didn't they receive Him? Why did they have to wait for the Holy Spirit after Jesus ascended into heaven?

We get a clue to the difference between these two events from Genesis 2:7: "And the LORD God formed man *of* the dust of the ground, and breathed into his nostrils the breath of life; and man became a living being." Just as God breathed the breath of life into Adam made from the dust, Jesus breathed the breath of eternal life into His disciples who had come to trust the finished redemptive work of Christ on the cross. It symbolized the regenerative work of the Holy Spirit mentioned in Ezekiel 37:14. The impartation of the Holy Spirit mentioned in Acts 2 is for taking the gospel to the ends of the earth. While John 20:22 points to the Holy Spirit's power to save, Acts 1:8 points to the power of the Holy Spirit to serve.

What does Pentecost mean? It means to impart the power of the Holy Spirit for the preaching of the gospel. The apostles, filled by the Holy Spirit, went about preaching Christ and His resurrection. If you and I are going to be witnesses for Christ, we need the power of the Holy Spirit. The prophet Zechariah understood that any worthwhile endeavor for God requires the aid of the Holy Spirit. He said, "Not by might nor by power, but by My Spirit."

Second, Pentecost means the exaltation of God, the Father. On the day of Pentecost, the disciples were filled with the Holy Spirit and began to speak the wonderful works of God in different known languages. In other words, they were worshipping God. The early church "continued daily with one accord in the temple and "praising God and having favor with all the people" (Acts 2:47). Worshipping or exalting God is an integral part of a Spirit-filled life. The apostle Paul exhorts us to be continuously filled with the Spirit, "speaking to one another in psalms and hymns and spiritual songs, singing and making melody in [our] hearts to the Lord" (Eph. 5:18–19).

If you are Spirit-filled, worshipping God should be as natural as breathing air. The Bible says, "Let everything that has breath praise the LORD" (Ps. 150:6). Under the new covenant, we do not offer animal sacrifices as part of our worship ritual; we offer the sacrifice of praise to God: that is, the fruit of our lips, giving thanks to His name (Heb. 13:15). Worship offered by a Spirit-filled person is more than what they do when in church. Worship is a lifestyle such that everything one does becomes an act of worship unto the Lord (Rom. 14:8; Col. 3:23).

The seventeenth-century Carmelite layman in Paris, famously known as Brother Lawrence, knew how to worship God and practice His presence in everything he did. He said, "The time of business does not with me differ from the time of prayer; and in the noise and clatter of my kitchen, while several persons are at the same time calling for different things, I possess God in as great tranquility as if I were upon my knees at the blessed sacrament."[36] So, on this Pentecost Sunday, resolve to be a worshipper of God in the Spirit.

Third, Pentecost means the proclamation of God, the Son. Being full of the Holy Spirit, Peter, standing with his fellow apostles, raised his voice and proclaimed Jesus Christ, His death on the cross, resurrection, and ascension into heaven. Luke's focus in the book of Acts was to show how the Holy Spirit empowered the apostles to preach the gospel even in adversity. Peter demonstrated to us through his preaching that the content of our proclamation is Jesus Christ; as the apostle Paul wrote, "We preach Christ crucified" (1 Cor. 1:23).

What does Pentecost mean? It means the impartation of God, the Holy Spirit, which is the inward work of God; it means the exaltation of God, the Father, which is the upward work of God; and it means the proclamation of God, the Son, which is the outward work of God. I pray that the meaning, message, and might of Pentecost will reverberate in your life and propel you to expect great things from God and attempt great things for God.

I challenge you to resolve to share Christ with others vocally through your words and visually through your works. Let your light shine in the world that you move about so people may know Jesus Christ, the giver of eternal life.

---

36. Brother Lawrence, *The Practice of the Presence of God the Best Rule of a Holy Life* (New York: Fleming H. Revell Company, n.d.), 18.

# The Golden Calf: The Formative Nature of Idolatry

And he received *the gold* from their hand, and he fashioned it with an engraving tool, and made a molded calf. Then they said, "This is your god, O Israel, that brought you out of the land of Egypt!" So when Aaron saw *it*, he built an altar before it. And Aaron made a proclamation and said, "Tomorrow *is* a feast to the LORD." Then they rose early on the next day, offered burnt offerings, and brought peace offerings; and the people sat down to eat and drink, and rose up to play.

—Exodus 32:4–6

The worship of the golden calf was a watershed event with disastrous results in the history of the children of Israel. Exodus 32 describes the incident in detail and its effects on the Israelites in the years that followed. Moses was on Sinai for forty days and forty nights. While he was gone, the Israelites were at the foot of Sinai, wondering what had happened to Moses. They became impatient and frustrated because their leader was gone, and they did not know when he would return.

So, the people gathered around Aaron and asked him to make gods that would go before them. In response, Aaron collected the golden jewelry from the people, melted it, and made a molded calf. The people looked at the golden calf and said, "This is your gods [plural in Hebrew] O Israel, that brought you out of the land of Egypt." They blasphemed the name of Yahweh by ascribing His mighty act of deliverance to the bovine gods of Egypt. It was also an act of blatant disobedience because God had instructed them through Moses not to make carved images of any kind nor to bow down to them (Ex. 20:4–5). Hundreds of years later, Jeroboam, the first king of the northern kingdom of Israel, caused the people of God to sin by sacrificing to the calves that he had made. He said, "Here are your gods, O Israel, which brought you up from the land of Israel" (1 Kings 12:28). Idolatry had become a constant practice among the Israelites, invoking the anger and chastisement of God.

Idol worship is an abomination in God's sight. From the golden calf story, one important lesson we learn is about the formative nature of idolatry. The Bible teaches that what we worship, we become. After describing the idols of the heathen that could not speak, hear, see, smell, handle, or walk, the psalmist said, "Those who make them are like them; so is everyone who trusts in them" (Ps. 115:4–8). "What people revere, they resemble, either for ruin or restoration."[37] The rebellious Israelites worshipped the golden calf and became like a "stiff-necked" cow (Ex. 32:8–9) and a stubborn heifer (Hosea 4:17). Though Exodus 32 does not explicitly state it, it is implied that the Israelites had also become dumb, deaf, and blind like the idols they worshipped (Isa. 6:9–10; Jer. 5:20–22). The prophet Jeremiah proclaimed to Judah: "Hear this now, O foolish people, without understanding, who have eyes and see not, and have ears and hear not" (Jer. 5:20–21). Theologian G. K. Beale notes that this "sensory-organ-malfunction language," when used in the Old Testament, refers exclusively to the sin of idol worship.[38]

---

37. G. K. Beale, *We Become What We Worship: A Biblical Theology of Idolatry* (Downers Grove: IVP Academic, 2008), 16.

38. Ibid., 41.

Though the Israelites did not bow before idols made of silver and gold in the days of Jesus, they were nonetheless steeped in idolatry because they put their trust in the vain traditions of men, money, power, position, and people instead of in God. As a result, Jesus equated them to dumb, deaf, and mute idols (Mark 4:12; John 12:40). In the parable of the sower, when Jesus' disciples asked Him why He spoke to the people in parables, He replied, "because seeing they do not see, and hearing they do not hear, nor do they understand" (Matt. 13:13–14). Jesus quoted them the prophecy of Isaiah to say that they had become like idols they worshipped—blind, deaf, and dumb.

Idolatry in our contemporary life is seen in the displacement of God by self-adoration and worship. We trust our careers, wealth, personal achievements, and what the world considers success to carry us through life. What pleases us is more important than what pleases God. Media and commentators on television, rather than the Word of God, have become the arbiters of truth. As the apostle Paul wrote, our foolish hearts have become darkened, and we have changed the glory of God into "an image made like corruptible man—and birds and four-footed animals and creeping things" (Rom. 1:23). For us who live in the West, "birds and four-footed animals and creeping things" represent all human-made and human-oriented objects of trust and loyalty.

John Calvin said that the human heart is a perpetual factory of idols.[39] The idols of our hearts have made us blind and deaf to the things of God. Just as the Israelites attributed their deliverance from Egypt to the golden calf instead of to Yahweh, we ascribe all glory and honor to the idols of our making instead of to the God who revealed Himself through nature, Scripture, and the person of Jesus Christ. It's time to

---

39. John Calvin, *Institutes of the Christian Religion*, trans. Henry Beveridge (Peabody: Hendrickson, 2008), 54.

take an inward look and see what idols are enshrined in our hearts. And because we become what we worship, let us get rid of the idols that lead us to ruin and trust in Jesus Christ alone. Let us give Him the glory due to His name and worship Him in the beauty of holiness (Ps. 29:2). When we do, we become more and more transformed into the image of Christ, for which purpose we are saved from darkness and made partakers of the divine nature (2 Peter 1:4). Our destiny is to resemble Christ, who loved us and gave Himself for us.

# The Cross and the Empty Tomb

Most assuredly, I say to you, unless a grain of wheat falls
into the ground and dies, it remains alone; but if it dies,
it produces much grain.

—John 12:24

On Good Friday each year, most Christians worldwide ponder
the death of Jesus Christ and its significance to their lives.
Though from a human perspective the greatest tragedy in all
human history was the crucifixion of Jesus Christ, the Son of
God, Christ-followers gratefully reflect on His death because
of the measureless and fathomless blessings that flow from it.
Jesus said, "Most assuredly, I say to you, unless a grain of wheat
falls into the ground and dies, it remains alone; but if it dies, it
produces much grain" (John 12:24).

Followers of Christ need not mourn His death. In the final
moments of His death on the cross, Jesus said to the women
who were mourning and lamenting: "Daughters of Jerusalem,
do not weep for Me, but weep for yourselves and for your
children" (Luke 23:28). Jesus knew very well that His
excruciatingly painful, atoning death pleased the Father who
sent Him to the earth to save "His people from their sins"
(Matt. 1:21). The Bible says, "It pleased the LORD to bruise
Him [Jesus]; He [Father] has put Him [Jesus] to grief. When
you make His soul an offering for sin, He shall see His seed,

He shall prolong His days, and the pleasure of the LORD shall prosper in His hand" (Isa. 53:10).

Jesus, the eternal seed, came down to the earth to die and produce innumerable descendants (much grain). Jesus vehemently resisted any suggestion of avoiding the cross. When Jesus told His disciples that He must go to Jerusalem and suffer, be killed, and be raised on the third day, Peter rebuked Him, saying, "Far be it from You, Lord; this shall not happen to You!" Jesus turned to Peter and said, "Get behind Me, Satan! You are an offense to Me, for you are not mindful of the things of God, but the things of men" (Matt. 16:21–23). In other words, Jesus reprimanded Peter for not seeing His death from a divine perspective. As Christians, we regard the death of Christ as a triumph, not a tragedy, because, to borrow an expression from the Puritan divine, John Owen, we see on the cross "the death of death in the death of Christ."[40] Jesus dealt with sin, the sting of death, on the cross so that death no longer has a grip of terror on those in Christ. Good Friday summons us to gaze reverently at the splendor of the cross on which Jesus died. The apostle Paul wrote, "But God forbid that I should boast except in the cross of our Lord Jesus Christ" (Gal. 6:14).

Jesus said that unless a grain of wheat falls to the ground and dies, it will not produce much grain. Jesus came to die and rise again from the grave to produce numerous offspring or followers. The cross was the necessary prelude to Christ's victory over death and the grave. Good Friday inevitably must lead to Easter! Jesus said to the two gloomy disciples of Christ who were on the road to Emmaus, "Ought not the Christ to have suffered these things and to enter into His glory?" (Luke 24:26). Indeed, the risen Savior has entered glory, giving us the

---

40. John Owen, *The Death of Death in the Death of Christ* (Carlisle: The Banner 0f Truth Trust, 2002), 1.

hope that all those who are dead in Christ shall also rise from their graves (1 Cor. 15:20; 1 Thess. 4:16).

The death and resurrection of Christ points to at least three empowering realities. First, we note that the resurrection of Christ points to the cessation of our old life. The apostle Paul wrote, "Knowing this, that our old man was crucified with Him [Christ], that the body of sin might be done away with, that we should no longer be slaves to sin" (Rom. 6:6). He said, "I have been crucified with Christ; it is no longer I who live" (Gal. 2:20). Even though historically, we did not die with Christ two thousand years ago, all who are in Christ are reckoned to have been dead with Him experientially. The Bible teaches that "our old man" was crucified with Christ so that we should no longer be slaves to sin (Rom. 6:6).

Second, the death and resurrection of Christ points to the initiation of our new life. Having been crucified with Christ, we have risen from our spiritual deadness with the newness of life in Christ. The Bible says, "Therefore, if anyone is in Christ, he is a new creation; old things have passed away; behold all things have become new" (2 Cor. 5:17).[41] This new life is qualitatively different because it is the life of the resurrected Christ coursing through us. We have put off the old man and put on the new man, "created according to God, in true righteousness and holiness" (Eph. 4:22–24). The apostle Paul put it this way: "It is no longer I who live, but Christ lives in me; and the life which I now live in the flesh I live by faith in the Son of God, who loved me and gave Himself for me" (Gal. 2:20). This new life in Christ gives us the power to overcome

---

41. In Greek, this verse reads, "If anyone is in Christ, new creation." The New International Version (NIV) renders it as, "Therefore, if anyone is in Christ, the new creation has come." For a person in Christ, the eschatological new creation has dawned upon him. Their rebirth by the Holy Spirit demonstrates that God will make all things new in the coming age. See Chris Bruno, *The Whole Message of the Bible in 16 Words* (Wheaton: Crossway, 2017), 40.

the mastery of sin and control of the old Adamic nature within us until the return of Christ. Not only that, the resurrection power of Christ in us empowers us to face the challenges of life with the confidence that "I can do all things through Christ who strengthens me" (Phil. 4:13).

Third, the death and resurrection of Christ points to the perpetuation of our eternal life. God said, "Behold I make all things new" (Rev. 21:5), which includes this earth on which we live presently. The eternal life that we have in Christ will continue beyond the grave. The promise of our resurrection gives us hope that we shall be with the Lord in a new domain in which the new heaven (New Jerusalem) will come down and fuse with the new earth, and God Himself will be with His people and be their God (Rev. 21:3). This final stage in which "God may be all in all" is called the eternal state.

As you contemplate on the cross and the empty tomb of Christ, I pray that the Holy Spirit will draw you to experience the blessing of the cross, which is salvation from your sins, and the empty tomb, which is the power to live triumphantly now and in the hereafter. You can have both blessings by believing in the Lord Jesus Christ as Lord and Savior. Will you take that step of faith today?

# Our God Forever and Forever

For this *is* God, our God forever and ever; He will be our guide *even* to death.

—Psalm 48:14

Psalm 48 is a beautiful worship song. The psalm begins by extolling the greatness of God. "Great is the LORD, and greatly to be praised. In the city of our God, in His holy mountain." It ends by exclaiming the goodness of God. "For this is God, our God forever and ever; He will be our guide even to death." In between these two exalting bookends, we find the psalmist pointing us to three truths about God's character: His presence (v. 3), lovingkindness (v. 9), and righteousness (vv.10–11).

When we are going through difficult times, it is comforting to know that the Lord is our refuge and strength in our midst. He hovers over us with His lovingkindness as a hen covers her chicks under its wings. Though Satan is allowed to create havoc in this world for the time being, God remains the Sovereign King of this universe and will rule the earth with righteousness and justice. These truths should lift our hearts from the fatigue of despair and keep us afloat with hope.

I want to draw your attention to the last verse of this psalm and highlight three powerful truths about the God of the Bible and their implications to our lives. We read: "For this is God, our God forever and ever; He will be our guide even to death" (Ps. 48:14).

First, we learn of the reality of God. God is not a figment of human imagination, nor is He, as Karl Marx said, the "opium of the people." God is the inescapable and transcendent cause of all reality. The Bible does not try to prove the existence of God, but rather takes His presence as an indisputable fact. The Bible begins with these words: "In the beginning God...." The central presupposition of the revealed Word of God is that God exists. This presupposition, rooted in divine revelation, explains all of reality inside and outside of our experience.

The reality of God explains the origin of the universe. Scientists of all stripes universally agree that our universe had a beginning. We know that nothing comes out of nothing; therefore, the beginning of the universe, known as the singularity, must have been put into motion by an external agent. The Bible calls this agent God, a personal, spiritual, self-existent, uncaused, and necessary being. The Bible's claim of the reality of God also explains the anthropic principle, which says that from the very start of the universe, all the cosmic constants had to be precisely fine-tuned to produce life on earth as we know it. Any minute change in these constants would have aborted a universe suitable for life. Only an intelligent and supreme God could have regulated these constants, as a conductor directs a symphony orchestra.

The biblical claim of the reality of God best explains the irreducible complexities we find in the biological world, both at the microscopic and macroscopic levels. A random collision of atoms and molecules or successive addition of building blocks could not have formed these irreducible complexities. The human genome, for instance, which codes for billions of bits of information and guides the transfer and translation of the encrypted message to produce various proteins in the cell, declares the handiwork of God, not the mindless and purposeless assembly of atoms and molecules from a primordial soup.

The reality of God affirms that God created us and put us on the earth for a purpose, which is to glorify Him (Isa. 43:7; Rev. 4:11). To glorify God does not mean that somehow, we can add to God's glory. He is infinitely glorious, so we cannot add to or subtract from His glory. But what we can do is reflect His glory in all that we do (John 17:4). God reveals His glory through both the saved and unsaved persons. Through the former, He shows His mercy, and through the latter, His justice.

Second, we learn of the eternality of God. "For this is God, our God forever and ever." The law of causality tells that every effect has a cause. The universe is an effect; therefore, it has a causal agent. The Bible calls this agent God. Who caused the existence of God? No one! As a necessary being, He transcends causality, for He always is, has been, and will be. He has no beginning and no end. He is forever and ever (Deut. 33:27; 1 Tim. 1:17). The eternality of God assures us that we can approach Him anytime and anywhere. He is always there to meet us at our point of need.

Third, we learn of the activity of God. "He will be our guide even to death." The God of the Bible is not the absentee God of deists such as Thomas Jefferson. The God of the Bible is very active, and He guides all that He has created toward their predetermined end. The writer of Hebrews reminds us that God in Christ is "upholding all things by the word of His power" (Heb. 1:3). This means that God guides and moves all things—people, nature, and history—toward their final destiny.

What this means for us is that our God is very much involved in our lives. He is not only a transcendent God, but He is also an immanent God. He says, "I will instruct you and teach you in the way you should go; I will guide you with My eye" (Ps. 32:8). Would you like to be guided by this God? If you would, you first need to make Him "your God." Our text says, "For this is God, our God." How do you make Him your

God? You do so by surrendering your life to Jesus Christ, who is the express image of God (Heb. 1:2). Call upon the name of the Lord Jesus Christ and believe in Him today. He will be your God, and you will be a part of His people.

# The Incarnate Word

In the beginning was the Word, and the Word was with God, and the Word was God.

—John 1:1

We hear many messages about Christ's first advent during the Christmas season and its implications to the world. An expression you are likely to hear often is, "And the Word became flesh and dwelt among us" (John 1:14). "Word," as used in John 1:1, is the translation of the Greek word *logos*. However, the term *logos* represents much more than the "words" that are spoken or written. Theologically, it carries a profound meaning, which will make the Christmas story transformative if we understand it rightly.

First, we need to know what the word *logos* meant in the Jewish context or to the Jewish mind. To the Jewish thinker, *logos* represented the divine word (or divine communication). In the parable of the sower, Jesus referred to the seed as the "word of God" (Luke 8:11). In several other biblical passages, we find God's communication as the "word of God" (2 Chron. 11:2; 17:3; Ps. 107:11; Prov. 30:5; Matt. 4:4; Mark 7:13; Luke 3:2; John 3:3; Acts 6:7; Eph. 6:17). Interestingly, during the Babylonian captivity, the Hebrew Scripture (Tanakh) was translated into Aramaic to benefit the Jews living in Babylon who were not fluent in Hebrew. The translated Tanakh was called Targum. Because the word *Yahweh* was so holy and transcendent, the translator avoided taking the name of God in vain by using the Aramaic term *memra*, which means "the word of God." For example, in Exodus 19:17, we read: "And Moses brought the people out of the camp to meet with God, and they stood at the foot of the mountain." In the Targum, it says that Moses brought the people to meet with *memra* or the word of God. Thus, theologically speaking, the term *logos* is synonymous with divine communication.

Second, to the ancient Jew, *logos* represented divine wisdom (*sophia*). *Logos* was the wisdom behind all that exists or is created. Philo (20 B.C.–A.D. 50), the Alexandrian Jewish philosopher, called the *logos* "the tiller by which the pilot of the universe steers all things." He also thought of *logos* as the mediator between God and man. Thus, *logos* or the word of God possessed creative powers. It not only said something, but it also did something. "Then God said, 'Let there be light;' and there was light" (Gen. 1:3). "The Lord by wisdom founded the earth; by understanding He established the heavens; by His knowledge the depths were broken up, and clouds drop down the dew" (Prov. 3:19–20).

But to grasp the full scope of the meaning of *logos*, we must also consider what the word meant to the Greeks. Heraclitus (560 B.C), who famously said, "One never steps into the same river twice," thought that *logos* is the mind that keeps the world from falling apart or becoming chaotic. *Logos* holds the universe in order. Plato believed that *logos* kept the planets in their courses. The New Testament theologian William Barclay argues that the apostle John brilliantly combined the Jewish and Greek understanding of the term *logos* to communicate with his audience that Jesus is the "creative power of God" and the "incarnate mind of God" Or "the mind of God became a man."[42]

In John 1:1–4, John gives us a more in-depth understanding of Jesus as the *logos*. First, we learn about the preeminence of

---

42. William Barclay, *New Testament Words* (Louisville: Westminster John Knox Press, 1974), 188.

Jesus. "In the beginning was the Word [*logos*]." The Greek word, *arche,* translated as "beginning," points to Jesus being first in time and importance. Second, we learn about the personality of Jesus. "And the Word was with God." Third, we learn about the deity of Jesus. "And the Word was God." Fourth, we learn of the eternality of Jesus. "He was in the beginning with God." Fifth, we learn about the creativity of Jesus Christ. "All things were made through Him, and without Him nothing was made that was made. In Him was life, and the life was the light of men" (John 1:3–4). For John, Jesus was the supreme and personal revelation of God.

Jesus Christ, the eternal *logos*, came down to the earth to reconcile us with God. This, indeed, is the beauty and the glory of Christmas. My prayer for you is that Jesus, the Word incarnate, will find His habitation in you and that you will experience the glory of Christmas.

# The Reciprocity of Divine Judgment

For with what judgment you judge, you will be judged;
and with the measure you use, it will be measured back
to you.

—Matthew 7:2

The Bible teaches that God's judgment is always true (Ps. 19:9; John 8:16; Rev. 16:7; 19:2). When Jesus was reviled by His enemies, He did not revile in return, but committed Himself to His Father in heaven, who judges righteously (1 Peter 2:23). The Father has appointed Jesus to be the judge of all (John 5:22; Acts 17:31). Because Jesus is one with the Father in nature (essence), His judgment represents the judgment of God, the Father. Jesus said, "I can of Myself do nothing. As I hear, I judge; and My judgment is righteous, because I do not seek My own will but the will of the Father who sent Me" (John 5:30).

God is the ultimate judge of all (2 Tim. 4:1, 8; Heb. 10:30; 12:23; 1 Peter 1:17). He does not judge us based on our appearance, but on the condition of our heart and His holy standard. In His earthly ministry, Jesus focused on saving the world, not judging the world (Luke 12:14; John 8:15). However, Jesus will return to be the judge of all (Acts 17:31). Because God in Christ is the only judge of all, when we judge people, we assume the prerogative of God and put ourselves at the risk of being judged by God (Rom. 2:1). Jesus said, "For with what judgment you judge, you will be judged, and with the measure you use, it will be measured back to you" (Matt. 7:2). The apostle Paul wrote, "Therefore judge nothing before the time, until the Lord comes, who will both bring to light the hidden things of darkness and reveal the counsels of the hearts" (1 Cor. 4:5).

History bears witness to the fact that God judges with equity (Ps. 98:9). In Isaiah 47, we read about God using Babylon's sinful inclinations to do evil as His instrument to punish Judah for its sins. But, when Babylon's cruelty toward Judah went out of bounds, God unleashed His fury and judgment on Babylon. Listen to what God said to Babylon: "For I was angry with my chosen people and punished them by letting them fall into your hands. But you, Babylon, showed them no mercy. You oppressed even the elderly. So, disaster will overtake you, and you won't be able to charm it away. Calamity will fall upon you, and you won't be able to buy your way out. A catastrophe will strike you suddenly, one for which you are not prepared" (Isa. 47: 6, 11 NLT). In Jeremiah 25, God says that Babylon was "His servant" to punish Judah and take them into captivity for seventy years. Then God says, "I will punish the king of Babylon and that nation, the land of the Chaldeans, for their iniquity" (Jer. 25:12 ESV).

Those who judge others outside biblically sanctioned church discipline settings (Matt. 18:15–20; 1 Cor. 5:1–7) will do so at their peril. They will not escape the reciprocity of God's judgment. Jesus said, "Judge not, and you shall not be judged. Condemn not, and you shall not be condemned. Forgive, and you will be forgiven" (Luke 6:37). God's reciprocity is evident when we judge (John 7:1–2), forgive (Matt. 6:145), and give (Luke 6:38).

The Bible says, "Do not be deceived, God is not mocked; for whatever a man sows, that he will also reap" (Gal. 6:7). We all suffer the effects of our sinful deeds irrespective of who we are. Therefore, the Bible encourages us to judge ourselves.

"For if we judge ourselves, we would not be judged" (1 Cor. 11:31). I pray that we would be quick to remove the plank from our own eyes before we try to take the speck from another's eye (Luke 6:42). When we judge ourselves, we will be drawn to the gospel because only in the gospel do we find the power for reconciliation and forgiveness.

# A Grand Reversal

And the LORD spoke to Moses, saying, "Speak to all the
congregation of the children of Israel, and say to them:
'You shall be holy, for I the LORD your God *am* holy.'"

—Leviticus 19:1–2

God said to the Israelites, "You shall be holy, for I the LORD
your God *am* holy" (Lev. 19:1). The apostle Peter repeats this
divine imperative when he quotes it to encourage us to be holy
in our conduct (1 Peter 1:14–16). Both in the Old and New
Testaments, holiness conveys the idea of being separated or
cut off from the unholy. It means to be separated from sin and
set apart for God. Personal holiness, therefore, is not an option
but an obligation. Oswald Chambers notes: "The destined end
of man is not happiness, nor health, but holiness."[43] The Bible
says, "Pursue peace with all people, and holiness, without
which no one will see the Lord" (Heb. 12:14).

Under the old covenant, there were three ritual states:
unclean, clean, and holy. These ritual states had nothing to do
with hygiene, but they governed what people could or could
not do or where they could or could not go. For example, a
ritually unclean person could not make a peace offering
(Lev. 7:20). Similarly, a person declared unclean due to
contracting leprosy was put outside the camp until cured of the
disease and made clean. Or a ceremonially unclean priest was

---

43. Oswald Chambers, *My Utmost For His Highest* (Westwood: Barbour and
Company, 1963), 180.

prohibited from offering sacrifices. Another critical characteristic of ritual holiness was that it was not indirectly transferable. For example, if a piece of meat dedicated for sacrifice (considered holy) was wrapped in a garment, and if the garment came in contact with another object, the holiness of the meat was not transferred from the garment to the third object.

On the other hand, a person who became unclean by contacting a dead body polluted everything he touched. Thus, uncleanness or defilement was transferable (Hag. 2:10–15).

When Jesus, the Holy Son of God, came into this world, He profoundly reversed the holiness transferability. In Matthew 8:3, we read that Jesus touched a leper and made him clean. In handling the leper, Jesus was not defiled; instead, the leper was made clean. In the village of Nain, Jesus saw a dead body being carried for burial, the only son of a widowed mother. Jesus was moved with compassion and said to her, "Do not weep." Then He went near the coffin and touched the bier and raised the dead man. Jesus did not become ceremonially unclean when he touched the dead body. Instead, the dead man was brought to life.

How are we to understand holiness under the new covenant? In Christ, holiness is the most transferable of all attributes of God. The holiness of God is not transferred, but we are made holy by becoming partakers of the divine nature (2 Peter 1:4). Under the old covenant, one was able to be ritually holy without being morally righteous. The relationship between God and people was based on a legal transaction. But in the new covenant, holiness is born out of a love relationship with God and a changed heart. Holiness works itself out from within and is manifested in our conduct. God's demands don't change, but He gives us the power to follow His commands through His indwelling Spirit. St. Augustine understood this truth well when he prayed: "Give what you command, and command what you will."[44]

At a practical level, holiness has to do with our public and private behavior. It is fascinating to note that right after God says, "You shall be holy, for I the LORD your God am holy," God instructs the Israelites, "Every one of you shall revere his mother and his father" (Lev. 19:2–3). The apostle Peter wastes no time connecting our behavior with holiness: "As He who called you is holy, you also be holy in all your conduct, because it is written, '*Be holy, for I am holy*'" (1 Peter 1:15–16).

The character of God determines how we behave and the standard for our behavior. That is why God's people who seek to live holy lives should seek to know God experientially and grow in the knowledge of God as revealed in the Scripture. Holiness makes God's people radically different from the unbelievers in their conduct and values. Peter calls God's people" a holy nation, His own special people (1 Peter 1:9). James calls them "unspotted from the world" (James 1:27).

Friend, God has chosen us before the foundation of the world that we should be "holy and blameless before him" (Eph. 1:4). Therefore, we can be holy in our conduct because God who called and dwells within us is Holy!

---

44. Augustine, *Confessions*, trans. and ed. Philip Burton (New York: Alfred A. Knopf, 2001), 239.

# DEVOTIONAL

For those who live according to the flesh set their minds on the things of the flesh, but those who live according to the Spirit the things of the Spirit.

—Romans 8:5

Man, made in the image of God, has a purpose—to be in relationship to God, who is there. Man forgets his purpose and thus he forgets who he is and what life means.

—Francis Schaeffer

# Is God a Fading Reality in Your Life?

Unless the God of my father, the God of Abraham and the Fear of Isaac, had been with me, surely now you would have sent me away empty-handed. God has seen my affliction and the labor of my hands, and rebuked *you* last night.

—Genesis 31:42

Can a self-existent, immutable, and omnipotent God fade in His person or power? No! But He may wane in our experience and consciousness. With each passing generation, human experience shows that there may be a lack of clarity in how that generation perceives God and a diminution in its understanding of God.

Genesis 31 captures a snippet of Jacob's life. After twenty years of lackeying for his uncle, Laban, Jacob had enough of his life of servitude. He decided to return to his home and his father, Isaac, in Canaan. One morning, Jacob packed up his belongings, and taking his wives, children, and livestock, left Laban without telling him. When Laban learned that Jacob had escaped, he pursued and caught up with him in the mountains of Gilead. During that encounter, an argument ensued between the two, and Jacob said: "Unless the God of my father, the God of Abraham and the Fear of Isaac, had been with me, surely now you would have sent me away empty-handed. God has seen my affliction and the labor of my hands, and rebuked you last night" (Gen. 31:42).

Notice how Jacob identified God's relationship with his grandfather, Abraham, and with his father, Isaac. To Abraham, God was the God of Abraham. Abraham was so close to God that the Bible gives him the appellation "friend of God" (James 2:3). God's relationship with Abraham was so intimate that He would not destroy Sodom without telling Abraham what He was about to do. God said: "Shall I hide from Abraham what I am doing, since Abraham shall surely become a great and mighty nation, and all the nations of the earth shall be blessed in him?" (Gen. 18:17–18). So, for Abraham, God was his *friend*.

In the next generation—Isaac's generation—God was the fear of Isaac. Isaac's relationship with God was different from Abraham's. Isaac knew that he was the inheritor of God's promises to Abraham, but his relationship with God was limited to fearing Him. Isaac enjoyed a comfortable life, living off his father's inheritance, eating tasty food, and drinking from the wells his father had dug years earlier. His life was not marked by any remarkable achievements. In the end, he was buried in a tomb that was paid for by his father. Compared to Abraham, Isaac's relationship with God was merely marked by awe for God. For Isaac, God was his *awe*.

By the time the third generation came around—Jacob's generation— God had faded in Jacob's experience such that He had descended to becoming the "God of my father." For Jacob, the supplanter and drifter, God morphed into being just a *provider* of him. Jacob had taken a utilitarian view: God would attend to his needs and make his life safe and secure. On his way to the house of Laban, Jacob made a vow: "If God will be with me and keep me in this way that I am going and give me bread to eat and clothing to put on, so that I come back to my father's house in peace, then the LORD shall be my God" (Gen. 28:20–21) Jacob was only interested in what God could give him. If God gave him all he asked for, then God would be "his God." For Jacob, God was his *provider*.

Today, many people live as Jacob lived, drifting along in life, living in servitude, and turning to God for what He can do for them. God is not their *friend* nor their *awe*; He is only their *provider*. The path upward from God being a *provider* to *awe* to a *friend* is only possible when God finds us as God found Jacob at the ford of Jabbok. At Jabbok, God, who had faded into a service provider in Jacob's life, wrestled with Jacob and became a life changer. He changed Jacob from a man of machinations into a person struggling with God and prevailing, seeing God face to face (Gen. 32:22–32). Jacob had an amazing epiphany.

Is God a fading reality in your life? If so, you can begin your journey back to God, where God can be your friend. Only God in Christ can make this possible. Jesus said to His disciples, "No longer do I call you servants…. but I have called you friends" (John 15:15). The road to friendship with God runs through Christ. Will you take that road by believing in Jesus Christ as your Savior and Lord?

# Quieted by God's Love

In that day it shall be said to Jerusalem: "Do not fear; Zion, let not your hands be weak. The LORD your God in your midst, the Mighty One, will save; He will rejoice over you with gladness, He will quiet *you* with His love, He will rejoice over you with singing."

—Zephaniah 3:16–17

One morning, I was meditating on Zephaniah 3:17 during my personal time with the Lord. Seven words leaped off this verse as a beam of light and refreshed my heart: "He will quiet you by His love" (ESV). Oh, how I needed to hear those words from the lover of my soul! When chaos, turmoil, anxiety, uncertainty, doubt, restlessness, and fear surround me like a vast ocean, I can still float like a balloon with the buoyancy of hope because the Lord will quiet me by His love.

The prophet Zephaniah warned the southern kingdom of Judah about the coming day of the Lord, in which He would judge Israel for oppressing the poor, not obeying the voice of God and receiving His correction, not trusting in the Lord, and not drawing near to Him (Zeph. 3:1–2). Having warned Israel, God hastened to assure His people that a faithful remnant (Jews and Gentiles) will remain when the fury of His judgment abates. This faithful remnant will come under the reign of the Messiah and worship Him in righteousness and truth (Zeph. 3:9–10). On that day of the fullness of the messianic rule on earth, God will dwell among His people and quiet them with His love.

But what does this beautiful messianic promise mean to us today? It means that we can now individually experience the blessing of God's kingdom— the quieting of our soul by God's love—when we come under the kingship, rule, and authority of Jesus Christ. He came to inaugurate the kingdom of God in our hearts now, which will find its consummate manifestation when Christ returns. During the present time, described as "already and not yet," all who are in Christ stand to experience and foretaste the presence, power, and provisions of God's rule in their lives while awaiting the fullness of God's kingdom.

God in Christ quiets us amid our troubles because we are the object of His love. His love for us is not conditioned by who we are, what we have, or what others say about us. We have peace and rest because we are the people of God, and He is our God.

Friend, I don't know what may be weighing on your heart or what anxieties you may be having at the moment. But you can count on God to quiet your soul, for you are the object of His love.

# God's Power Is Made Perfect in Weakness

And He [God] said to me, "My grace is sufficient for you, for My strength is made perfect in weakness." Therefore most gladly I will rather boast in my infirmities, that the power of Christ may rest upon me.

—2 Corinthians 12:9

This text summarizes one of the dominant themes of this epistle of Paul. The apostle Paul was afflicted by a "thorn in the flesh," which he implored the Lord three times to remove from him.[45] But God comforted him, saying, "My grace is sufficient for you, for my power is made perfect in weakness."

We must make two observations to interpret the meaning and application of this text correctly. First, though the possessive pronoun "My" is not found in some manuscripts, especially the best ones, the word "strength" refers to the "power of Christ." "My" does not refer to Paul's inherent power or strength. Furthermore, the sufficiency of God's grace

---

45. There is no unanimous agreement among scholars about what Paul meant by "a thorn in the flesh." Some of the most popular theories about Paul's thorn in the flesh included a chronic eye problem, speech impediment, and other physical ailments. I believe that the context of 2 Corinthians 12:7 indicates what the thorn in the flesh was. Paul said it was a messenger sent by Satan to "buffet" him. He then identifies this messenger as "infirmities" such as persecutions, reproaches, distresses, and constant opposition to his preaching of the gospel (2 Cor. 12:10).

and the perfection of His power stated in 2 Corinthians 12:9 is in the "present indicative active," meaning that Paul was simultaneously experiencing these divine graces while writing this letter. A literal translation of the verse might be: "And He has said to me, 'sufficing to you is the grace of Me, for [My] power is being perfected in weakness.'"

Second, the key to correctly understanding and applying this text are the words "made perfect." The Greek verb *teleioutai* translated as "made perfect" does not mean that the power of Christ is somehow deficient and needs to be perfected. The power of Christ has no inherent deficiency. One cannot add to or delete from the power of Christ. Yes, sometimes our lack of faith may hinder the manifestation of God's power (Matt. 6:5–6), but never causes a diminution in His power. The Lord's power is complete, from beginning to end, and cannot be made perfect or more powerful.

So how are we to understand the meaning and application of these words in this verse? The word *teleioutai* should be taken to mean "attain a purpose, bring to an end, accomplish a predetermined purpose, or achieve a goal." Jesus used this same word to declare that His work of atonement was brought to its finish: before He commended His Spirit to the Father, He said, "It is finished]" (John 19:30). In John 17:4, Jesus said, "I have finished the work you gave me to do."

What goal or purpose was God accomplishing with Paul? I suggest that the goal was to bring Paul to the point of utter weakness and dependency. When Paul came to that point, God's purpose or task was finished. But why get him to the point of utter weakness? For one thing, the power of Christ was made demonstrably evident in his infirmity. The Lord allowed Satan to harass Paul so that he would remain humble, not become conceited because of the beatific vision he had of God of the third heaven and stay dependent on Him. God needed to keep Paul humble and dependent on Him lest he lift himself and become unfit for the Master's service.

God is always attracted to weakness. Unless we decrease, Christ cannot increase in us or be made visible to others. God's power shines brightly when our "self" gets out of the way, and we become obscure. We are unfit for the Lord's service if we think we can lick our wounds or lift ourselves by our bootstraps. But when we are reduced to utter nothingness, then the *purpose* of God is reached.

It is very instructive to note that the words "And He said to me" are in the past perfect tense, which describes an action in the past but with results that continuing into the present. This suggests that what God said to Paul in the first century still holds true for us who live in the twenty-first century. Its truthfulness remains unchanged! Unanswered prayers may be a mystery to us but not to God. In His sovereign grace, He uses our infirmities and weaknesses to glorify Himself in ways we may never fully comprehend.

# Should We Be Thankful or Grateful to God?

> In everything give thanks; for this is the will of God in Christ Jesus for you.
>
> —1 Thessalonians 5:18

Thanksgiving is an important day on our national calendar. On that day, we gather with our families to express our gratitude and thanks to God for His benevolence and blessings throughout the year. In 1621, the English pilgrims of Plymouth and Wampanoag Indians gathered together to thank God for the bountiful harvest they had that year. The New England colonists regularly observed a day of thanksgiving and prayer for divine blessings such as "military victory or the end of a drought." On October 3, 1863, President Abraham Lincoln proclaimed Thursday, November 26, as the National Day of Thanksgiving. Since that time, we have set aside the last Thursday of November as the day of thanksgiving.

The apostle Paul wrote, "In everything give thanks; for this is the will of God in Christ Jesus for you" (1 Thess. 5:18). It is interesting to note that the Bible uses the words "thanks," "thanksgiving," or "thankfulness" to describe our response to God's favor and grace toward us. The Bible does not say "be grateful to God" for what He has done. Whenever we see the words "grateful" or "gratitude" in an English translation of the Bible as they relate to our response to God, the original word in Hebrew or Greek more accurately means to be thankful or joyful.

I recognize that we use "gratitude" and "thanks" interchangeably to express our appreciation to God. But technically, thankfulness is more appropriate than gratitude when referring to our response to God's goodness. The reason is that gratitude carries a debtor's obligation with it, requiring one to reciprocate in kind for a favor received from another. It is customary in some parts of our country to say "much obliged" instead of "thank you" when a person gets something good from another. Gratitude invokes what social psychologists call "the law of reciprocity." For example, if someone invited you for dinner, you most likely want to reciprocate by asking that person to dinner with you.

Can we apply this law of reciprocity to the grace we have received from the Lord? The psalmist asked, "What shall I render to the LORD for all His benefits?" He answered his own question, saying, "I will offer to you the sacrifice of thanksgiving, and will call upon the name of the LORD" (Ps. 116:12, 17). The apostle Paul, quoting Job 41:11, exclaimed: "Who has given a gift to him [God] that he might be repaid?" (Rom. 11:35 ESV) Nobody! It is because "from him [God] and through him and to him are all things. To him be glory forever" (Rom. 11:36 ESV). We can give nothing to God in payment for His goodness because everything we have already belongs to Him. As theologian John Piper noted, even if we could pay back God for what He has done, "we would only succeed in turning grace into a business transaction."[46]

Let us make every day a Thanksgiving Day and approach God not with a debtor's ethic but with a thankful heart for God's gracious gifts. "Therefore by Him let us continually offer the sacrifice of praise to God, that is, the fruit of our lips,

---

46. John Piper, *A Godward Life; Savoring the Supremacy of God in All of Life* (Sisters: Multnomah Publishers, 1997), 36.

giving thanks to His name. But do not forget to do good and to share, for with such sacrifices God is well pleased" (Heb. 13:15–16). Let us thank God for giving us His Son, Jesus Christ, in whom we are made complete; for making us, who are poor, rich in Christ, and for God's promise to meet our needs according to Christ's riches in glory. When we are thankful to God for what He has done, our thanksgiving also finds a tangible and God-pleasing expression—sharing what we have with those in need.

# Other-Minded Thanksgiving

We give thanks to God always for you all, making
mention of you in our prayers, remembering without
ceasing your work of faith, labor of love, and patience of
hope in our Lord Jesus Christ in the sight of our God
and Father, knowing, beloved brethren, your election by
God.

—1 Thessalonians 1:2–4

There is an old French proverb that says, "Gratitude is the
memory of the heart." William Thayer (1820–1898), American
historian and writer, wrote, "Where there is no memory of the
heart, there is an absence of grateful feelings. Thankfulness is
an expression of a grateful feeling. Character is essentially
defective without this element of gratitude."[47]

Is your heart filled with grateful feelings? Do you remember
what the Lord has done? God's will for our lives is that we give
thanks to God in everything. The apostle Paul wrote, "In
everything, give thanks; for this is the will of God in Christ
Jesus concerning you" (1 Thess. 5:18). The Bible teaches that
giving thanks is a sacrifice that truly honors God (Ps. 50:23).
To fail to thank God for His benefits is to trample His grace.

When we think of thanksgiving, we invariably think of
giving thanks to God for all the blessings He has bestowed on

---

47. William M. Thayer, *Gaining Favor With God And Man* (San Antonio:
Mantle Ministries, 1989), 338. Mr. Thayer originally published the book in
1893.

us. The psalmist asked: "What shall I render to the LORD for all His benefits toward me?" (Ps. 116:12). I want to encourage you to thank God for what He has done and is doing in the lives of your friends, family, and colleagues.

In 1 Thessalonians 1:2–10, the apostle Paul models for us what I call "others-minded thanksgiving." He wrote, "We give thanks to God always for you all." Paul and his partners in the ministry—Silas and Timothy—were motivated to thank God for the believers at Thessalonica. You will agree that it is quite natural for us to be self-minded when giving thanks to God: that is, to give thanks for what He has done for us. But it takes a profound sense of community and unity with members of the body of Christ to give thanks to God for others. In 1Thessalonians 1, the apostle Paul gives us three expressions of others-minded thanksgiving.

First, we can thank God for others by our supplication. Paul wrote, "We give thanks to God always for you all, making mention of you in our prayers." The Greek word *prosuche* refers to general prayer, but in this case, it was a prayer of thanksgiving, mentioning the believers in Thessalonica. Paul prayed for them always. Let us not forget to take time to pray, making mention of our neighbors, friends, coworkers, church family, and spiritual leaders. Praying for others is a beautiful expression of others-minded thanksgiving to God.

Second, we can thank God for others by our recollection. Paul wrote, "Remembering without ceasing your work of faith, and labor of love, and patience of hope in our Lord Jesus Christ." Paul took the time to remember what God was doing in the lives of the believers at Thessalonica. Their faith was not a dead faith, but a living faith. Their love was expressed in action. Their patience was rooted in the blessed hope of the sure return of Jesus Christ. Paul was quick to remember their love, faith, and labor for Christ.

Can you recall one or two things God has been doing for His glory in the lives of people you commonly associate with?

The psalmist said, "Bless the LORD, O my soul and forget not all His benefits" (Ps. 103:2). The benefits of God include what He is doing in the lives of others around you. So, make it a point to identify one or two specific things God has done or is doing in the lives of at least three people close to you and thank the Lord for His goodness and faithfulness toward them. This is also an excellent time to remember those who are in need that you can help tangibly. The Bible says, "Do not neglect to do good and to share what you have, for such sacrifices are pleasing to God" (Heb. 13:16 ESV).

Third, we can thank God for others by our commendation. In verses 6–10, the apostle Paul commends the Christians at Thessalonica for their imitation of Christ, representing a joyful life and proclamation of the transforming gospel. While Paul thanked the Lord for what God was doing in the lives of Christians at Thessalonica, he made sure to commend their progress in the faith. Take the time to commend the Christian virtues we find in those close to us and thank God for them. We can make our commendation by a telephone call, a short note, an email, or a personal conversation.

Shakespeare's Hamlet says, "Beggar that I am, I am even poor in thanks."[48] Let us not be "poor" in giving thanks to God for those who have had a positive impact on us. May the Lord help us to engage in others-minded thanksgiving through our supplication, recollection, and commendation. Like the apostle Paul, let us say to those around us, "I thank my God upon every remembrance of you" (Phil. 1:3).

---

48. *Hamlet* II, ii, 286.

# Growing in Love

So he answered and said, "You shall love the LORD your God with all your heart, with all your soul, with all your strength, and with all your mind, and your neighbor as yourself."

—Luke 10:27

On May 5, 2000, millions of people around the globe unwittingly opened an email with the subject line "I LOVE YOU" and an attachment entitled "LOVE-LETTER-FOR-YOU." When the attachment was opened, it activated a computer virus that corrupted their document, image, and audio files. The virus also sent a copy of itself to all the addresses in the user's address book. Computer experts estimated that this virus caused $5–$10 billion in damage worldwide. This all happened because those who opened this email were fascinated to read that someone loved them and wanted to know who it was.

We all want to love and be loved. Indeed, love is an intense expression of our being. This should not be surprising, for we are born with the capacity to love because God, who created us in His image, is love (1 John 4:8). Jesus said: "You shall love the LORD your God with all your heart, with all your soul, with all your strength, and with all your mind, and your neighbor as yourself" (Luke 10:27).

Our ability to love others or seek their greater good, irrespective of who they are, flows from our love for God. Loving God and loving others are inextricably linked; we cannot do one without the other (1 John 4:20–21). How do we grow in loving God and others? St. Bernard of Clairvaux (1090–1153), a French abbot who founded the Cistercian order, helps answer this question. In his treatise *On Loving God*, he wrote of the four stages or degrees of love.[49]

The first stage of love is to love oneself for self's sake. This is selfish love, whereby a person, like a newborn infant, only thinks of self-gratification and is preoccupied with selfish interests. The way to keep in check this selfish love, according to St. Bernard, is by loving our neighbor, knowing that God is the source of love, and trusting Him for our personal needs.

The second stage of love is to love God for self's sake. Though we may think that we are self-made and can stand on our own, the reality is that sometimes we run into storms of life that move us to seek God's help. Our unmet needs drive us to God, and in the process, we experience His goodness. We soon learn that we cannot live independent of God and begin to love Him, even if that love serves as a means for meeting our needs.

In the third stage of love, we love God for God's sake. As we experience the goodness and grace of God, we learn who God is and love Him for Himself (Ps. 49:18). "No longer do we love God because of our necessity, but because we have tasted and seen how gracious the Lord is."[50] Once we start loving God for Himself, it becomes easier to love our neighbor, for "whosoever loves God aright loves all God's creatures."[51]

The fourth stage of love is to love oneself for God's sake. At this stage, our will and affections are subsumed in God so

49. Richard J. Foster and James B. Smith, eds; *Devotional Classics* (New York: HarperCollins Publishers, 1980), 40.

50. Robert Imperato, *Early And Medieval Christian Spirituality* (New York: University Press of America, 2002), 115.

51. Ibid.

that His will becomes ours. St. Bernard wrote, "Blessed are we who experience the fourth degree of love wherein we love ourselves for God's sake."[52] As a drop of water poured into wine loses itself, so we forget ourselves when we are transmuted into the will of God. We desire none but God, and whatever we do, we do for His sake (Ps. 73:25). At this point, we genuinely love God with all our hearts, soul, mind, and strength.

Is it possible for us to love God and our neighbor perfectly in this life? Not really! Even in our redeemed state, we still live with a fallen nature and are subject to the cares and vicissitudes of life. We must await the return of Christ and our glorification for perfection. We must still seek to grow in loving God, others, and ourselves in obedience to the command of Christ. It is a journey that begins by embracing God's love lavished upon us on the cross. The Bible says, "We love Him because He first loved us" (1 John 4:19).

The power to love others in a giving, forgiving, and unchanging way is a gift of the Holy Spirit (Rom. 5:5; Gal. 5:22). We make progress in this journey by living a relinquished life: that is, dying daily to self (1 Cor. 15:31), whereby we can say, "I have been crucified with Christ; it is no longer I who live, but Christ lives in me; and the life which I now live in the flesh I live by faith in the Son of God, who loved me and gave Himself for me." (Gal. 2:20).

---

52. Richard J. Foster and James B. Smith, eds; *Devotional Classics*, 42.

# Always Pray

Pray without Ceasing.

—1 Thessalonians 5:17

Of all the activities we can engage in, the one activity that moves the very heart of God is praying. Prayer changes things. Certain things happen in history only when we pray. E. M. Bounds wrote:

> This [prayer] is the high calling of the [people] of the church, and no calling is so engaging, so engrossing and so valuable that we can afford to relieve Christian men from the all-important vocation of secret prayer. Nothing whatever can take the place of prayer. Nothing whatever can atone for the neglect of praying. This is uppermost, first in point of importance and first in point of time. No man is so high in position, or in grace, to be exempt from an obligation to pray. No man is too big to pray, no matter who he is, nor what office he fills. The king on his throne is as much obligated to pray as the peasant in his cottage. None is so high and exalted in this world or so lowly and obscure as to be excused from praying.[53]

During the COVID pandemic, many Christians worldwide earnestly prayed for God to restrain the pandemic. The Bible

---

53. E. M. Bounds, *The Complete Works Of E. M. Bounds On Prayer* (Grand Rapids: Baker Book House, 1990), 393–394.

teaches that we must constantly pray (1 Thess. 5:17). Let the soothing aroma of our prayers, praise, and pleas continue to reach the nostrils of God. One day, as I was praying for India and our nation, the Lord led me to develop the word "prayer" into an acrostic. I am aware of the several helpful acrostics developed by others about prayer, and I thank the Lord for those aids. I trust you will find my acrostic below useful.

**P**raising: Prayer, by nature, is seeking an audience with the Sovereign King of the universe. As such, our prayer would be incomplete if it did not include words exalting the One to whom we are praying. When the Sanhedrin threatened Peter and John with imprisonment and punishment if they did not stop proclaiming Jesus, they went to their companions to pray. They prayed together, saying, "Lord, You are God, who made heaven and earth and the sea, and all that is in them" (Acts 4:24). Daniel began His prayer for those in captivity with these words of exaltation: "O Lord, great and awesome God, who keeps His covenant and mercy with those who love Him..." (Dan. 9:4).

**R**epenting: The prayer that moves the heart of God is one in which the petitioners admit their sinfulness and desperate need of God. Daniel prayed for Judah while he was in captivity in Babylon (Dan. 9). He began his prayer by admitting his sins and the sins of his people (Dan. 9:5). Repentance is a necessary condition for answered prayers (Ps. 66:18).

**A**sking: At the fundamental level, prayer is asking—nothing more and nothing less (Matt. 7:8; 21:22; Mark 11:24; Luke 11:10; John 16:24; James 4:3; 1 John 3:22). The inviolable condition for receiving from God is asking. "You do not have because you do not ask" (James 4:2).

**Y**ielding: Many are people's plans, but only God's counsel will come to pass (Prov. 19:21). In the end, we must be willing to yield our will to the will of God. Jesus exemplified this profoundly in His prayer in Gethsemane. In that prayer, He succinctly demonstrated the principle of submission. He prayed: "O My Father, if it is possible, let this cup pass from Me; nevertheless, not as I will, but as You will" (Matt. 26:39). As we yield our will to God by the aid of the Holy Spirit, we learn to pray according to God's will (1 John 5:14).

Expecting: Based on our history with God, we must expect God to respond to our prayers. In our prayer, we must remember and echo what God has done for us in the past. When the Moabites and the Ammonites went against Jehoshaphat, Jehoshaphat sought the Lord. In his prayer, he recalled what the Lord had done for Israel. He prayed: "Are you not our God, who drove out the inhabitants of this land before Your people Israel and gave it to the descendants of Abraham Your friend forever?" (2 Chron. 20:7). Jehoshaphat expected God to act based on his prior experience with God.

Resting: At any given time, the end of our prayer is when we come to rest in Christ, believing that He has heard our prayer. When we cast our burden on the Lord, the inevitable result should be a sense of relief and repose (Matt. 11:28–29). Jesus demonstrated this principle in His prayer at the tomb of Lazarus: "Father, I thank you that You have heard Me. And I know that You always hear Me" (John 11:40). What faithfulness, restfulness, and thankfulness!

Let us keep asking the Lord, who alone can grant what we ask according to His will.

# Are You Feeling Abandoned by God?

Be still, and know that I *am* God; I will be exalted among
the nations, I will be exalted in the earth!

—Psalm 46:10

We experience God in many ways. In general, there are two
pathways by which we experience Him: the cataphatic (or
*positive way*) and the apophatic (or *negative way*). These terms
refer to two ways of approaching God and experiencing Him,
and they "have a long history of usage in religious thought."[54]

The cataphatic path focuses on experiencing God through
the "richness of our created world," relating with other people,
participating in church functions, engaging in worship, and a
host of other activities in which we affirm the presence of God
(Pss. 16:11; 22:3). Most Christians are familiar with this avenue
of experiencing God's presence, comfort, and direction.[55]

But an infinite God is not limited to the cataphatic pathway
of knowing Him. It is a grave error to think that we can fully
capture an infinite God with our finite faculties and
experiences. The truth is that many times we find ourselves
traversing through what St. John of the Cross called "The dark
night of the soul." In such moments, God is beyond the reach

---

54. Sandra Cook, *Dark Nigh Journey: Inward Repatterning Toward a Life
Centered in God* (Wallingford: Pendle Hill Publications, 1993), 4.

55. Ibid.

of words, expressions, prayers, or anything we can do to tangibly experience Him. We may even feel abandoned by God. In such moments, silence before Him is the most appropriate response (Ps. 46:10). This is the apophatic pathway of experiencing God.

The apophatic pathway is not sufficiently appreciated by contemporary evangelicalism. I believe we should be open to both cataphatic and apophatic paths of experiencing God. Sandra Cronk captures the richness of the apophatic pathway: "The dark night is a time of preparation for a life lived more fully centered in God. In the stripping and emptiness, we discover that God bursts beyond all our previous avenues of knowing."[56] If you are presently traveling the apophatic pathway, take courage. God is stripping all the places, things, and people you have depended on for your security and meaning so He can fill that empty space with Himself (Col. 2:10).

---

56. Ibid., 5.

# God's Plan for Our Provision

And my God shall supply all your need according to His riches in glory by Christ Jesus.

—Philippians 4:19

Have you ever wondered what plan God has to provide for your needs? Wonder no more! Under the new covenant, God's primary means of supplying our needs fall into five categories:

**Working**— God created man for work (Gen. 1:26; 2:5; 1 Tim. 5:8). The primary means of providing for our needs is employment. "If anyone will not work, neither shall he eat" (2 Thess. 3:10).

**Sharing**—The church, which is the body of Christ on earth, is mandated to care for the poor and those in need (Acts 2:45; Rom. 15:25–27; 2 Cor. 8:1–4; 9:1–9; 1 Tim. 5:16; James 1:27).

**Bearing**—Christians are exhorted to bear one another's burdens and thus fulfill the law of Christ (Gal. 6:2). The Greek word *baros*, translated as "burdens," in Galatians 6:2, means a crushing weight. If someone is under unbearable weight, we are to go to their side and lift that load. We are urged not to hoard God's resources but rather to share them with those in need (1 Tim. 6:17–18; Eph. 4:28).

**Honoring**—Children are to honor their parents (Eph. 6:2). When children are small, they are instructed to obey their parents (Eph. 6:1). When they are young adults, they are to respect their parents (Heb. 12:9). But when they are older, they are to honor their parents. An important way of honoring is by taking care of parents in their old age if need be (Matt. 15:1–9). A son or daughter who fails to care for a parent in need is cursed and is considered worse than an infidel (1 Tim. 5:8).

**Parenting**—This involves a wide range of responsibilities. One aspect of responsible parenthood, as it relates to meeting material needs, is leaving an inheritance for the children (2 Cor. 12:14). Godly parents should endeavor to leave a portion of their estate for the care of their children.

Nowhere in the New Testament are we instructed to look to the government (Caesar, in Christ's day) for meeting our needs. God is our source, and He has prescribed five specific ways to meet our needs. If a government has a system to care for the poor, that is pleasing in God's sight.

# I Love You, Dad

Behold, the LORD'S hand is not shortened, that it cannot save; Nor His ear heavy that it cannot hear.

—Isaiah 59:1

You may have seen or heard the commercial about a hearing aid in which a son says to his father, "I love you, dad." Because the father cannot hear him well, he asks, "What?" The son says, "I love you, Dad," a second time. Again, the father asks, "What?" At this point, the commercial describes the superiority and cost-effectiveness of the hearing device, and the father buys the latest hearing aid. As the commercial ends, the son says to his father, "I love you, Dad." To the son's dismay, the father asks, "What?" as if he did not hear what had been said. Again, the son says, "I love you, Dad." But this time, the father responds, "I heard you the first time; I wanted to hear it again."

"I heard you the first time; I wanted to hear it again." What a heart-warming statement! When I heard that, I could not help thinking of my Father in heaven. He, too, hears me the first time I tell Him how much I love Him. If I do not feel that He heard me, I should not lose heart, because He heard me the first time and wants to hear from me again how much I love Him. I cannot depend on my feelings for divine affirmation. Feelings are fleeting and have no reality in themselves.

Victor Edman said, "Never doubt in the dark what God told you in the light."[57] So let us go by what God teaches us in the light of His Word. The Bible says, "The LORD'S arm is not too weak to save you, nor is his ear too deaf to hear you call" (Isa. 59:1 NLT). God takes pleasure when we adore Him and tell Him that we love Him. The Bible says, "The LORD takes pleasure in His people; He will beautify the meek with salvation" (Ps. 149:4). "The LORD has set apart for Himself him who is godly; the LORD will hear when I call to Him" (Ps. 4:3). It is good, pleasant, and beautiful to praise the Lord and extol His virtues (Pss. 106:1; 135:3; 147:1).

Given what we learn in the light of God's Word (the Bible), we can be confident that He always hears us the first time when we say, "I love You." And He wants to hear it again!

---

57. "Quote by Victor Raymond Edman," Christian Central Network, accessed June 1, 2022, https://christiancentral.net/quotes/victor-raymond-edman-never-doubt-dark/.

# Man Is Incurably Religious

> He has made everything beautiful in its time. Also He has put eternity in their hearts, except that no one can find out the work that God does from beginning to end.
>
> —Ecclesiastes 3:11

During Donald Trump's presidency, I saw a video clip on Facebook showing a man from India worshiping President Trump, whom he regarded as a god. He was very devoted to Trump and had built a small shrine in his home to offer his prayers to Trump. While it was amusing to watch this video clip, it reminded me of one of the fundamental characteristics of human nature: man is incurably religious.

There is a God-made vacuum in every human. The Bible says that God has put eternity in our hearts (Eccl. 3:11). This God-made vacuum can only be filled by the God of the Bible who has revealed Himself in nature, history, and ultimately in the person of Jesus Christ. St. Augustine rightly said, "You [God] stir us up to take delight in your praise; for you have made us for yourself, and our heart is restless till it finds its rest in you."[58] If the God of the Bible does not fill this vacuum in our hearts, we will fill it with counterfeit gods because we are incurably and inescapably religious.

The Hindu man who was seen worshipping President Trump was simply practicing a basic tenet of Hinduism. In Hinduism, it is not unusual for someone to worship a human

---

58. Augustine, *Confessions*, 5.

being, for Hinduism is a pantheistic belief system that says, "All is god and god is all." Furthermore, the distinction between the divine and human is blurred to the point that one overlaps the other. Hinduism recognizes Brahman as the ultimate reality: without form, impersonal, eternal, infinite, unknowable, and pure consciousness. Brahman is the only reality, and everything outside of Brahman is mere illusion or *maya*. We only see things as they appear to be but not as they are in themselves. All things, including humans, are mere expressions of Brahman, for Brahman pervades everything.

In contrast to Brahman, which is unknowable and indistinguishable from creation, the Bible's God is knowable and transcendent. He is distinct from and dimensionally beyond all that He has created, yet immanent. He is not distant from us, but rather is involved with His creation. He upholds all things by His power (Heb. 1:3). In other words, He is guiding and moving all that He has created toward their predetermined end.

It is possible that this Hindu man may have seen President Trump as an avatar or manifestation of one of the Hindu gods who has come down in a human form. It is a profound error to equate the Hindu concept of the avatar to the biblical idea of incarnation. An avatar in Hinduism is a part of a god, usually Vishnu, taking an animal's or human's appearance without becoming one. Furthermore, an avatar is repeatable, and once the mission of an avatar is completed, it reverts to its original existence.

The biblical concept of incarnation differs from the avatar of Hinduism. In the incarnation, God became a man (God incarnate) in the person of Jesus Christ, never to revert to His pre-incarnate state. The second person of the Trinity, Jesus Christ, added to Himself the true human nature which He did not have before incarnation. Jesus did not merely appear to be human; He was fully human and fully God (God-man). He became one of us (Heb. 2:17).

Moreover, Jesus, who is seated now at the Father's right hand, continues to be God-man, for He never divested His human nature when He ascended to heaven. He will forever remain God-man. The Bible says, "there is one God and one Mediator between God and men, the Man Christ Jesus" (1 Tim. 2:5). Because God became flesh and identified Himself with us, He understands our needs, concerns, weaknesses, and infirmities. The Bible teaches that we have a great High Priest in Jesus. "For we do not have a High Priest who cannot sympathize with our weaknesses but was in all *points* tempted as *we are, yet* without sin" (Heb. 4:15). This means we can boldly approach the "throne of grace, that we may obtain mercy and find grace to help in time of need" (Heb. 4:16).

Do you know this Jesus Christ who came down from heaven to give His life for your redemption? Will you come to Christ with all fears, anxieties, burdens, and tears? You will find rest and relief in Him. I pray that you will repent of your sins and surrender your life to the living Christ. He is eager to come into your heart.

# Cast All Your Anxieties on the Lord

Therefore humble yourselves under the mighty hand of God, that He may exalt you in due time, casting all your care upon Him, for He cares for you. Be sober, be vigilant; because your adversary the devil walks about like a roaring lion, seeking whom he may devour. Resist him, steadfast in the faith, knowing that the same sufferings are experienced by your brotherhood in the world. But may the God of all grace, who called us to His eternal glory by Christ Jesus, after you have suffered a while, perfect, establish, strengthen, and settle you.

—1 Peter 5:6–10

The apostle Peter wrote this letter in A.D. 62–63 from Rome, primarily to Christians living in five Roman provinces of Asia Minor, known today as Turkey. These Christ-followers were going through various forms of persecution at the hands of the Roman rulers, so Peter wrote this letter to encourage them to endure persecution for the glory of God. In 1 Peter 4:12, he writes, "Dear friends, do not be surprised at the fiery ordeal that has come on you to test you, as though something strange were happening to you. But rejoice inasmuch as you participate in the sufferings of Christ, so that you may be overjoyed when His glory is revealed."

The pandemic of Coronavirus has caused much suffering to people around the world. The body of Christ—the church—is no exception to this worldwide suffering. In our community in Delaware, every family has had its share of trials in the last few years in one form or the other, some related to COVID and others not. It is an understatement to say that many in our society are anxiety-ridden in the face of what they are going through economically, physically, relationally, politically, and socially.

As I meditated on chapter five in the context of the hardships we are going through, I was encouraged by Peter's exhortation in 1 Peter 5:7: "Cast all your anxiety on Him because He cares for you." If there ever was a time in our spiritual walk to learn to cast our burdens on the Lord, it is now. We must cast our burden on Him with humility because God cares for us, and we cannot bear the weight of our cares on our own. We need God's "mighty hand" to have the weight lifted from our shoulders. The apostle Paul trumpets the same encouragement when he says, "Do not be anxious about anything, but in every situation, by prayer and petition, with thanksgiving, present your requests to God. And the peace of God, which transcends all understanding, will guard your hearts and your minds in Christ Jesus" (Phil. 4:4).

What strengthens me most to face my daily challenges with hope is Peter's encouragement in 1 Peter 5:9–10. We learn three truths about the trials we experience in our Christian pilgrimage in these two verses.

First, we learn of the commonality of our suffering. Peter writes, "Resist him [the devil], steadfast in the faith, knowing that the same sufferings are experienced by your brotherhood in the world" (1 Peter 5:9). When we face suffering, it is so easy for us to privatize our problems, become self-centered, and believe that we are the only ones going through tough times. We must not forget that we are a part of the community of believers worldwide enduring similar, if not greater, hardships. Persecution and suffering are common traits of our spiritual journey. We must expect them, embrace them, and learn to bear them.

Second, we learn of the temporality of our suffering. Peter punctuated his encouragement with these words of hope: "After you have suffered a little while. . ." Yes, we will face difficulties and hardships in life, but God will interpose our suffering with times of reprieve and rest. Our suffering has a point of termination. Even Jesus did not suffer on the cross forever; He bore our sins and suffered for 7–8 hours for our redemption. Peter strikes a resounding note of hope, saying, "After you have suffered a little while," there will be a breakthrough. If you are going through a difficult time, resist the devil who seeks to derail you in your faith by planting seeds of doubt, despair, and depression. Stand firm in the faith: that is, on the promises and truths given to us in God's Word (the Bible). Soon, the Lord will cut through your encircling gloom and lead you into the bright light of His glory and grace.

Third, we learn of the functionality of our suffering. We read: "And the God of grace. . . will Himself restore you and make you strong, firm and steadfast. To Him be the power for ever and ever. Amen" (1 Peter 5:10–11). Our God is not capricious in His acts, nor is He sadistic in inflicting hardships on His people. In fact, "As a father pities his children, so the LORD pities those who fear Him" (Ps. 103:13). God is not the author of evil, but He allows suffering to make us mature and to equip us for good works. In 1 Peter 5:10–11, Peter gives us the fourfold function of afflictions: (1) to make us perfect (*katartizo*) or suitable for God's work; (2) to establish (*sterizo*) us as steadfast; (3) to make us strong (*sthenoo*) (4) to settle (*themeleeoo*) us as unwavering. These are traits of growing in maturity and being effective in Christian service.

Perhaps one of the most important reasons God allows us to go through hardships is to draw us unto Himself. David said, "It is good for me that I have been afflicted, that I may learn Your statutes" (Ps. 119:71). The most severe loss in one's life is to be estranged from God. So, in His grace, sometimes God allows troubles to draw us unto Himself. In his book titled *The Problem of Pain*, C. S. Lewis writes, "God whispers to us in our pleasures, speaks in our conscience, but shouts in our pains: it is His megaphone to rouse a deaf world."[59] Is it possible that God is trying to "rouse your deaf ear" through your difficulties?

Peter concludes by appealing to us to stand fast in the grace he witnessed and testified in his letter. When everything is said and done, the grace of God is all that matters and all that is needed. By faith in Christ, we have access to this grace in which we are to stand (Rom. 5:2). So let us boldly enter the gracious presence of God, cast away our burdens, and seek the mercy and help available to us in our time of need (Heb. 4:16).

---

59. C. S. Lewis, *The Problem of Pain* (New York: HarperCollins Publishers, 1940), 91.

# The Virtue of Forbearance

Do you despise the riches of His goodness, forbearance, and longsuffering, not knowing that the goodness of God leads you to repentance?

—Romans 2:4

Whom [Jesus Christ] God set forth as a propitiation by His blood, through faith, to demonstrate His righteousness, because in His forbearance God passed over the sins that were previously committed.

—Romans 3:25

"Forbearance" is not a word we commonly use in our conversations. Though it is rare in our terminology, it holds rich meaning and profound theological implications. The apostle Paul exhorts: "Therefore, as *the* elect of God, holy and beloved, put on tender mercies, kindness, humility, meekness, longsuffering; bearing with one another, and forgiving one another, if anyone has a complaint against another; even as Christ forgave you, so you also *must do*" (Col. 3:12-13). In most English translations of this passage, "forbearing" is substituted by the word "bearing," but the meaning is the same. Considering Paul's exhortation, I want to briefly touch on three aspects of the virtue of forbearance: its meaning, model, and manifestation.

**Meaning:** The word "forbearance" was coined in the sixteenth century to convey the idea of refraining from enforcing an obligation or a debt that is due. It means to hold back an action that is right and legally justified. In other words, forbearance signifies the postponement of the enforcement of a legal right. Though this word is related to "patience," it is more than patience, longsuffering, or tolerance. It should be noted that the noun "forbearance" (Greek: *anochē*) appears only twice in the New Testament (Romans 2:4; 3:25), and in both cases, it is about the forbearance of God.

A sterling example of the virtue of forbearance is found in Genesis 26:12–24. Isaac, son of Abraham, lived in Gerar, a region ruled by Abimelech, the Philistine king. Isaac was a wealthy man with lots of livestock and servants. During this time, his shepherds drew water for their sustenance from the wells his father had dug years earlier. But the Philistines became envious of Isaac's riches and got back at him by throwing dirt and debris into his wells. Abimelech ordered Isaac to move away from Gerar, so he moved with his flocks and servants to a nearby valley. There he reopened the wells his father had previously dug when he was alive. Again, the shepherds of Gerar quarreled with Isaac's shepherds, saying, "The water is ours." Though these wells belonged to Isaac, he chose to exercise forbearance and move to a different place to dig a well. Isaac could have argued and fought with the shepherds of Gerar for his right to use his father's wells, but he didn't. Instead, in forbearance, he moved on to another location, which he called Rehoboth, meaning "now the Lord has made room for us."

**Model:** Our supreme model of forbearance is God. The Bible says that God, in His forbearance, "passed over" the sins of people who lived before Christ so that He might demonstrate that He is both "just and the justifier of the one who has faith in Jesus" (Rom. 3:25–26). Though God's justice demanded that He swiftly punish the guilty and exact a full payment for their sins, He restrained Himself for a specific time. He did not ignore or wink at their sins but simply "overlooked" them for the time being, given the future atoning death of Christ on the cross when full payment for their sins would be made. In the meantime, the animal sacrifices they offered served not to expiate their sins, but to foreshadow the effectual sacrifice of the Lamb of God that was to come for the remission of their sins.

God continues to show forbearance today by not imposing the wages of our sin (death) immediately; instead, He allows us to repent and turn to Him for salvation (Rom. 2:4). But soon, His forbearance will come to an end, at which moment He shall return to judge sinners and pour His retribution on the wicked (Acts 17:30–31).

**Manifestation:** We are never more like Christ than when we show forbearance (Phil. 2:5). The apostle Peter wrote, "For to this you were called, because Christ also suffered for us, leaving us an example, that you should follow His steps… who, when He was reviled did not revile in return; when He suffered, He did not threaten, but committed Himself to Him who judges righteously" (1 Peter 2: 21-23). During our earthly pilgrimage, we will face unjust opposition, conflict, and hostility. In such situations, instead of fighting to stay our ground, sometimes a more Christlike response would be to show forbearance and believe that God will make room for us elsewhere. Yes, embracing pain and loss is a manifestation of forbearance!

Our natural inclination is to fight for our rights and entitlements. But it is only by the Holy Spirit or the Spirit of Christ that we can supernaturally practice forbearance (Gal. 5:22). Jesus said, "Take My yoke upon you and learn from Me, for I am gentle and lowly in heart, and you will find rest for your souls. For My yoke is easy and My burden is light" (Matt. 11:29–30). The yoke of forbearance is easy because Christ carries the weight. That makes all the difference!

I pray that you will seek to show forbearance toward others in the love of Christ and the power of the Holy Spirit (Eph. 4:2).

# A Prayer of Repentance and Contrition

Then I set my face toward the Lord God to make request by prayer and supplications, with fasting, sackcloth, and ashes.

—Daniel 9:3

One morning, I was meditating on the prayer of Daniel recorded in Daniel 9:3–19. When Daniel realized that Jerusalem's desolation would last for seventy years, he turned to God for His intervention. He prayed with contrition and self-abasement, confessing his sins and the sins of his people. Daniel acknowledged that the Israelites had rebelled against God and turned away from His commandments and laws. In his prayer, he extolled God's righteousness, justice, mercy, and readiness to forgive.

More importantly, Daniel acknowledged that the Israelites' exile was a just punishment for sinning against God. He prayed, "All Israel has disobeyed your instructions and turned away, refusing to listen to your voice. So now the solemn curses and judgments written in the law of Moses, the servant of God, have been poured down on us because of our sin" (Dan. 9:11 NLT). God heard Daniel's prayer, spoke to Him through Gabriel, and revealed to him the events that would take place.

We, as a nation, have rejected God and turned our backs on Him. Violence, injustice, lawlessness, falsehood, debauchery, and desecration of life and family sanctity abound. The hope of America rests only in God. It is time for us to embody the creed inscribed on our coin: "In God we trust." Let us pray fervently for our nation, confessing our sins and unfaithfulness toward God. Let us pray that God will give us leaders who are willing to turn to God for help, leaders who are committed to upholding law and order (Rom. 13:1–7). We need leaders who will commit to protecting our nation's sovereignty (Acts 17:26) and promoting an atmosphere of tranquility in which Christians can practice their faith and engage in public life without compromising their convictions (1 Tim. 2:1–2).

The present course that we are on in America is a sure prescription for destruction. We must change the course of our direction. "O Lord, hear! O Lord, forgive! O Lord, listen and act! Do not delay for Your own sake, [our] God, for Your [nation] and Your people" (Dan. 9:19).

# Perfect Peace

You will keep *him* in perfect peace, *whose* mind is stayed *on You*, because he trusts in You.

—Isaiah. 26:3

Often, we quote this familiar verse from the Bible to encourage ourselves and others: "You will keep *him* in perfect peace, *whose* mind is stayed *on You*, because he trusts in You" (Isa. 26:3). Peace, it seems, is in short supply personally, nationally, and internationally. People scurry around the world looking for peace, and invariably they end up looking for it in all the wrong places. At the end of their frantic search, they return home more frustrated and disenchanted.

Just as David longed for a cup of water from Bethlehem when he was at the cave of Adullam and the garrison of the Philistines was in Bethlehem (2 Sam. 23:13–15), we long for peace. In Isaiah 26:3, God has promised peace for those who are in a covenant relationship with Him. It is a blessing that God is willing and eager to lavish upon His people. Three truths are worth noting about this matchless blessing.

First, the peace of God is a qualified blessing. Every promise in the Bible is conditional, and God's peace is no exception. It is the portion and inheritance of those who trust God and live their lives dependent on Him. The key to God's peace: "Because he trusts in You." The apostle Paul wrote, "And the life which I now live in the flesh I live by faith in the Son of God, who loved me and gave Himself for me"

149

(Gal. 2:20b). The Christian life is a dependent life in which we put our whole weight on God.

Second, the peace of God is an assisted blessing. "You will keep *him* in perfect peace, *whose* mind is stayed *on You*." The New Living Translation reads: "You will keep in perfect peace all who trust in you, all whose thoughts are fixed on you." A cursory reading of this verse suggests that we must strive to keep our minds on God to enjoy divine peace. If God's peace depends on our striving or "staying" our mind on Him, we are bound to fail. We have no hope. But don't lose heart. This verse's grammatical structure is a "passive participle," which means that the action of "staying" or "fixing" our mind on God is not something we do, but God does it for us. In other words, when we live in total dependence on God, God will cause our minds to stay or rest on Himself. This means that Christian life is not a life of trying but trusting. It is not a matter of striving but submitting to God.

Third, the peace of God is a guarded blessing. "You will keep *him* in perfect peace." The adjective "perfect" is not added here because there is an inherent deficiency in God's peace." There is no deficiency. God's peace is perfect because it guards against the assaults of our adversary, the devil (1 Peter 5:8). The devil cannot steal God's peace. God Himself will be the bulwark protecting His peace granted to us.

Lasting peace is a supernatural gift, for its source is the God of peace (Heb. 13:20). This God of peace has revealed Himself to us in the person of Jesus Christ. Seven hundred years before Jesus Christ graced the landscape of human history, the prophet Isaiah identified Him as the "Prince of Peace" (Isa. 9:6). And this Jesus said, "Peace I leave with you, My peace I give you; not as the world gives do I give to you. Let not your heart be troubled, neither let it be afraid" (John 14:27).

The peace God gives us "surpasses all understanding" and guards our hearts and minds even when we go through troubles and turmoil. It flows out of Christ's presence in us.

Some time ago, I read a story about a king who offered a prize to the artist who would paint the perfect picture of peace. Many artists submitted their paintings of "perfect peace." The king looked at all of them and picked two as the finalists. One was a painting of a serene lake by a luscious meadow and a flock of sheep grazing peacefully on the grassy field. All who saw this painting thought it was going to be the winner. The other painting depicted a tumultuous waterfall cascading down a rocky precipice; the crowd could almost feel its cold, penetrating spray. Dark and stormy clouds covered the sky. The scene did not look peaceful at all. But when the king looked, he saw a tender tree clung to the rocks at the waterfall's edge. On one of its branches that leaned over the tumultuous waters, there was a little bird nest. Inside, the mother bird was content, undisturbed, and peacefully rested on her eggs with her eyes closed, her wings covering her little ones. She manifested what it means to have peace amid the storm.

Friend, you can have this peace if you trust Jesus Christ, the Prince of Peace. You may be going through a storm right now, but you can have His peace amid your storms. Trust in the all-sufficiency of Christ, and you will have His "Perfect Peace."

# Water from Bethlehem

And David said with longing, "Oh, that someone would give me a drink of the water from the well of Bethlehem, which is by the gate!"

—2 Samuel 23:15

In this narrative, King David recalled an experience he had when he was being pursued by Saul (1 Sam. 22:1–5). It is also possible that this event occurred later in David's early days as king when waging a campaign against the Philistines. Whenever it happened, David and his men were hiding in the cave of Adullam in the Shephelah region, ten miles southeast of Gath, between the Philistine land and Israel. The Philistines set up their camp in the Valley of Rephaim in preparation for a battle with the Israelites.

While David was hiding in the cave of Adullam, he suddenly had an irresistible desire for a drink of water from the well at the gate of Bethlehem. "Oh, that someone would give me a drink of water from the well of Bethlehem, which is by the gate!" When three of his men heard this, they broke through the Philistine camp without regard for their lives, drew water from the well at the gate of Bethlehem, and brought it to David. But to their astonishment, David would not drink the water but poured it out to the Lord, saying, "Far be it from me, O LORD, that I should do this! Is *this* not the blood of the men who went in jeopardy of their lives?" (2 Sam. 23:17). It was a powerful and moving display of holy reverence toward God by David for his men's selfless and sacrificial bravery.

This short narrative teaches that one of the most important expressions of our relatedness to God is our longing for Him. David longed for water from Bethlehem. We don't know what exactly motivated him to want a drink of water from Bethlehem. It may be that he was thirsty. Or perhaps he longed for his birthplace, Bethlehem. Whatever the reason, his longing for water from Bethlehem is a beautiful picture of the deepest longing of every soul, which no earthly experience can satisfy (Jer. 2:13; John 4:13–14; 7:37–38). C. S. Lewis said: "Creatures are not born with desires unless satisfaction for those desires exists."[60] For example, a baby feels hunger, which is satisfied by something called "food."

Every temporal desire is fulfilled in part or whole by something that exists in the material world. However, Lewis argued that if we find a passion that no human experience can fully satisfy, the most probable explanation is that we are made for God, who alone can satisfy it.[61]

Whether we realize it or not, our deepest longing is not material but spiritual. There is a God-made vacuum in every person which only He can fill. St. Augustine said, "You [God] stir us up to take delight in your praise; for you have made us for yourself, and our heart is restless till it finds its rest in you."[62] The prophet Jeremiah lamented: "For My people have committed two evils; they have forsaken Me, the fountain of living waters, and hewed out cisterns for themselves, broken cisterns that can hold no water" (Jer. 2:13). Any effort to fill this deep-seated vacuum apart from God is like hewing broken cisterns that can hold no water. Jesus said to the Samaritan woman at Jacob's well: "Whoever drinks of this water will thirst again, but whoever drinks of the water that I shall give him will never thirst. But the water that I shall give him will

---

60. C. S. Lewis, *Mere Christianity*, 120.

61. Ibid.

62. Augustine, *Confessions*, 5.

become in him a fountain of water springing up into everlasting life" (John 4:13–14). Only God in Christ can satisfy our deepest longing. David longed for water, but only Jesus can give the living water we desperately need.

Do you long for God more than anything else in this world? Do you long for Christ, who is the giver of living water? The psalmist wrote, "As a deer pants for flowing streams, so pants my soul for you, O God" (Ps. 42:1 ESV). David expressed his thirst for God, saying, "My soul thirsts for you...as in a dry and weary land where there is no water" (Ps. 63:1 ESV). Just as the David's men brought the water by breaking through the stronghold of the Philistines, Jesus, the son of David, broke through the defenses of Satan by offering His blood on the cross for our sins and conquering the grave. Because of Jesus' death and triumphant resurrection, we have access to the living water He provides through the Holy Spirit who dwells in us (John 7:37–38).

Malcolm Muggeridge described the satisfying power of the living water that Christ offers as follows:

> I may, I suppose, regard myself, or pass for being, as a relatively successful man. People occasionally stare at me in the streets–that's fame. I can fairly easily earn enough to qualify for admission to the higher slopes of the Internal Revenue–that's success. Furnished with money and a little fame even the elderly, if they care to, may partake of trendy diversions– that's pleasure. It might happen once in a while that something I said or wrote was sufficiently heeded to persuade myself that it represented a serious impact on our time–that's fulfillment. Yet I say to you — and I beg you to believe me–multiply these tiny triumphs by a million, add them all together, and they are nothing–less than nothing, a positive impediment–measured against one draught of

that living water Christ offers to the spiritually thirsty, irrespective of who or what they are.[63]

George Eliot, the English novelist, wrote: "It seems to me we can never give up longing and wishing while we are still alive. There are certain things we feel to be beautiful and good, and we must hunger for them."[64] You may be languishing in the "cave of Adullam" of difficult circumstances, but don't give up longing. The most beautiful and greatest good you can long for in your present life situation is God Himself. Seek God in Christ and regard Him as your exceeding reward! Receive from Him the living water that He freely offers irrespective of your station in life. Let Christ fill the void in your life and mold you to become the person He purposed you to be.

63. "Malcolm Muggeridge on Faith," Apologetics 315, accessed February 24, 2021, https://apologetics315.com/2010/06/sunday-quote-malcolm-muggeridge-on-faith/.

64. "George Eliot Quotes," BrainyQuote, accessed July 22, 2021, https://www.brainyquote.com/quotes/george_eliot_402277.

# We Can Trust God for Guidance

I will instruct you and teach you in the way you should go; I will guide you with My eye. Do not be like the horse or like the mule, which have no understanding, which must be harnessed with bit and bridle, else they will not come near you.

—Psalm 32:8–9

Have you ever wondered whether you could trust God for guidance when you come to what is commonly called the "fork in the road" decision point? We all have experienced such decision points: should I buy a PC or a Mac, go to an in-state university or an out-of-state university, accept or decline an invitation. The list goes on! In Psalm 32, verses 8 and 9, God says, "I will instruct you and teach you in the way you should go; I will guide you with My eye. Do not be like the horse or like the mule, which have no understanding, which must be harnessed with bit and bridle, else they will not come near you."

In these two verses, we learn that every person whose sin is forgiven and is reconciled to God can rest assured of divine guidance when needed. We are given in these verses the promise of divine guidance, the process of divine guidance, and the preconditions of divine guidance.

First, we have the promise of divine guidance. We can be confident that God will guide us when we seek Him in the hour of need. God says, "I will instruct you in the way you should go. I will guide you with My eye." God is willing to show us the right path and say, "This is the way, walk in it" (Isa. 30:21 ESV). When the apostle Paul was traveling through the regions of Galatia preaching the gospel, he wanted to go to Bithynia in Asia Minor, but the Holy Spirit forbade him. Instead, the Holy Spirit guided him, through a vision, to go to Macedonia.

Second, in our text, we are given the process of divine guidance. God guides us in many ways, but here we learn of three specific ways: illumination, instruction, and intervention. "I will instruct you in the way you should go." The Hebrew word translated "instruct" means to have wisdom, prudence, insight, and understanding. God guides us by giving us comprehension. That is, the ability to look at our life situation with insight. Today's problem is not a lack of information but the inability to comprehend and sift through the alternatives and make the right choices affecting our relationships, finances, family, career, and other issues that we face in life. Such comprehension is given to us by the Holy Spirit. He is called the Spirit of wisdom. The Bible says, "If any of you lacks wisdom, let him ask of God, who gives to all liberally and without reproach, and it will be given to him" (James 1:5). The Holy Spirit leads us into all truth. He is not the Spirit of confusion, but of clarity and illumination.

Another way God guides us is by instructing us through His Word. "I will teach you in the way you should go." The term "teach" comes from Hebrew, which conveys the idea of pointing a person where they must go. The noun form of this word is the Hebrew word "Torah," which means instruction or direction. The Bible says that all "Scripture is given by inspiration of God and is profitable for doctrine, for reproof, for correction, for instruction in righteousness that the man of God may be complete thoroughly equipped for every good work (2 Tim. 3:16, 17). The Bible has something to say on virtually every issue confronting us directly, inferentially, or through overarching principles. That's why the Bible says, "Your word is a lamp to my feet and a light to my path" (Ps. 119:105). If we need to sense the guidance of God, we need to give ourselves to reading and obeying the Word of God (the Bible). As we live in obedience to the Word of God, we become more attuned and sensitive to divine guidance.

Yet another way God guides us is by intervening in our lives in various ways to keep us from falling. "I will guide you with My eye." Just as the father keeps his eye on his child and intervenes when necessary to keep the child from hurt, our Father continually has His eye on us. He may intervene through godly counselors, parents, mentors, or life circumstances. One of the most brilliant men of the twentieth century was Albert Schweitzer. He excelled as a musician, a medical doctor, and a theologian. He was best known for his work as a medical missionary in Africa. But early in his life, he was not sure what God wanted him to do. God gave him so much talent, but what was His will? While cleaning his desk at the university where he was teaching, he came across a magazine of the Paris Missionary Society. It was addressed to his friend but was put on his desk by mistake. In that magazine, he read an article on the needs of the Congo mission. After he read that article, he realized his search for God's will was over. He went to the Congo and lived one of the most extraordinary lives imaginable.

Finally, we learn of the preconditions of divine guidance. God says don't be like a horse or a mule. A horse is known for impatience and a tendency to jump the gun. A mule is known for self-will. What this means is that we must walk in step with God. We must be in step with God's timing. That requires being patient with God. Once, the distinguished writer and pastor Frank Boreham had a friend visit him during his early years of ministry in New Zealand. As they sat together on the verandah and looked across the plains and the beautiful mountains, Boreham asked the visiting pastor this question:

Can a man be reasonably sure that in the hour of perplexity, he will be rightly led? "I am certain of it," the pastor friend exclaimed, "if he will but give God time!"[65]

Give God time. Don't go ahead of Him. Equally important is to resist being a mule and being stubborn with God. When God shows us clearly what step to take, we must move in faith. Often, God guides us one step at a time. As He unfolds each step to us, we must move forward in faith and in step with God.

Cardinal John Newman was a nineteenth-century Roman Catholic bishop from England. Before his conversion to Catholicism, he served as a vicar in the Church of England. Newman knew that his ministry was in England but was not sure how it would take shape. He went to the Mediterranean and Italy in search of a direction for his life. While in Rome, he met with the Pope but was still very restless for lack of direction. On his return to England, his ship was held up for a week in the straits of Bonifacio for lack of wind. During that time, he cried out to God for direction and penned these words: "Lead kindly light amidst encircling gloom, lead Thou me on. The night is dark, and I am far from home; lead Thou me on. Keep Thou my feet; I do not ask to see the distant scene, one step enough for me."[66]

Friend, if you are struggling for direction, I want to assure you that God wants to guide you, and He will do it one step at a time. You don't need to see the distant scene; all you need to see is the next step to take. God will show that to you as you look to Him.

---

65. F. W. Boreham, "The Man who Saved Gandhi: Part 6," The Official F W Boreham Blog Site, accessed July 26, 2022, http://fwboreham. blogspot.com/2006_02_26_archive.html.

66. John H. Newman, "Lead Kindly Light," Timeless Truths, accessed April 8, 2022, https://library.timelesstruths.org/music/ Lead_Kindly_Light/.

# Praise and Worship

I will worship toward Your holy temple, and praise Your
name for Your lovingkindness and Your truth; for You
have magnified Your word above all Your name.

—Psalm 138:2

A few years ago, as I sat in the Minneapolis airport waiting for
my flight to Philadelphia, I thought about a question that a
friend had asked me a couple of days earlier: Is there a
difference between praise and worship? I want to share what I
eventually wrote to him in reply.

Etymologically, "praise" and "worship" are different and
convey different meanings. "Praise" in Hebrew and Greek
refers to extolling the virtues of the object of praise. Such
adoration is directed toward God in a religious setting and is
expressed by singing hymns and psalms. At the heart of praise
is the idea of voicing the merits, greatness, nobility, or virtues
of the object of praise.

"Worship," on the other hand, presupposes a difference in
status between the worshipper and the one worshipped. In
Greek and Hebrew, worship conveys the idea of rendering
obeisance by an inferior to a superior. At the heart of worship
is an attitude of deference expressed by falling prostrate or
bowing down before the one worshipped, such as a king or
God.

In our Western culture, we don't bow to any person;
therefore, we have trivialized the historical and theological
meaning of worship and reduced it to primarily singing songs

of praise to God. But, of course, biblical worship is more than a matter of gesture or body movement; it is a Spirit-empowered and truthful expression of one's relationship to God as a wholly dependent creature. Such a worshipful response entails every aspect of one's life. William Temple (1881–1944) defines worship as follows:

> Worship is the submission of all our nature to God. It is the quickening of conscience by His holiness; the nourishment of mind with His truth; the purifying of imagination by His beauty; the opening of the heart to His love; the surrender of the will to His purpose – and all of this gathered up in adoration, the most selfless emotion of which our nature is capable and therefore the chief remedy for that self-centeredness which is our original sin and the source of all actual sin.[67]

In practice, praise and worship go together, with the latter's scope reaching far beyond verbalizing praises to God in a church service. What is more important is that God wants us to be worshippers, for when we worship Him in spirit and truth (John 4:23), we do that for which we are created. So, be a worshipper.

---

67. William Temple, *Readings in St. John's Gospel: First and Second Series* (London: Pendlebury Press Limited, 1945), 67. Kindle.

# Whatever Became of Hymns?

And do not be drunk with wine, in which is dissipation; but be filled with the Spirit, speaking to one another in psalms and hymns and spiritual songs, singing and making melody in your heart to the Lord, giving thanks always for all things to God the Father in the name of our Lord Jesus Christ, submitting to one another in the fear of God.

—Ephesians 5:18–21

Almost five hundred years before Christ, Pythagoras proposed that the revolutions of the heavenly bodies create musical tones that blend to fill the universe with a grand harmonious song. It sounds far-fetched, but it is true. According to the late astronomer Edward Nather of the University of Texas, "the stars are humming to themselves in the dark." Astronomers now recognize that most stars vibrate at resonant frequencies, like musical instruments, and sing in the dark. Astronomers can determine a star's mass, rotation rate, and magnetic field by hearing its sounds.

If all of nature "sings" and "worships" God with joy, how much more should we, who are redeemed by God and filled with His Spirit, worship the Lord with singing? In fact, one way we demonstrate the fullness of the Spirit is by singing worship songs. The Bible says, "Be filled with the Spirit, addressing one another in psalms, hymns and spiritual songs, singing and making melody to the Lord in your heart" (Eph. 5:18–19, ESV). In the parallel text recorded in Colossians 3:16, we read: "Let the word of Christ dwell in you richly, teaching and admonishing one another in all wisdom, singing psalms and hymns and spiritual songs, with thankfulness in your hearts to God."

When we are controlled and enthralled by the Spirit of God and His Word, we spontaneously burst forth in singing psalms, hymns, and songs in a way that glorifies the Lord and edifies those who hear them. In this verse, "psalms" refers to the Psalter or the book of Psalms in the Old Testament set to music and accompanied by stringed instruments. "Hymns" refer to songs of praise directed toward God, voicing His worthiness, greatness, holiness, and character. "Spiritual songs" are simply songs with or without musical accompaniment.

In worship, we are summoned to extol the virtues of God (Pss. 68:4; 145:1; Phil. 2:5–11). The focus of worship is God and His attributes. Worship is not about us or our needs. One of the early hymns sung in the first-century apostolic church is recorded in Philippians 2:5–11. This beautiful hymn, sung by the early Christians, was entirely centered on Christ—His incarnation, identification with fallen humanity, atoning death on the cross, resurrection, and exaltation. In Revelation, we read of the four living beings and twenty-four elders falling before the Lamb and singing a new song about the worthiness of the Lamb of God and His sacrificial death for the redemption of people from every tribe and language. This song also points to the glorious truth that God in Christ has caused us to become a kingdom of priests for God (Rev. 5:8–14). It is all about God—His power and riches, wisdom and strength, honor, and glory. St. Augustine rightly defined a worship song or hymn as a praise song centered on God and sung for His glory. The New Testament scholar Richard Trench wrote, "A hymn must always be more or less of a *Magnificat*, a direct address of praise and glory to God."[68]

By this standard, how do the contemporary worship choruses compare with the great hymns of the English-speaking church? Most modern praise-and-worship songs tend to be anthropocentric with few exceptions and are bereft of good theological content or expressions of the gospel's beauty. More accurately, these choruses should be called "prayers" to God expressing felt needs rather than songs focused on God and His greatness. For example, take the popular contemporary song, "One Thing Remains (Your love never fails)," which makes you unsure of this chorus's focus. There is no mention of Jesus Christ or God. Essentially, the chorus repeats the phrase "Your love never fails, never gives up, never runs out" ad nauseam. One might as well sing this chorus to a girlfriend or boyfriend.

In contrast, consider the familiar hymn of the church, "Blessed Assurance." From the three stanzas of this beloved hymn, we learn of the certainty of our salvation in Christ, our regeneration by the Holy Spirit, the cleansing power of the blood of Christ, and the blessed hope of seeing Him when He shall return. The hymn ends with a call to rest in our Savior while watching and waiting for His appearance. Thus, this hymn touches on the doctrines of salvation, the Holy Spirit, atonement, and the second coming of Christ. It is safe to say that if ever the Bible and Christian books are destroyed from the face of the earth, and only a handful of hymnals are left, one could still reconstruct the cardinal doctrines of our faith from these hymnals. Ralph Earle observes: "Hymns like 'Holy, Holy, Holy,' 'All Hail the Power of Jesus' Name,' 'Majestic

---

68. Richard C. Trench, *Synonyms of the New Testament*. Ninth edition, 1880 (Grand Rapids: Wm . B. Eerdmans, 1974), 298. Quoted in Ralph Earle, *Word Meanings in the New Testament* (Peabody: Hendrickson Publishers, 1986), 323.

Sweetness,' or 'Come, Thou Almighty King' point people toward God. That is what is needed at least one hour a week."[69]

Many churches today are abandoning traditional hymns in favor of contemporary choruses. In a survey conducted by *Christianity Today*, 52% of the respondents said they sing mostly modern worship choruses. In my view, these churches are missing out on the richness of the hymns of the church. In 1956, Elisabeth Elliot, wife of Jim Elliott, who died a martyr's death in Ecuador, waited with "bated breath" to find out if her husband was dead or alive. The hymn "How Firm a Foundation," based on Isaiah 43:1–2, sustained and comforted her immensely during that difficult time.

> Fear not, I am with thee, oh, be not dismayed,
> For I am thy God, and will still give thee aid;
> I'll strengthen thee, help thee, and cause thee to stand,
> Upheld by My gracious, omnipotent hand.
>
> When through the deep waters I call thee to go,
> The rivers of sorrow shall not overflow;
> For I will be with thee thy trouble to bless,
> And sanctify to thee thy deepest distress.
>
> The soul that on Jesus doth lean for repose,
> I will not, I will not desert to his foes;
> That soul, though all hell should endeavor to shake,
> I'll never, no never, no never forsake.

To be fair, one occasionally comes across a gem of a worshipful contemporary song such as "You Are God Alone," which focuses entirely on God and His attributes. This song makes no mention of "me," "my," or "I," but is wholly centered on what God is—His self-sufficiency, eternality, sovereignty, immutability, or unchangeableness, omnipotence, and absolute worthiness. Understand me: I am not suggesting that hymns are the "sacred cows" of the church. I am saying

69. Ibid.

that whether we choose to sing choruses or hymns in worship, let us make sure that our songs are instructive and explicitly focused on the greatness of God and His acts in history.

Keep in mind that worship presupposes a difference in status between the worshipper and the one worshipped. Worship conveys the idea of an inferior obeying a superior by falling prostrate or bowing down before the one worshipped, such as a king or God. Because we don't bow to any person in the West, we tend to trivialize worship's historical and theological meaning and reduce it to singing choruses of prayers expressing felt needs. Of course, biblical worship is more than a matter of gesture or movement of the body; it is a Spirit-empowered and Spirit-directed response to divine revelation and an expression of one's relationship to God as a wholly dependent creature. Such a worshipful response involves every aspect of one's life.

God invites us to give Him the glory due to His name and worship Him in the beauty of holiness (Ps. 29:2). God sees our worship as "beautiful" when we render it to Him with utmost devotion, awe for His purity, and a life that reflects the character of God.

# A Mighty Fortress Is Our God

Then the LORD spoke to Moses, saying, "Speak to the children of Israel, and say to them: 'When you cross the Jordan into the land of Canaan, then you shall appoint cities to be cities of refuge for you, that the manslayer who kills any person accidentally may flee there.'"

—Numbers 35:9–11

In 1529, Martin Luther penned the song titled "A Mighty Fortress Is Our God," which soon became the battle hymn of the Reformation. This hymn echoes Hebrews 6:18: the faithfulness of God should encourage all who have fled to God for refuge to take hold of the hope that is set before them. Whenever I hear this hymn, I am reminded of the cities of refuge God instructed Moses to designate for anyone who unintentionally killed another person. We read about these cities in Numbers 35, Deuteronomy 19, and Joshua 20. These cities were among the 48 cities allotted to the Levites.

The cities of refuge were established to provide temporary asylum to anyone who killed a person unintentionally until the manslayer's innocence or guilt was determined. The purpose was to ensure that the avenger (usually a relative of the victim) would not take the life of the accused unjustly or in haste if the murder were committed by accident. These cities of refuge were not meant to shelter a person who took the life of another intentionally. For crimes committed with premeditation, the punishment was life for life, eye for an eye, tooth for tooth, hand for hand, foot for foot, burn for burn, wound for wound, and stripe for stripe (Ex. 21:24–25).

When we examine the meaning of the names of these cities of refuge and their intended purpose, we may see them as pictures or pointers of three wonderful works of God's grace and mercy toward us through Jesus Christ. First, these cities of refuge picture that in Jesus Christ, we have divine protection. The manslayer would run to one of these cities of refuge for safety until a determination was made whether the murder was committed intentionally or unintentionally. On the east side of the Jordan River were three cities—Kadesh, Shechem, and Hebron. On the west side of the Jordan River were three cities—Bezer, Ramoth, and Golan.

These cities of refuge show that, in Jesus, we have protection from divine condemnation. Kadesh means righteousness. In Christ, we have the security of His righteousness to stand before a holy God. Shechem means shoulder. Christ protects us as our burden bearer. Hebron means fellowship. Through Christ, we have the protection of fellowship with the Father. Bezer means fortification. In Christ, we have a fortress never failing. Ramoth means high place. In Christ, we have the protection of being seated in heavenly places. Golan means joy. In Christ, we have the safety of the joy of the Lord. Yes, Jesus is our refuge. He said, "Come to Me, all you who labor and are heavy laden, and I will give you rest" (Matt. 11:28).

These cities of refuge were accessible to Israelites, strangers, and sojourners. A manslayer who sought refuge in the city could get into it within a day's journey from any point of the conquered land in Canaan. The protection that Jesus gives is accessible to all who run to Him, both Jew and Gentile. Jesus said, "All that the Father gives Me will come to Me, and the one who comes to Me I will by no means cast out" (John 6:37). Yes, Jesus Christ is our protection. We can be safe in Him.

Second, these cities of refuge picture that in Jesus Christ, we have divine adjudication. If the manslayer had killed a person intentionally, his punishment was death—life for life. Therefore, to make sure that a death punishment was not imposed unjustly on one who was not guilty of intentional murder, God put a process of adjudication into place. The accused who sought refuge in the city would be taken to the city gate entrance or to the city where he had lived and would be tried by the elders of that community. If he were found not guilty of intentional murder, he would be escorted back into the city of refuge and allowed to stay there until the reigning high priest's death. If he ever left the city and its immediate surrounding before the death of the high priest, then the avenger could apprehend and slay the accused.

It is interesting to note that the Hebrew word for "avenger" is *ga-al*. The same word refers to a kinsman-redeemer or one who buys back a relative's property from another. In the case of the manslayer in the city of refuge, the avenger sought to redeem his relative's life by taking the life of the manslayer. While the blood avenger could not touch the accused as long as he was in the city of refuge, what absolved him of his crime was not his exile in the city of refuge but the death of the high priest. The death of the high priest removed the guilt associated with his unintentional killing.

In Jesus, we have not only protection from divine condemnation but also the adjudication of our sins. The big difference is that we have the adjudication of both our intentional and unintentional sins in Christ. The means of this adjudication is not our trial but the trial of Jesus in our place. Jesus, our great High Priest, bore our sins—past, present, and future—and by His death on the cross redeemed us from the penalty and guilt of our sins. The Bible says, "There is therefore now no condemnation to those who are in Christ Jesus, who do not walk according to the flesh, but according to the Spirit" (Rom. 8:1). If you are in Christ, you are set free.

Third, these cities of refuge picture that in Jesus Christ, we have divine restoration. After the high priest's death, the accused, who remained in the city of refuge, was allowed to return to his former land safely. He was released from exile and restored to his community. He no longer lived in fear of being killed by the blood avenger. The Bible says, being justified by faith, we have peace with God through our Lord Jesus Christ (Rom. 5:1). Through Christ, we are reconciled to the Father and are no longer in enmity with Him. Not only that, in Christ, we become heirs of God and joint heirs with Christ (Rom. 8:17). Our lost inheritance is restored. All that we have forfeited in the first Adam are regained in Christ, the last Adam.

Is Jesus Christ your "mighty fortress and bulwark never failing?" If He is not, run to Him in faith today. In Him alone we find our protection, our adjudication, and our restoration. I pray that the Holy Spirit will draw you to turn to Christ for your safety.

# Cure for the Heart

Come to Me, all *you* who labor and are heavy laden, and
I will give you rest. Take My yoke upon you and learn
from Me, for I am gentle and lowly in heart, and you will
find rest for your souls. For My yoke *is* easy and My
burden is light.

—Matthew 11:28–30

"Life is largely a matter of luggage," said Frank Boreham. "So
soon as a child can toddle, he displays an insatiable passion for
carrying things."[70] It seems that the "law of life's luggage" has
turned us into creatures of burden with a load to carry
wherever we go. In Matthew 11:28, Jesus said, "Come to Me,
all you who labor and are heavy laden, and I will give you rest."
There are three movements to our journey toward relief that
God in Christ offers to all who labor and are heavy-laden.

The first movement in our journey toward relief is the
divine invitation. Jesus said, "Come to Me, all you who labor
and are heavy laden." Jesus tenderly extends an invitation to
every weary soul to find repose in Him. The God of the Bible
is a God who relentlessly beckons us to enter His rest. God
said to Noah, "Come into the ark, you and all your household"
(Gen. 7:1). He invited Noah to enter the ark for safety from
the flood, which would destroy the whole earth. In Isaiah 55:1,
we read of God's invitation to all who are thirsty,
impoverished, hungry, and dissatisfied with life to come to

---

70. F. W. Boreham, *The Luggage of Life* (Grand Rapids: Kregel, 1995), 3.

Him and find satisfaction and relief from their burdens free of charge. The Lord invites all who are laden with the guilt of sin, saying, "Come now, and let us reason together...Though your sins are like scarlet, they shall be as white as snow; though they are red like crimson, they shall be as wool" (Isa. 1:18).

Jesus invites all who labor and are heavy-laden to come to Him and find rest (Matt. 11:28). Irrespective of the type of baggage you carry on your shoulders right now, the first step you can take is to respond to the divine invitation— "Come to Me." Jesus said, "All that the Father gives Me will come to Me, and the one who comes to Me I will by no means cast out" (John 6:37).

The second movement in our journey toward relief is the divine evaluation. Jesus said, "Come to Me, all you who labor and are heavy laden." Jesus accurately diagnoses our predicament—we labor and are heavy-laden. The word labor means to toil, grow weary, tired, and exhausted. It also refers to the grief and despair associated with such labor. In Luke 5:5, the apostle Peter used this word to refer to his toil as a fisherman. He said, "Master, we have toiled all night and caught nothing." The apostle Paul used the Greek word *kopiao* to describe the labors of a Christian worker: He wrote, "And we urge you, brethren, to recognize those who labor among you, and are over you in the Lord and admonish you" (1 Thess. 5:12). In this fallen world, we toil, and in the sweat of our face, we eat bread (Gen. 3:17–19).

The word "heavy laden" means to bear a load like that of a cargo ship. In its historical context, this word refers to the unbearable burden of satisfying the demands of the Mosaic law and the oral traditions of the Pharisees and Scribes (Luke 11:46; Acts 15:10). At the Jerusalem council held in A. D. 49, the apostle Peter told those who came together: "Now therefore, why do you test God by putting a yoke on the neck of the disciples which neither our fathers nor we were able to bear?" (Acts 15:10). In the immediate context of Matthew

11:28, the expression "heavy laden" points to the physical, relational, emotional, financial, and spiritual burdens we bear in life.

In his book *The Pilgrim's Progress*, John Bunyan began his iconic story with these inimitable words: "As I walked through the wilderness of this world, I lighted on a certain place, where was a Den, and I laid me down in that place to sleep. And as I slept, I dreamed a Dream. I dreamed, and behold I saw a man clothed with rags, standing in a certain place, with this face from his own house, a Book in his hand, and a great Burden upon his back."[71] In his dream, John Bunyan saw a man burdened by his sins and the resultant condemnation and judgment of God. This, indeed, is the heaviest burden that all unsaved persons carry on their back. King David lamented, saying, "My guilt overwhelms me—it is a burden too heavy to bear. My wounds fester and stink because of my foolish sins" (Ps. 38:4–5 NLT). Jesus invites every soul burdened with sin to come to Him for relief. He bore our sins in His own body on the cross so that we might live in freedom and wholeness (1 Peter 2:24).

The third movement in our journey toward relief is divine restoration. Jesus said, "Take My yoke upon you and learn from Me, for I am gentle and lowly in heart, and you will find rest for your souls. For My yoke is easy and My burden is light." We find true repose and restoration when we are harnessed to Christ and submit to Him. Paradoxically, the rest that Christ offers comes not by displacing our burden but by replacing our burden with His. His yoke (burden) is easy in that we are relieved from the unbearable burden of fulfilling the law for our justification, for Christ is the "end of the law for righteousness to everyone who believes" (Rom. 10:4). The burden that Jesus gives is light because He empowers us to do

---

71. John Bunyan, *The Pilgrim's Progress* (Uhrichsville, Ohio: Barbour and Company, 1989), 1.

what He demands of us. Just as an experienced ox guides an inexperienced ox when they are yoked together, Jesus shows us to walk the "highway of holiness" with peace and rest.

When Alexander Maclaren, the great Scottish preacher, was a young boy, he took a job in Glasgow a few miles away from home. After working through the week, he would return home for the weekend. To reach home, he had to pass through a ravine. At the end of the first week of work, when he came to the edge of the ravine, he was gripped with overwhelming fear. As he stood there motionless, suddenly he heard a voice calling him, "Alex, it's your dad. I came to walk through the ravine with you." You can imagine the relief, confidence, and rest Maclaren felt at that moment.[72]

Friend, I don't know what burdens and fears are weighing you down right now. But Jesus is calling you, saying, "I am here to walk with you through your valley. Cast your care on me. I will bear your burden." There remains a rest (Sabbath) for all who trust Jesus (Heb. 4:9). I pray you, therefore, to obey the voice of God and enter His rest by faith.

---

72. Lloyd John Ogilvie, *God's best for My Life* (Eugene: Harvest House Publishers, 1981), 12.

# Expect the Unexpected

And behold, there was a woman who had a spirit of infirmity eighteen years, and was bent over and could in no way raise *herself* up. But when Jesus saw her, He called *her* to *Him* and said to her, "Woman, you are loosed from your infirmity." And He laid *His* hands on her, and immediately she was made straight, and glorified God.

—Luke 13:11–13

In the summer of 1968, I was a freshman in college and desperately needed a summer job. It was my first summer in America, and I did not know how to find a summer job. I had no family or relatives to help me. I had no money to stay on campus for the summer and had to vacate my dorm soon. I had no place to go. I was utterly helpless and without cash except for a few dollars. As I was packing my meager belongings, which amounted to just two suitcases, something unexpected happened. I received a phone call from my roommate, who had gone to his home for the summer. He called to know whether I had found a job or a place to stay. When I told him that I found neither, he invited me to come to his home and stay with him for the summer. I had just enough money to take a train and go to his place. His parents helped me find a summer job.

Nothing can be more thrilling than experiencing an unexpected blessing. In Luke 13, we read the story of a woman who was crippled for eighteen years. She was bent over and could not fully straighten herself. One day, something unexpected happened. Jesus saw her in a crowd, called her over, and said to her: "Woman, you are freed from your disability." He laid His hands on her, and she was made straight. This daughter of Abraham unexpectedly was freed from her infirmity, and she glorified God. Perhaps you need an unexpected breakthrough in your life. Maybe it is in your finances, health, employment, relationships, family affairs, or emotional well-being.

As covenant children of God, we can expect an unexpected blessing for three good reasons. First, we can expect an unexpected blessing because the Lord sees us. The Bible says, "Jesus saw her." Jesus saw her need, helplessness, and heartache. While the people around her paid no attention to her, Jesus zeroed in on her. In Genesis 16, we read the story of Hagar fleeing from Sarai. She was pregnant with a child and found herself by a spring of water in the wilderness. Unexpectedly, the angel of the Lord appeared and comforted her in her hour of need. She called the Lord who spoke to her "the God who sees." God said to Moses in the wilderness of Midian, "I have surely seen the oppression of my people who are in Egypt and have heard their cry."

People that you love may pass you by. Others may never see the teardrops in your eyes or feel the heartache you bear. But the Lord sees you and wants to meet you at the point of your need.

Second, we can expect an unexpected blessing because the Lord summons us. Jesus not only saw this disabled woman, but He called her. When the people around saw her as a distraction and a nuisance, Jesus saw her as a woman of great value and called her out. It must have been music to her ears. God said to Moses, "I know you by name." God said to Jeremiah that He knew him before he was conceived in his mother's womb. God said to Israel that He called him by his name and made him His own. The Bible says that the Lord knows all who belong to Him. He knows you by your name.

Jesus is in the business of calling people to Himself. He said, "Come to Me, all you who labor and are heavy laden, and I will give you rest." Jesus is calling you to find rest and deliverance in Him. He summons all who need His touch. Draw near to Him, and He will draw near to you.

Third, we can expect an unexpected blessing because the Lord straightens us. Jesus touched this woman, and her misaligned body was realigned and restored. The Bible says God will make the crooked places straight. He will make the rough places smooth. He can break in pieces the gates of bronze and cut the bars of iron. This means that whatever is crooked and misaligned in our lives, God can straighten it. He can smoothen the rough patches in our lives. He can dismantle what we consider an insurmountable obstacle to our progress. All we need is one touch of the Master. He is ready and willing to touch and straighten us.

Let's expect an unexpected blessing this week, this month, or this year. Remember, the Lord sees us; the Lord summons us; the Lord straightens us. Jesus is calling you. Will you respond to His call?

# Getting Through Your Wilderness

So I have looked for You in the sanctuary, to see Your
power and Your glory. Because Your lovingkindness is
better than life, my lips shall praise You. Thus I will bless
You while I live; I will lift up my hands in Your name.
My soul shall be satisfied as with marrow and fatness,
and my mouth shall praise You with joyful lips.

—Psalm 63:2–5

Victor Frankl, who pioneered a branch of psychiatry known as
"logotherapy," was a Holocaust survivor. His father, mother,
and brother died in the camp. One day, the Nazi soldiers
barged into his cell and stripped him of his clothes. As he stood
before them naked and emaciated, they tried to take from his
finger his last possession—his wedding ring. As they were
removing his wedding ring, he thought to himself: "You can
take away all I have, my dignity, and my life. But one thing you
can't take away from me is my freedom to choose how I react
to what is happening to me."[73] He called the freedom to choose
one's attitude the last of all human freedoms.[74]

---

73. Charles R. Swindoll, *Man to Man* (Grand Rapids: Zondervan, 1996),
63.

74. Victor E. Frankl, *Man's Search For Meaning* (Boston: Beacon Press,
2006), 66.

In Psalm 63, we find David in the wilderness of Judea fleeing from his son, Absalom, who was trying to overthrow David and take over the kingdom of Israel. David and his six hundred men were in the wilderness—weary, thirsty, hungry, and running for their lives. Even though his hope of returning to Jerusalem looked bleak, David refused to fall into self-pity. Instead, he fixed his mind on God. He became theocentric or God-centered.

Perhaps you are going through a wilderness right now, and you are weary and exhausted because of the trials and challenges life has thrown at you. How will you exercise the last of all human freedoms – the freedom to choose how you will react to your situation? From Psalm 63:2–5, I would like to suggest three ways you can respond to your wilderness.

First, seek the Lord. In verse 1, we read about David's thirsting and longing for God. Instead of becoming self-centered, David chose to be God-centered and seek the Lord. The Bible says, "Seek the LORD while He may be found, call upon Him while He is near" (Isa. 55:6). Just as a silversmith stays close to the refining fire, God is most near us when we go through fiery trials and sufferings. The psalmist said, "The LORD is near to all who call upon Him, to all who call upon Him in truth" (Ps. 145:18). Whatever life situation you may be in right now, seek the Lord. He is right in the thick of your life situation.

Second, remember the Lord. In verse 2, David said to himself: "In the sanctuary, I have seen you and witnessed your power and splendor" (NET) David remembered his past experiences with God, of seeing His power and glory. He was sure that God would come through again. When Jehoshaphat, king of Judah, was attacked by the Moabites and Syrians, he remembered how God delivered His people in the past. Having recalled what God had done in the past, He prayed to God, saying: "O our God, will You not judge them? For we have no power against this great multitude that is coming against us; nor do we know that to do, but our eyes are upon You" (2 Chron. 20:12).

Forgetfulness may be a blessing at times, but it can be an impediment when it comes to our relationship with God. When the Israelites were journeying through the wilderness, they repeatedly angered God by not remembering the miracles He had done for them. As a result of their forgetfulness, they complained and murmured against God. In times of difficulties, remember what God has done for you in the past and be confident that He will do it again. The psalmist said: "Bless the LORD O my soul, and forget not all His benefits" (Ps. 103:2).

Third, worship the Lord. In verses 3–5, David worshiped the Lord for His lovingkindness. With joyful lips and his hands lifted, he worshipped God. When the apostle Paul and Silas were in a Jail in Philippi bound with chains, they began to worship God, and God descended upon them and broke their chains. The Bible says God inhabits the praises of His people (Ps.22:3). We invoke His presence when we worship Him, and every yoke and bondage is broken in His presence. Seeking the Lord, remembering the Lord, and worshipping the Lord when going through a wilderness are only possible when we trust the all-sufficiency of God.

David was wandering in a dry and thirsty land. He was tired. He longed to quench his thirst and find rest for His soul. Hundreds of years later, the great son of David, Jesus, appeared on the landscape of history. He, too, experienced hunger, thirst, the wilderness of temptation, and suffering on the cross, but He triumphed over them. He said, "Come to Me, all you who labor and are heavy laden, and I will give you rest" (Matt. 11:28). He also said, "If anyone thirsts, let him come to Me and drink. He who believes in Me, as the Scripture has said, out of his heart will flow rivers of living water" (John 7:37b–38). Turn to Christ and find rest for your weary soul. He will see you through your wilderness.

# Honoring God

A son honors *his* father, and a servant *his* master. If then I am the Father, where *is* My honor? And if I *am* a Master, where *is* My reverence? says the LORD of hosts to you priests who despise My name. Yet you say, "In what way have we despised Your name?"

—Malachi 1:6

As Christians, one of the questions we struggle with is how to honor God. How do we glorify God? Through the prophet Malachi, God said to the exiles who returned from their Babylonian captivity: "A son honors *his* father, and servant *his* master. If I am your Father, where *is* My honor? If I *am* your Master, where *is* My reverence?" Malachi was the last of the Old Testament prophets who ministered to the people of Israel. His name means "Messenger of God." Malachi came on to the scene almost a hundred years after Haggai and Zachariah. While Haggai and Zachariah focused on motivating the exiles to rebuild the temple of God, Malachi focused on calling the exiles to return from their moral and spiritual backsliding to serve the Lord in holiness. Though the temple was rebuilt, and the divine order of worship was reestablished, these exiles wearied God by their self-righteousness, ungodliness, and unholy mixed marriages. In other words, they had a form of godliness without power and external rituals without an intimate relationship with God.[75]

From God's indictment of the exiles recorded in Malachi 1 and 2, we learn at least three ways we should honor God and bring joy to His heart. First, we should honor God in our worship. In chapter 1, God expressed His utter displeasure at the unholy sacrifices offered by the priests. They sacrificed lame, stolen, blemished, blind, and sick animals on the altar of God. The psalmist wrote, "Give unto the LORD glory due to His name; Worship the LORD in the beauty of holiness" (Ps. 29:2). But that's not what they were doing!

Today, we don't offer animal sacrifices to God in worship. The Old Testament priesthood and animal sacrifices foreshadowed the superior priesthood and sacrifice of Jesus Christ. As our great High Priest, Jesus offered Himself for us as a Lamb without blemish and spot. Today, because of Jesus' perfect sacrifice, we do not offer animal sacrifices to God in worship; instead, we offer our bodies as a living sacrifice, holy, acceptable to God, through our worship (Rom. 12:1). What this means is that we offer to God all that we are; and whatever we do, we do unto the Lord to please Him—in our work, in our finances, in our devotional life, in our marriage, in our relationship with others--the list goes on. This is what Jesus meant when He said that the Father seeks those who worship Him in spirit and in truth.

Second, we must honor God in our walk. In chapter 2, we read how the priests and the people dishonored God in their walk or conduct. The priests were supposed to serve as messengers of God and instruct the people about the things of God. Instead, they departed from the ways of God and caused many to stumble at the law. They corrupted the covenant of God by expecting its privileges without fulfilling its conditions.

---

75. G. Campbell Morgan, *Handbook for Bible Teachers and Preachers* (Grand Rapids: Baker Book House, 1995), 174.

The people profaned the holy institution of marriage by marrying heathen women. During the time of Ezra, the exiles repented of this abomination; however, by the time Malachi came to the scene, they had relapsed into mixed marriages. Not only that, but the people also dealt treacherously with their wives by divorcing them. The altar of God was covered with the tears of women subject to the violence of divorce.

Again, we take our cue from Jesus, the great High Priest and supreme messenger of God, when it comes to honoring God in our walk. Unlike the priests of Malachi's days, Jesus never deviated from the will of the Father who sent Him. He faithfully finished the work that the Father gave Him to do. Jesus said, "I have glorified You on earth. I have finished the work You gave me to do...I have given to them (disciples) the words which You have given Me and they have received them" (John 17:4, 8). The Bible says, "As you, therefore, have received Christ Jesus the Lord, so walk in Him" (Col. 2:6).

What does it mean to walk in Christ? It means to organize our lives around the pattern Jesus set for us. We honor God when we faithfully do the work that God has given us. We honor God when we walk worthy of the Lord, pleasing Him in all we do and increasing in the knowledge of God (Col. 1:10). We honor God when our actions in and outside the home are motivated by our love for God (Eph. 5:2).

Third, we must honor God in our words. The exiles dishonored God with their cynical, arrogant, and self-righteous words. They repudiated God's charges with the word "wherein" and sought to justify their actions seven times. They accused God of endorsing the actions of evil men. The priests disdained the temple of God for having to eat the left-over meats of blemished animals sacrificed on the altar.

Jesus said that by our words, we are justified, and by our words, we are condemned (Matt. 12:37). Jesus never challenged the will of His Father in heaven. His attitude was, "Not My will but Thine." We dishonor God when we accuse

God of being evil and question His justice. May our prayer be, "Let the words of my mouth and the meditations of my heart be acceptable in Your sight, O LORD, my strength and my Redeemer" (Ps. 19:14). We must honor God with our words that flow from a heart that is right with Him.

Is Malachi's message applicable to us today? Absolutely. Today, many are engaged in unholy worship, unruly walk, and speaking untruthful words, just as in his days. Malachi pleaded with the exiles, saying, "But now entreat God's favor, that He may be gracious to us" (Mal. 1:9). God's favor came to us through Jesus Christ, God's only Son. We must turn to Him in repentance and faith as the first step toward honoring God in our worship, our walk, and our words. Jesus alone is the pathway to glorifying God. He said, "He who does not honor the Son does not honor the Father who sent Him" (John 5:23).

# The Peril of Losing Self Control

He who is slow to anger is better than the mighty, and He who rules his spirit than he who takes a city.

—Proverbs 16:32

But the fruit of the Spirit is love, joy, peace, longsuffering, kindness, goodness, faithfulness, gentleness, self-control. Against such there is no law.

—Galatians 5:22

On the night of the 94th Academy Awards, Will Smith became world-famous, not for winning the Oscar for his performance in the movie "King Richard," but for slapping the face of comedian Chris Rock before millions of viewers around the globe. As John Nolte noted in his column, at that infamous moment, Will Smith "blew up 30 years of goodwill in 30 seconds." Nolte continued: "His obituary will lead with The Slap. Then, future biographers will stop in their tracks to detail The Slap."[76]

Smith notoriously failed the test of self-control, which every member of Adam's race will take at one time or the other. Will Smith's stock precipitously plummeted for his lack of self-

---

76. "Nolte: Will Smith Blew Up 30 Years of Good Will," Breitbart, accessed June 14, 2022, https://www.breitbart.com/entertainment/2022/03/29/nolte-will-smith-blew-up-30-years-of-goodwill-in-30-seconds/.

control, while Chris Rock's stock took a meteoric rise for his self-control. Will Smith failed to show discretion and be slow to anger. His inability to overlook the transgression of Chris Rock took the better of him, making him an object of mockery. The Bible says, "The discretion of a man makes him slow to anger, and his glory is to overlook a transgression" (Prov. 19:11).

History is replete with tragic lives of men and women who suffered grievous losses for a lack of self-control. A classic example is the world conqueror, Alexander the Great (356 B.C. to 323 B.C.). He came to power at age 20. Within ten years, he extended his rule over three continents, from Greece to India in the east and Egypt in the south. He died at age 32, marked by a lack of self-control and uncontrollable anger. In a fit of rage, Alexander killed his best friend Cleitus with a spear, and many historians believe that he had done so in a fit of drunkenness. Thus, Alexander went down in history as a man who conquered most of the known world but could not conquer his own spirit.

The Bible teaches, "He who is slow to anger is better than the mighty, and He who rules his spirit than he who takes a city" (Prov. 16:32). C. S. Lewis calls self-control or temperance a cardinal virtue.[77] The word "cardinal" comes from the Latin *cardinalis*, meaning the hinge of a door. Just as the hinge of a door is pivotal for ensuring the proper functioning of the door, cardinal virtues such as temperance are vital to ensuring the smooth operation of society. People who disregard the virtue of temperance will do so at their peril. The Bible says, "He who is slow to wrath has great understanding. But he who is impulsive exalts folly" (Prov. 14:29).

Jesus said, "Blessed are the meek, for they shall inherit the earth" (Matt. 5:5). The Greek word *praus*, translated as "meek," refers to one's dependence on God to adjudicate any injustice

---

77. C. S. Lewis, *Mere Christianity*, 74.

shown toward them, knowing that God can use the injury inflicted to sanctify them. Martin Lloyd Jones defines "meekness" as follows: "Meekness is essentially a true view of oneself, expressing itself in attitude and conduct with respect to others."[78] When we see ourselves as sinners with nothing to boast about, we treat others with tolerance, patience, and kindness. "Meekness," says R. T. Kendall, "is easier described by what it is not rather than what it is. It is the opposite of self-righteousness, arrogance, haughtiness, smugness, and defensiveness. Meekness is unpretentiousness, gentleness, sweetness, and the grace to be utterly self-effacing."[79]

The supreme paragon of self-control and meekness was Jesus Christ. When Jesus was reviled, He did not retaliate. When He suffered, He did not threaten, but rather committed Himself to the Father, who judges righteously (1 Peter 2:23). The night before His crucifixion, Jesus appeared before Caiaphas, the high priest. While Caiaphas was questioning Jesus in the presence of the chief priests and the elders, some people spat on Jesus' face and beat Him. Others struck Him with the palm of their hands, saying, "Prophecy to us, Christ! Who is the one who struck You." Jesus could have retaliated by calling twelve legions of angels—72,000 angels—to decimate the priests instantly. But He did not. Instead, Jesus exercised self-control to accomplish the redemptive mission for which He came into the world.

We learn from the Gospels that Jesus could show righteous anger when it was appropriate and yet not sin, as in the case of cleansing the temple. But Jesus never expressed anger or engaged in retaliation when people reviled His person or His character. Jesus' meekness was strength under control.

---

78. Martyn Lloyd-Jones, *Studies In The Sermon On The Mount* (Grand Rapids: WM. B. Eerdmans Publishing Company, 1972), 68.

79. R. T. Kendall, *The Sermon on the Mount* (Minneapolis: Chosen, 2011), 35.

Every one of us is guilty of not exercising self-control at one time or the other. And we have all seen how a lack of self-control has nullified the good we have done. So, while Will Smith's slapping of Chris Rock in the sight of millions of Americans was deplorable, his loss of self-control was typical of the human experience. As it is often said, "But for the grace of God, there go I." Is there hope for Will Smith? Certainly! What can he do to atone for his obnoxious misbehavior? To start, he must ask Chris Rock to forgive him for his offense.

But most important, Will Smith must repent of his sin and ask forgiveness of God, who alone can atone for our sins based on what Jesus Christ has done on the cross. The God of the Bible is the God of the second chance. The Bible says, "If we say that we have no sin, we deceive ourselves, and the truth is not in us. If we confess our sins, He is faithful and just to forgive us our sins and to cleanse us from all unrighteousness" (1 John 1:8–9). If Will Smith turns to God in repentance and receives Jesus as Lord and Savior, God will forgive him and empower him to live a new and victorious life.

As followers of Christ, how do we abound in self-control? We cannot manufacture meekness by self-effort. The source of humility and self-control is Jesus Christ. Jesus said, "Take my yoke upon you and learn from Me, for I am gentle and lowly in heart, and you will find rest for your souls" (Matt. 11:29). The metaphor of a yoke in the Old Testament refers to the law, which the people could not bear because the law told people what to do but could not empower them to do what it demanded. But when we are yoked with Christ, we can bear what Jesus commands us to do because He empowers us to do what He commands.

Just as an inexperienced ox is yoked with an experienced ox for training purposes, we must be yoked with Christ, who is the end of the law. Jesus fulfilled all the demands of the law and condemned sin by living a sinless life. As such, all who are in Christ and walk according to the Spirit stand before God as having fulfilled the righteous requirements of the law (Rom. 8:4). We become yoked with Christ when we are baptized into Christ by the Holy Spirit at the point of our conversion (Gal. 3:26–27). We become the dwelling place of God through the Holy Spirit. As we live our lives controlled by the Holy Spirit, we begin to bear the fruit of the Spirit. One aspect of the fruit of the Holy Spirit is self-control (Gal. 5:22).

So then, self-control is not controlling self by the self; it is controlling self by the Holy Spirit. The Bible says that we are to put on the Lord Jesus Christ and make no provision for the flesh to fulfill the flesh (Rom. 5:16). "Put on the Lord Jesus Christ" refers to the idea of partaking in the divine nature. The apostle Peter writes: "Grace and peace be multiplied to you in the knowledge of God and of Jesus our Lord, as His divine power has given to us all things that *pertain* to life and godliness, through the knowledge of Him who called us by glory and virtue, by which have been given to us exceedingly great and precious promises, that through these you may be partakers of the divine nature, having escaped the corruption *that is* in the world through lust." (2 Peter 1:2–4).

The key to gaining self-control is to come to the knowledge of God and of Jesus Christ our Lord. Do you know Christ personally as Lord? In the next verse (2 Peter 1:5), Peter informs us that the virtue of the knowledge of God is the building block of self-control, which in turn is the building block of patience. Paradoxically, the path toward self-control is to lose control of one's "self" to Christ. If you do not know Jesus Christ as Lord and Savior, I pray you will respond to the gospel and surrender your life to Christ. He will usher you into a new dimension of living.

# Meeting with God

Then the LORD said to Moses, "Come up to Me on the mountain and be there; and I will give you tablets of stone, and the law and commandments which I have written, that you may teach them."

—Exodus 24:12

Meeting with God and spending time with Him in prayer is necessary for our spiritual formation. In Exodus 24:12, we read, "Then the Lord said to Moses, 'Come up to Me on the mountain and be there; and I will give you tablets of stone, and the law of commandments which I have written, that you may teach them.'" Earlier, God invited Moses, Aaron, Nadab, Abihu, and seventy of Israel's elders to come up the mountain to be with Him. They went up and saw the God of Israel. Moffat's translation puts it this way: "They saw the God of Israel, through something, like a pavement of blue sapphire under his feet, clear as the sky itself." Elsewhere in the Bible, God said to Moses, "You cannot see My face; for no man shall see Me, and live" (Ex. 33:20).

If no one can see the face of God and live, that means though Moses and his companions were in the presence of God, they did not have a beatific vision of God—a direct, unveiled, and glorious sight of God, because no human can withstand such a view of God on this side of heaven. But it is safe to say that they were in the visible and manifest presence of God.

God, in His sovereign grace, chose to reveal Himself to us in the person of Jesus Christ, who was the "brightness of His glory and the express image of His person" (Heb. 1:3). The disciples who walked, talked, and ate with Jesus saw the face of God even though His glory was veiled. But now, by the Holy Spirit who dwells in us, we can see the glory of God as we are being transformed into His image from glory to glory (1 Cor. 2:17). From the passage in Exodus, we learn three truths concerning meeting with God.

First, we learn of God's invitation. God said to Moses, "Come up to Me." God invited Moses to separate himself from his companions and go up to be with Him alone. Moses needed to disassociate himself from the others who were with him on the mountain and be with God alone. Jesus always prayed to His Father alone. We don't read about Jesus praying with His disciples in common prayer. He sent the multitudes away and went up on a mountain by Himself to pray (Matt. 14:23; John 6:15).

Even in the final moments of His earthly life, Jesus went to pray alone in Gethsemane. He said to His disciples (Peter, James, and John), "Sit here while I go and pray over there" (Matt. 26:36). Jesus did not call His three closest disciples and hold their hands to pray. He went to be alone with His heavenly Father. We, too, must cultivate the habit of being alone with God, which requires us to separate ourselves from people and things intentionally. God's invitation to be with Him stands: "Let us therefore come boldly to the throne of grace, that we may obtain mercy and find grace to help in time of need" (Heb. 4:14). Yes, the early church engaged in group prayer (Acts 12:5; 13:1–3), but taking time to be alone with the Lord is biblical and follows the pattern set by Jesus Christ.

Second, we learn of God's injunction. God said to Moses, "Come up to Me on the mountain and be there." If Moses was on the mountain before God, was he not there already? What was the point in saying "be there?" The point was that a person might be on the top of a mountain, but his or her mind might be elsewhere. In essence, God told Moses to stand before Him with undivided attention, fully present in body, spirit, and mind.

If we want to hear from God during our time with Him, we must be "there" in His presence—fully present, not allowing our mind to gather wool or be distracted by what may be going on around us. We must ignore the chores we have to do, emails to answer, errands to run, people to visit, and all the rest. These distractions keep us from being "there" before God.

Third, we learn of God's instruction. God said to Moses, "I will give you tablets of stone, and the law and commandments which I have written that you may teach them." We can only guess how God might have communicated with Moses. But we do know from Scripture that Moses had the experience of hearing the voice of God (Ex. 19:19). Can God speak to us today audibly? He certainly can if He wants to. But more likely than not, we hear from God through His Word, which is reliable and trustworthy (2 Peter 1:19).

As we sit in the presence of God, we must sit with God's Word (the Bible) so that we can hear what He has to say to us through His Word. St. Augustine said: "When the Bible speaks, God speaks." God can also speak to us by bringing to our attention a promise to claim, a sin to forsake, a command to obey, or a word for our encouragement. In the end, to hear from God is to follow what He tells us to do. Listening and following God's instruction go hand in hand (Rom. 2:13; James 1:22).

Let us say yes to God's invitation to go up the mountain to be with Him, respond to His injunction to be "there" to hear what He has to say through His Word, and to follow His instructions diligently.

# The Mother Who Lent Her Son to the Lord

Then she made a vow and said, "O LORD of hosts, if You will indeed look on the affliction of Your maidservant and remember me, and not forget Your maidservant, but will give Your maidservant a male child, then I will give him to the LORD all the days of his life, and no razor shall come upon his head."

—1 Samuel 1:11

And Samuel judged Israel all the days of his life.

—1 Samuel 7:15

John Wesley, the founder of the Methodist Church, famously said, "Give me one hundred preachers who fear nothing but sin and desire nothing but God, and I care not a straw whether they are clergymen or laymen, such alone will shake the gates of hell and set up the kingdom of heaven on earth."[80] The person who was most influential in his life was his mother, Susannah Wesley. Susannah was not an educated woman, but she was a person of deep piety and godliness. Once, when she was asked how to judge an unlawful pleasure, she answered: "Whatever weakens your reason, impairs the tenderness of your conscience, obscures your sense of God, takes away your

---

80. "John Wesley Quotes," BrainyQuote, accessed April 27, 2022, https://www.brainyquote.com/quotes/john_wesley_524891.

relish for spiritual things, whatever increases the authority of the body over the mind, that thing is a sin to you, however innocent it may seem in itself."[81] Few theologians could have matched her definition of sin with such erudition.

The influence of a mother on a person's life cannot be underestimated. The poet William Ross Wallace said, "The hand that rocks the cradle is the hand that rules the world."[82] In 1 Samuel 1 and 2, we learn of a mother named Hannah whose hands rocked the cradle of a baby boy—Samuel—who went on to become Israel's first prophet, priest, and judge (1 Sam. 7:15). The Bible profiles her as a mother who lent her son to the Lord. From her biography, we learn five salient characteristics of a godly mother.

First, a godly mother is known for her prayerfulness. The Bible says that Hannah prayed to the Lord for a son. She prayed continually and never gave up. Though her lips moved, her voice was not heard, for she spoke in her heart. But God heard her voice loudly and clearly. Another godly mother was Susannah Wesley. Often, she would pull her long apron over her head to form a tent. It was her tent of meeting with God, and she would spend hours praying for her husband and children. Much of John Wesley's success as a preacher was attributed to the prayers of his mother.

Second, a godly mother is known for her tearfulness. Hannah wept before God in anguish. She poured out her soul before Him with tears. Shedding tears for divine intervention is like sowing seeds to ensure a good harvest. The Bible says, "Those who sow in tears shall reap in joy" (Ps. 126:5). Jesus offered prayers and supplications with "vehement cries and tears" (Heb. 5:7). From the cross, Jesus said to the women who

81. "Defining Sin: Susanna Wesley," Southern Nazarene University, accessed June 3, 2022, http://home.snu.edu/~hculbert/sin.htm.

82. William R. Wallace, "The Hand That Rocks the Cradle," PotW.org, accessed April 27, 2022, http://www.potw.org/archive/potw391.html.

were weeping for Him: "Daughters of Jerusalem, do not weep for Me, but weep for yourselves and for your children" (Luke 23:28). There is no more excellent gift for a son or a daughter than to have a mother who sows for her children with tears. I was blessed to have the advantage of such a mother myself.

Third, a godly mother is known for her faithfulness. Hannah was faithful in the sense that she trusted God to provide her with a son. She raised her empty hands of faith toward God for a child. Hannah made a vow to the Lord that if He blessed her with a son, she would lend him to the Lord for the rest of his life. And she kept her vow. I was blessed to have a godly grandmother whose husband died when she was pregnant with my father. After my father, her only child, was born, she dedicated him to the Lord's work. She remained unmarried for the rest of her life—more than sixty years—and faithfully served the Lord until He took her home. I thank the Lord for her life and the influence it had on me. A godly mother is known for her faithfulness.

Fourth, a godly mother is known for her worshipfulness. When Eli, the priest, assured Hannah that the Lord would grant her petition, she got up, ate, and was no longer sad. The following day, she worshipped the Lord and returned to her home in Ramah. After Samuel was born, Hannah nursed him, and when Samuel was weaned, she took him to the house of God at Shiloh and worshipped the Lord. She offered the required animal sacrifice to the Lord, but more importantly, she worshipped God by dedicating her most precious possession, her son, to Him. John Stott, the late Anglican pastor, wrote, "Worship is a response to the biblical revelation."[83] Hannah learned that God was able to open her womb and bless her with a child. In response to the revelation

---

83. John Stott, *The Living Church: Convictions of a Lifelong Pastor* (Downers Grove: IVP Books, 2007), 35.

of God's goodness and greatness, she worshipped God. A godly mother is known for her worshipfulness.

Fifth, a godly mother is known for her joyfulness. Hannah said, "My heart rejoices in the LORD; my horn is exalted in the LORD. I smile at my enemies because I rejoice in your salvation" (1 Sam. 2:1). It is interesting to note that Hannah's story begins with her weeping and ends with her rejoicing. The Bible says, "Weeping may endure for a night, but joy comes in the morning" (Ps. 30:5). The Lord turned Hannah's weeping into dancing. A godly mother is marked by joy in the Lord even when life is rough because the joy is rooted in God.

The Bible teaches that Hannah's son, Samuel, prefigured Jesus Christ, the greatest prophet, priest, and judge of them all. He supremely modeled for us a life of prayerfulness, tearfulness, faithfulness, worshipfulness, and joyfulness. I pray that every mother reading this musing will turn to Christ, who alone can empower her to possess these spiritual virtues and model them before her children.

# Everybody Is Praying
# These Days

When Jesus heard it, He marveled, and said to those who
followed, "Assuredly, I say to you, I have not found such
great faith, not even in Israel!"

—Matthew 8:10

What constitutes an effective prayer? Is it the length of our
prayer? The intonation of our prayer? The profundity of our
prayer? The simplicity of our prayer? Or is it the structure of
our prayer? Who is sufficient to render a judgment on the
quality of our prayer on this side of heaven?

The only one who is qualified to judge the effectiveness of
prayer is Jesus. And He has done just that. In connection with
prayer, only twice did Jesus commend a person for their prayer
in the Gospels. In Matthew 8, Jesus praised a Roman centurion
for his petition, saying, "Assuredly, I say to you, I have not
found such great faith, not even in Israel." His prayer was great
because it was a prayer of great faith. In Matthew 15:28, Jesus
commended the prayer of a Canaanite woman, saying, "O
woman, great is your faith! Let it be to you as you desire."
Again, her prayer was great because it was a prayer of great
faith.

Fundamentally prayer is asking—nothing more, nothing
less. Jesus said, "Ask, and it will be given to you" (Matt. 7:7).
So, if prayer is asking, then how should we go about asking?
Of course, the answer is we must ask in faith (Matt. 21:22). The

story of the Roman Centurion and the Canaanite woman reveals three ingredients of a prayer of great faith. It is instructive to note and practice them in our lives.

First, we offer a prayer of great faith when we pray confidently. The centurion said to Jesus, "I am not worthy that You should come under my roof. But only speak a word, and my servant will be healed." You and I have been given authority by Jesus Christ to come boldly before the throne of grace (Heb. 4:16). So, we must ask with confidence (Luke 9:1) without a doubt (James 1:6).

Second, we offer a prayer of great faith when we pray humbly. The Canaanite woman approached Jesus with humility and self-deprecation. She fell at Jesus' feet for His mercy. When we pray, we must pray humbly for God's mercy. God is not a cosmic bellhop at our beck and call. He does what he pleases for His glory.

Third, we offer a prayer of great faith when we pray tenaciously. The Canaanite woman asked Jesus persistently for the healing of her daughter. When Jesus said "ask," He meant, "keep on asking." Don't give up.

The shortest prayer recorded in the Bible is in Matthew 14:30—just two words. Peter asked the Lord, "Save me!" And the result was astounding. So, don't try to impress God with fancy words, length of your prayer, or by invoking the names of Abraham, Isaac, Jacob, Daniel, or any other mortals in the Bible. Just go to the Lord and ask in faith what you need confidently, humbly, and tenaciously. You will be surprised by the results.

# Are You Ready to Be Shown?

The LORD is near to those who have a broken heart, and saves such as have a contrite spirit.

—Psalm 34:18

I recently stumbled onto a video of a noted author and speaker, the late Elizabeth Elliott. Her first husband was Jim Elliott, killed in 1956 while contacting the Auca Indians of eastern Ecuador. In her speech, she talked about a dear woman she affectionately called "Mom Cunningham." She was Elizabeth's encourager since both had been widowed at the time they met. One day, while they were having tea together, Mom Cunningham shared with Elizabeth Elliott the heartaches and pain she had suffered in her life, all the things she could have done but did not do, and things she did not do that should have been done. Then she said, "I prayed, Oh Lord, why didn't you show me.? And the Lord said because you weren't ready to be shown." Elizabeth Elliott said that was a revelation to her.[84]

We often ask God for His guidance, but we seem to hit a brick wall because we "aren't ready to be shown." We pray, "Teach me Your ways, O LORD, and lead me in a smooth path" (Ps. 27:11). But we are not "ready to be shown" the way

84. Elizabeth Elliott, "Make Yourself Small," accessed June 19, 2021, https://www.youtube.com/watch?v=tFnMLUUfoLY.

we must go. We pray, "Search me O God, and know my heart" (Ps. 139:23). But are we "ready to be shown" the condition of our hearts? Next time, when you go to the Lord in prayer, be humble and meek to see what God wants to show you and submit to His will to walk the path He directs. "The LORD is near to those who have a broken heart, and saves such as have a contrite spirit" (Ps. 34:18)

Elizabeth Elliott quoted a statement made by the renowned German philosopher Johann Wolfgang Goethe, which I believe should be etched on every heart: "I do not know myself, and God forbid that I should."[85] In our natural state, we don't want to confront our true selves. I pray that the Lord will shatter our visage of self-importance and give us the virtue of humility to see what He wants to show us. Then we will be "ready to be shown."

85. "Johann Wolfgang von Goethe Quotes" BrainyQuote, accessed May 1, 2022, https://www.brainyquote.com/authors/johann-wolfgang-von-goeth-quotes.

# Consider the Dandelions

So why do you worry about clothing? Consider the lilies
of the field, how they grow: they neither toil nor spin;
and yet I say to you that even Solomon in all his glory
was not arrayed like one of these.

—Matthew 6:28–29

While taking my morning walk in a park in Texas, I
experienced a special worshipful moment when I saw the green
meadow filled with beautiful dandelions. Suddenly, I was
reminded of Jesus' words of encouragement to His disciples.
He said: "Why do you worry about clothing? Consider the lilies
of the field, how they grow: they neither toil nor spin; and yet
I say to you that even Solomon in all his glory was not arrayed
like one of these.

"Now if God so clothes the grass of the field which today
is, and tomorrow is thrown into the oven, will He not much
more clothe you, O you of little faith?" (Matt. 6:30). These
assuring words of Christ propelled me to praise and worship
Him, reminding myself that if He arrays the dandelions with
beauty and clothes the grass of the field, will He not care for
me, I who am more valuable than they? Indeed, it was a
transcendental moment for me.

Jesus' assurance to His disciples was an expression of God's
"special grace" toward those who are in Christ. Some
theologians call it "God's love of complacency." R. C. Sproul
notes: "God's love of complacency has to do with His
redemptive love that is focused chiefly on His beloved Son, yet

spills out to those who are in Christ. God has a special love for the redeemed that He does not have for the rest of the world."[86] So, when Jesus said to His disciples, "Do not worry about your life," He was assuring them of His special grace and love for meeting their physical needs. When Paul was battling a "thorn in the flesh," God extended His special grace to him, saying, "My grace is sufficient for you" (2 Cor. 12:9). We must distinguish God's special grace from His common grace, which He bestows on all people without distinction (Matt. 5:45).

What worries your soul today? Is it a problem of lack of finances? Is it loneliness? Is it your poor health? Is it the break-up of your family? Or are you troubled about the trials you are going through at your place of employment? If you are in Christ, do not worry. As a follower of Christ, you have access to God's special grace. The Lord who turned water into wine and fed five thousand with five loaves of bread and two fish can give you your daily provisions.

The Lord who showed His grace to the widow at Zarephath and took care of her financial problem can also solve yours. The Lord who sent ravens to feed Elijah can providentially sustain you through the dry seasons of your life. (1 Kings 17:1–7). While the unbelievers worry about what to eat, drink, or wear, we in Christ should leave the "worrying" to our Father in heaven because He knows all our needs. We should seek first the kingdom of God and His righteousness. Attend to the matters at hand today, for we have enough troubles to be concerned about today; therefore, there is no need to worry today about tomorrow's problems; tomorrow will take care of itself. Martin Luther understood what it means not to worry about tomorrow. He wrote: "He who believes in God is not careful for the morrow, but labors joyfully and with a great heart. 'For He giveth His beloved, as in sleep.' They must work

---

86. R. C. Sproul, *Everyone's A Theologian: An Introduction to Systematic Theology* (Orlando: Ligonier Ministries, 2014), chapter 38. Kindle.

and watch, yet never be careful or anxious, but commit all to Him, and live in serene tranquility with a quiet heart, as one who sleeps safely and quietly."[87]

Jesus' encouragement not to worry is not an endorsement of leading a life of slothfulness. In Luke 10:1–8, we read that when Jesus sent His seventy followers, two by two, into every city and place to preach the gospel of the kingdom, He told them not to be concerned about their essential needs while doing God's work. Why? Jesus said, "The laborer is worthy of his wages," meaning because they were going to do the work of God, God would take care of their needs through the people to whom they would be ministering.

Jesus' point was that when we do what we must, trusting in God's goodness and faithfulness, we can be sure God will meet our needs, for we are more precious than the lilies of the field and the birds in the air. The Bible says, "Whoever works his land will have plenty of bread, but he who follows worthless pursuits will have plenty of poverty" (Prov. 28:19 ESV).

---

87. "Martin Luther Quotes," Inspirational Stories, accessed May 3, 2022, https://www.inspirationalstories.com/quotes/faith-is-a-living-daring-confidence-in-of-martin-luther-quote/.

# The Mountain-Moving Faith

So Jesus answered and said to them, "Assuredly, I say to you, if you have faith and do not doubt, you will not only do what was done to the fig tree, but also if you say to this mountain, 'Be removed and be cast into the sea,' it will be done. And whatever things you ask in prayer, believing, you will receive."

—Matthew 21:21–22

The Christian life is a life of faith. We are saved by faith (Eph 2:8), and we live by faith (2 Cor. 5:7). The Bible says, "Whatever is not from faith is sin" (Rom. 14:23).

The historical context of this text is the Passion Week. Jesus and His disciples were on their way to Jerusalem from Bethany. Jesus was hungry, and seeing a fig tree by the road, He came to it, hoping to satisfy His hunger. Unfortunately, the tree was full of foliage but did not have any figs. Interestingly, Mark records the same event with the additional detail: it was not the season for figs. Yet, Jesus cursed the tree, saying, "Let no fruit grow on you ever again" (Matt. 21:19). One might wonder why Jesus cursed the tree, knowing it was not time for the fruit to appear.

Some Bible scholars believe that the fig tree Jesus cursed might have been the variety mentioned in Isaiah 28:4, where the first-ripe figs appear before the leaves cover the tree.[88] Because the fig tree was full of leaves, Jesus might have expected to see some fruit. Others believe that this fig tree was the typical variety found in Palestine in which six weeks before the fruit appears, the tree produces precursors of the figs, called the *taqsh*. Ancient farmers often ate these almond-like knobs when hungry. Thus, it is supposed that Jesus may have expected to see the *taqsh* to eat.[89]

After cleansing the temple in Jerusalem, Jesus and His disciples returned to Bethany. When they passed by the fig tree that Jesus cursed, they were astounded to see it withered to its roots. Jesus told His disciples that they could do even greater things, such as casting a mountain into the sea. The hill in view was Mount Olivet and the sea, the Dead Sea. Jesus used an ancient Hebrew metaphor or figure of speech to convey that one can accomplish what seems impossible to the human experience by faith.

So, how does one go about demonstrating the mountain-moving faith? First, we show mountain-moving faith by trusting the power of God. It is not positive thinking, nor is it some abstract force to tap into to do extraordinary feats. Mountain-moving faith is trusting in God to do great things, with no doubt. God in Christ is the object of our faith (Mark 11:22). Jesus said, "If you have faith and do not doubt" (Matt. 21:21). The apostle James encourages us to "ask in faith, without doubting, for he who doubts is like a wave of the sea driven and tossed by the wind" (James 1:6). God in Christ is also the giver and perfecter of our faith (Heb. 12:2).

Life presents us with mountains of all sorts—financial needs, marriage problems, wayward children, joblessness,

---

88. John Phillips, *Exploring The Gospels: Matthew* (Neptune, NJ: Loizeaux, 1999), 407

89. F. F. Bruce, *The Hard Sayings of Jesus* (Downers Grove: InterVarsity Press, 1983), 209.

intractable illness, or emotional upheavals. No matter how big the mountain may be, as Charles Spurgeon wrote, "faith finds a way around it, through it, or over it; and so in effect removes it."[90] We show mountain-moving faith by trusting in the power of God.

Second, we show mountain-moving faith by keeping the commandments of God. Great faith is the inheritance of those who obey the precepts of God revealed in His Word. The apostle John wrote: "And whatever we ask we receive from Him because we keep His commandments and do the things that are pleasing in His sight" (1 John 3:22). Mountain-moving faith is not demonstrated by "naming and claiming." It is exercised by those who live in obedience to the revealed will of God. Where do we find the commandments of God? In the Bible, the Word of God. They are given to us so we may walk in the ways of God and please Him. Are you living your life in obedience to the divine precepts given to us in His Word?

Third, we show mountain-moving faith by knowing the will of God. Jesus said, "Whatever things you ask in prayer, believing, you will receive." The primary condition for receiving what we ask God is faith. The "whatever" in Jesus' promise is limited to whatever we request in His will. The apostle John wrote, "Now this is the confidence that we have in Him, that if we ask anything according to His will, He hears us. And if we know that He hears us, whatever we ask, we know that we have the petitions that we have asked of Him" (1 John 5:14–15). The apostle James admonishes: "You ask and do not receive, because you ask amiss, that you may spend on your pleasures" (James 4:3).

We can know the will of God from His Word, the Scripture, and by trusting in the Holy Spirit to reveal to us the mind of God. The Spirit intercedes on behalf of us according to God's

---

90. Charles Spurgeon, *The Gospel of Matthew* (Grand Rapids: Fleming H. Revell, 1987), 240.

will (Rom. 8:27). Therefore, even if we do not know what to pray for, we can trust the Holy Spirit to guide us in praying for that which is in the will of God.

God will not grant us mountain-moving faith for self-promotion or personal glory. During Jesus' temptation in the wilderness, the devil challenged Him to turn stones into bread to satisfy His hunger. Jesus refused to use His powers to feed Himself, but He did not hesitate to use His ability to feed five thousand people with five loaves of bread and two fish.

Jesus said, "If you have faith as a mustard seed, you will say to this mountain, 'Move from here to there,' and it will move; and nothing will be impossible for you" (Matt. 17:20). The power of mountain-moving faith lies not in its size or quantity but the object of our faith. We can attempt great things for God by trusting the power of God, keeping the commandments of God, and knowing the will of God.

# True Worship

An altar of earth you shall make for Me, and you shall sacrifice on it your burnt offerings and your peace offerings, your sheep and your oxen. In every place where I record My name I will come to you, and I will bless you. And if you make Me an altar of stone, you shall not build it of hewn stone; for if you use your tool on it, you have profaned it. Nor shall you go up by steps to My altar, that your nakedness may not be exposed on it.

—Exodus 20:24–26

How should we approach God in worship? What form of worship is God-pleasing? These are questions worthy of our reflection. Two months after the Israelites had left Egypt, they reached the wilderness of Sinai and camped at the foot of the mountain. Moses went up to the mountain to meet with God. The Lord reminded Moses about the great miracles He performed before Pharaoh to display His glory and said that if the people of Israel would obey His voice and keep His commandments, they would be to Him a "kingdom of priests and a holy nation" (Ex. 19:6).

Three days later, Moses went up to the mountain at God's command to receive what we usually call the ten commandments from Him. In addition to the ten commandments, God expressly instructed Moses to build for Him an altar made of earth to offer burnt offerings and peace offerings of sheep and oxen. Furthermore, if stones were to be used for creating the altar, God told Moses that it should be with stones not hewn with tools, lest the altar be profaned. And God instructed Moses not to build steps to the altar so that people would not see bare legs and feet. God gave these specific instructions to distinguish worship to the God of Israel (Yahweh) from worship offered to Canaanite or heathen gods.

From these three verses, we learn three truths regarding true worship. First, we must worship the Lord in surrender. The word "altar" in Hebrew is *zawbakh*, which means "to slaughter an animal." The altar was for offering a burnt sacrifice, which involves burning the animal on the altar all night until it is turned to ashes. Every part of the animal is burned. Nothing is spared.

True worship involves a total surrender of every area of our lives—our body, relationships, finances, marriage, employment, ministries, and Christian service—to the Lord. Nothing is to be spared. The Bible calls this total surrender "a living sacrifice, holy, acceptable to God, which is our reasonable service" (Rom. 12:1). Have you surrendered your life—all of it—to the lordship of Christ as an act of worship? As an old cliché puts it, "The problem with a 'living sacrifice' is that it tends to crawl off the altar." Therefore, we must surrender our lives to God repeatedly.

Second, we must worship the Lord in reverence. God instructed Moses that he should not use stones hewn with tools when building the altar. No human craftsmanship was to be employed. This directive is strange but fascinating! The Canaanites built their altars with stones hewn with tools. They sought to impress their gods with their craftsmanship and hewn stones with various designs carved on them. God said to Moses that He was not impressed by the altar's form and structure but by the worshiper's reverence to God.

God wants worshippers to approach Him just as they are, not trying to impress Him with their works. When we seek to impress God with our labor, we are profaning His name. A

DEVOTIONAL

stanza of the hymn titled "Rock of Ages" beautifully captures what our attitude should be when we approach God in worship: "Not the labors of my hands can fulfill thy law's demands; nothing in my hand I bring; simply to the cross I cling."[91] Reverence to God leads to self-abandonment before Him.

Third, we must worship the Lord in holiness. God told Moses not to build steps to the altar lest people see his legs or feet (nakedness). Because God is holy, we must be sure that we do not worship Him in spiritual nakedness (Rev. 3:17–18). We must be clothed with the white garment—His righteousness—that God provides us through Christ so that the shame of our nakedness is not revealed. To worship God in holiness is to honor Him wearing the righteousness of Christ.

Do you worship the Lord wearing the attire of Christ's righteousness? The Bible calls us to worship the Lord in the beauty of holiness (1 Chron. 16:29; Pss. 29:2; 96:9). Our worship of God is acceptable when we worship rightly. Therefore, let us worship the Lord in surrender, reverence, and holiness. God is pleased with such adoration.

91. "Rock of Ages, Cleft for Me," Hymnary.Org, accessed May 2, 2022, https://hymnary.org/text/rock_of_ages_cleft_for_me_let_me_hide.

# BEHAVIORAL

Let your light so shine before men, that they may see your
good works and glorify your Father in heaven.

—Matthew 5:16

There are two things to do about the Gospel—believe it and
behave it.

—Susannah Wesley

# Bearing One Another's Burden

Bear one another's burdens, and so fulfill the law of Christ.

—Galatians 6:2

Life is burdensome. Irrespective of who we are and what we have, we all must carry our share of burdens that come from mere existence. Sometimes, however, the load of life comes to us as natural disasters and pestilences such as COVID. But in every life situation, regardless of their magnitude, we can be sure that God is willing and able to come to our aid as our burden-bearer if we turn to Him. Our deliverance from nature's destructive forces comes not from human-made or human-oriented innovations, but from God, who is the Creator and Sovereign King of the universe. He is faithful toward His covenant children and is mindful of their plight. The Bible says, "But you are a tower of refuge to the poor, O LORD, a tower of refuge to the needy in distress. You are a refuge from the storm and shelter from the heat" (Isa. 25:4a NLT).

While God is "a very present help in trouble," He is also the God of means, who uses our weak and broken faculties to do what He wills. For example, He wills us to perform acts of compassion, thus bearing the burden of others. The apostle Paul exhorts: "Bear one another's burdens, and so fulfill the law of Christ" (Gal. 6:2). The Greek word *baros,* translated as "burdens," means to be weighed down or "pressed down by a crushing weight." When a person is under a crushing weight due to an unforeseen life situation, we should be willing and prepared to come to their aid and lift that pressing weight, lest it crush that person to the ground. Paul used this word in 2 Corinthians 1:8 to describe his crushing burden: "We were burdened beyond measure, above strength, so that we despaired even of life."

In bearing one another's burdens, says Paul, we fulfill the law of Christ—the law of love. Jesus said, "You shall love the LORD your God with all your heart, with all your soul, and with all your mind. This is *the* first and great commandment. And *the* second is like it: 'You shall love your neighbor as yourself.' On these two commandments hang all the Law and the Prophets" (Matt. 22:37–40). Jesus said that there is no "other commandment greater than these" (Mark 12:31). Indeed, the edifice of Christianity and our faith rests on these two immutable pillars.

The law of Christ is the antidote to the Darwinian "survival of the fittest" concept, and it compels us to distribute a load of life by bearing one another's burdens. One day, the revered Indian missionary Sadhu Sunder Singh, who is believed to have died in the foothills of the Himalayas, was traveling with a companion through the Himalayan Mountains. As they made their way through a treacherous passage, they came across a person lying unconscious in the snow. Sunder Singh wanted to help this person, but his companion refused, saying, "We shall lose our lives if we burden ourselves with him." But Sunder Singh would not think of leaving the man to die in the snow. Disregarding the safety of his own life, Sunder Singh chose to lift the man and carry him on his back. But his traveling companion bid him farewell and moved on to save himself.

As Sunder Singh carried the man on his back, the heat from Sunder Singh's body began to warm the man, and he revived.

Soon, both were able to walk together. As they went along, they caught up with Sunder Singh's former companion, who lay dead, frozen in the snow. Jesus said, "If you cling to your life, you will lose it; but if you give up your life for me, you will find it" (Matt. 10:39 NLT).[92]

I encourage you to ask God what He would have you do to help that person in your circle of friends who is being crushed by an unbearable burden. Once, the convener of a missionary meeting in England, having heard of the spiritual needs of India, remarked: "There is a gold mine in India, but it seems almost as deep as the center of the earth. Who will venture to explore it?" William Carey (1761–1834), the renowned missionary to India, responded: "I will venture to go down, but remember you must hold the ropes."[93] An effective way you can hold the ropes of those venturing to go to places to help the needy is by assisting them financially.

92. "Sadhu Sunder Singh Essential Writings," Spirituality Practice, accessed May 2, 2022, https://www.spiritualityandpractice.com/book-reviews/excerpts/view/14866.

93. George Harvey Trull, ed., *Missionary Studies For The Sunday-School: First Series* (Philadelphia: The Sunday School Times Company, 1904), 33.

# The Anatomy of Submission

He went a little farther and fell on His face, and prayed, saying, "O My Father, if it is possible, let this cup pass from Me; nevertheless, not as I will, but as You *will*."

—Matthew 26:39

Again, a second time, He went away and prayed, saying, "O My Father, if this cup cannot pass away from Me unless I drink it, Your will be done."

—Matthew 26:42

So Jesus said to Peter, "Put your sword into the sheath. Shall I not drink the cup which My Father has given Me?"

—John 18:11

The discipline of submission is the rudder of a life rooted in Christ. It sets the course and direction of our lives and brings us to a place where God can transform us. As bondslaves of Christ, we must submit to the Lord Jesus Christ in all matters of faith and conduct. The spirit of submission is a Christian virtue. We are called to submit to one another in fear of God (Eph. 5:21) and the elders who hold spiritual leadership over us (1 Tim. 5:17; 1 Peter 5:5). The Bible teaches that it is God's will that we submit to every ordinance of man, whether they be kings or governors, for the Lord's sake (1 Peter 2:13–15). Above all, we are to submit to God (James 4:7).

Submitting to God is not a natural disposition. In our unregenerate state, we are inclined to be self-willed and to want to have our own way. The Bible teaches that unregenerate people have no fear of God, are unjust, unyielding, and devoid of understanding (Rom. 3:10–18). Submission to God is a virtue that flows out of a heart regenerated and controlled by the Holy Spirit (Eph. 5:17–21). It is essential to differentiate submission from obedience. Obedience refers to obeying or following an order either willingly or unwillingly. On the other hand, submission points to volitionally yielding to another person out of respect, deference, affection, persuasion, and status of the person to whom one is submitting.

The supreme and unparalleled model of submission to God's will was Jesus Christ. He manifested it by willingly coming down from heaven and identifying with us. His incarnation was an act of divine condescension in submission to His Father's will for redeeming His people from their sins. He "who being in the form of God did not consider it robbery to be equal with God, but made Himself of no reputation [*kenosis:* emptied Himself], taking the form of a bondservant, and coming in the likeness of men" (Phil. 2:6). God the Father, attested to Jesus' submission when He said, "This is My beloved Son in whom I am well pleased" (Matt. 3:17).

Jesus Himself repeatedly affirmed His submission to His Father's will. He said: "My food is to do the will of Him who sent Me, and to finish His work" (John 4:34). "I do not seek My own will but the will of the Father who sent Me" (John 5:30). "I have come down from heaven, not to do My own will, but the will of Him who sent Me" (John 6:38). "He who sent Me is with Me. The Father has not left Me alone, for I always do those things that please Him" (John 8:29). The writer of Hebrews wrote, "Though He [Jesus] was a Son, yet He learned obedience by the things which He suffered" (Heb. 5:8).

In His state of incarnation, Jesus obediently suffered and fulfilled all righteousness for our redemption. In His prayer in the Garden of Gethsemane, Jesus provides us a window to peer into the anatomy of submission. We learn that the act of submission moves progressively through three stages: communication, abdication, and obligation.

The first stage of submission is communicating one's will. Jesus prayed, "O My Father, if it is possible, let this cup pass from Me" (Matt. 26:39). According to Mark, Jesus prayed, Abba, Father, all things are possible for You. Take this cup away from Me" (Mark 14:36). Luke renders it, "Father, if it is Your will, take this cup away from Me" (Luke 22:42). Jesus knew very well that it was the Father's will for Him to come down from heaven and drink the cup of divine judgment for our sake.

In Caesarea Philippi, when Jesus told His disciples about His impending death and resurrection, Peter was upset about what was to happen to Christ. So, he protested, saying, "Far be it from You, Lord; this shall not happen to You!" (Matt. 16:22). Jesus rebuked Peter, saying, "Get behind Me, Satan! You are an offense to Me, for you are not mindful of the things of God, but the things of men" (Matt. 16:23). All three gospel writers (Mathew, Mark, and Luke) record this event. Jesus knew very well that His journey to the cross was according to God's will and purpose (Acts 2:23). Jesus was the "Lamb slain from the foundation of the world" (Rev. 5:12; 13:8).[94]

Yet, as the incarnate Lord, Jesus did not hesitate to communicate His wish that the Father spare Him, if possible, from going to the cross. Then, Jesus hastened to add, "nevertheless, not as I will, but as You will." The apostle Paul pleaded with God three times to remove "a thorn in the flesh," which he called "a messenger of Satan to buffet me." But when

---

94. The expression "Lamb slain from the foundation of the world" means long before the creation of the world, God, the Father, decided that His Son, Jesus Christ, should die for the sins of the world. In other words, Jesus Christ, the second person of the Trinity, was given the assignment to be the sacrificial Lamb for the atonement of our sins.

Paul received God's assurance that he would experience God's gracious strength amid his affliction, he rejoiced, saying, "Therefore most gladly I will rather boast in my infirmities, that the power of Christ may rest upon me" (2 Cor. 12:7–10).

There is nothing wrong in telling God your desire and wishes; but do so recognizing that, in the end, His plan and purpose will prevail (Prov. 20:18). We are encouraged to make our requests known to God with thanksgiving (Phil. 4:5). Though Jesus knew what God's will concerning His mission was, He prayed, "Let this cup pass from Me." It is lovely to pray always within the will of God; that should be our aim. But sometimes, we fail to know what the will of God is when we make our requests known to God. Thank God for the Holy Spirit who knows how to make intercession for us according to the will of God (Rom. 8:26–28). We need not be afraid of letting God know our desires.

The second stage of submission is abdicating one's will. Jesus prayed a second and third time, saying, "O My Father, if this cup cannot pass away from Me unless I drink it, Your will be done" (Matt. 26:42, 44). Knowing that the determined will of the Father was for Jesus to drink the cup, He irretrievably abdicated His will to the Father. He prayed: "Your will be done."

When the angel Gabriel informed Mary that she would bring forth a Son and call His name Jesus, her immediate reaction was wonderment about how this was possible, since she hadn't had a sexual relationship with a man. But after hearing how she would conceive a Son by the Holy Spirit, she responded, saying, "Behold the maidservant of the Lord! Let it be to me according to your word" (Luke 1:38). Mary surrendered her will to the will of God. For a Christian, to abdicate one's will means to reach the point where they can humbly say, "It is no longer I who live, but Christ lives in me" (Gal. 2:20). Another way of saying it is, "Christ must increase, but I must decrease" (John 3:30).

The third stage of submission is obligating one's will. Jesus said to Peter in the Garden of Gethsemane, "Put your sword into the sheath. Shall I not drink the cup which My Father has given Me?" (John 18:11). Jesus moved from communicating His will to abdicating His will to obligating His will to do what the Father had given Him to do—to drink the cup. In other words, Jesus was determined to perform the assignment the Father had given Him, and nothing was going to stop Him. At this stage of submission, our will is subsumed in God's will, such that His will becomes our delightful obligation.

It is worth noting that Jesus' submission to the Father did not stop when He ascended to heaven. The Bible teaches that Christ will subject Himself to the Father at the consummation of salvation history, "that God may be all in all" (1 Cor. 15:28). This subordination of Christ to the Father is not in being but in function, because Christ is one with the Father and the Holy Spirit. All three persons of the Trinity are equal in essence or nature, with different activities known as the "economy of the Trinity."

At the heart of submission are self-denial and servanthood (Mark 8:34; 9:35). Paradoxically, submission frees us from the bondage of always having our way. Richard Foster captures the essence of this freedom well:

> In submission, we are at last free to value other people. Their dreams and plans become important to us. We have entered into a new, wonderful, glorious freedom— the freedom to give our rights for the good of others. For the first time we can love people unconditionally. We have given up the right to demand that they return our love. No longer do we feel that we have to be treated in a certain way. We rejoice in their successes. We feel genuine sorrow in their failures. It is of little consequence that our plans are frustrated if their plans

succeed. We discover that it is far better to serve our neighbor than to have our own way.[95]

Submitting to God is an act of will, made possible by the Holy Spirit (Phil. 2:13; Heb. 13:21). Let the prayer of Thomas à Kempis (1380–1471) be on our lips continually as an expression of our submission to God: "Give what Thou wilt, so much as Thou wilt, when Thou wilt. Do with me as Thou knowest best, and as best shall please Thee, and as shall be most to Thine honor. Place me where Thou wilt, and freely work Thy will with me in all things. I am Thy servant, ready for all things; for I desire to live not to myself but to Thee."[96]

---

95. Richard J. Foster, *Celebration of Discipline: The Path to Spiritual Growth* (San Francisco: Harper & Row, 1988), 112.

96. Thomas à Kempis, *The Imitation of Christ*, Book 3, XV (2).

# A Sad Epitaph – Part 1

So Saul died for his unfaithfulness which he had committed against the LORD, because he did not keep the word of the LORD, and also because he consulted a medium for guidance.

—1 Chronicles 10:13

Stephen Covey, the author of *The 7 Habits of Highly Effective People,* identifies four basic needs of all humans. They are to live, to love, to earn, and to leave a legacy. We all want our family, friends, relatives, and associates to remember us by the legacy we leave behind. Therefore, it is reasonable to say that an epitaph inscribed on a tombstone captures that person's focus and mission well.

In 1 Chronicles 10:13, we read about the epitaph of Saul, the first king of Israel, written by God. "So Saul died for his unfaithfulness which he had committed against the Lord, because he did not keep the word of the Lord, and also because he consulted a medium for guidance. But he did not inquire of the Lord; therefore, He killed him and turned the kingdom over to David the son of Jesse."

Earlier, the Scripture describes Saul as a choice young man, tall and handsome, more handsome than any among the children of Israel. God put His Spirit on Saul to prophesy just as the other prophets in his day. This gifted young man was God's answer to the people of Israel who had rejected God to be their king and wanted an earthly king over them.

Saul had a great beginning. But during his reign, he experienced three crises of faithfulness that caused him to lose his kingdom and die on the battlefield by suicide. From I Samuel and 1 Chronicles, we learn that Saul expressed his crises of faithfulness in three specific ways. It is instructive to know what they were so that we may guard against the pernicious evil of unfaithfulness by the grace of God.

First, we learn that our unfaithfulness toward God finds expression in our recklessness. In 1 Samuel 13, we read that after Samuel anointed Saul to be the king of Israel, Samuel instructed Saul to go to Gilgal and wait for him seven days to make sacrifices and peace offerings to the Lord. There was a garrison of the Philistines near Gilgal called the hill of the Lord or Gibeah Elohim. While Saul was waiting for Samuel at Gilgal, the Philistines gathered to fight Saul and his men. When Saul saw 30,000 chariots and 6,000 horsemen of the Philistines encroaching upon him and his men, the men of Israel ran away in fear and hid in caves, thickets, and pits. Saul became distraught that Samuel had not yet come to offer the sacrifices. So, Saul took upon himself the duty of offering the burnt sacrifices to the Lord. Saul recklessly usurped the power of a priest and trespassed against the Lord. He did not uphold the holiness of God amid the children of Israel. As a result, God rejected him to be the king of Israel.

Offering a sacrifice to the Lord was a divinely established order of worship, but the problem was that Saul offered it in disobedience to the expressed command of God. His heart was not in the right place. This tells us that we can engage in activities that may appear right and noble on the surface, but they are viewed as reckless by God when done in disobedience to God's revealed will. The Bible says to worship the Lord in the beauty of holiness (Ps. 96:9). Put it differently, praise the Lord in the attire of "holiness." Saul did not worship God in righteousness and truth. He was reckless in his worship.

Similarly, Moses was reckless in not hollowing the Lord before the children of Israel at the waters of Meribah. Instead of speaking to the rock, Moses struck the rock foolishly and in desperation. As a result, he forfeited the opportunity to enter the Promised Land. Friend, examine yourself if you are reckless before God by rendering Him your service in disobedience to His revealed will. It may be that your motive is not pure in your worship, charity, service, or a host of other activities. If so, what appears to be an acceptable service turns into a reckless act before God.

Second, we learn that our unfaithfulness toward God finds expression in our rebelliousness. Saul's next crisis of faithfulness occurred when God told him to destroy the Amalekites and all their possessions (1 Sam. 15). He was to spare nothing. But Saul spared king Agag and the choice livestock of the Amalekites. He destroyed only that which was despised and worthless. He was partially obedient, but in the eyes of God, his partial obedience was still disobedience. The Bible says that Saul feared his people and obeyed their voices. He considered the opinion of people more important than obeying the word of God.

God is looking for people who follow Him without reservation, so He may display Himself strongly on their behalf (2 Chron.16:9). For example, God said of Caleb: "My servant Caleb, because he has a different spirit in him and has followed Me fully, I will bring into the land where he went, and his descendants shall inherit it" (Num. 14:24). Friend, are you following the Lord without reservation, even if it costs you?

In 2 Kings 5, we read about the Syrian commander, Naaman, who went to see the prophet Elisha for healing from leprosy. Elisha did not even bother to meet with Naaman. He told Naaman through a messenger to go and dip in Jordan seven times. Naaman was furious that Elisha asked him to immerse himself in a dirty river like Jordan and was about to return home. But at the urging of his servant, Naaman went and dipped seven times, and his flesh was made clean.

Imagine if he had dipped only six times and had returned home because he was not healed. It would have been his great loss. Because he fully obeyed the prophet, he returned home a cured man. Maybe you are on the verge of giving up because you have not seen the result of your obedience yet. But don't give up. Follow the Lord wholeheartedly. What God desires from us more than anything is obedience to His revealed will.

In Part 2 of this musing, we will investigate Saul's third crisis of faithfulness and explore how we can guard against the pernicious evil of unfaithfulness toward God.

# A Sad Epitaph – Part 2

And when Saul inquired of the LORD, the LORD did not answer him, either by dreams or by Urim or by the prophets.

—1 Samuel 28:6

In "A Sad Epitaph – Part 1," we considered two crises of faithfulness that Saul, the first king of Israel, had faced, and how he expressed his unfaithfulness toward God. In his first crisis of faithfulness, he trespassed the command of God and usurped the authority of a priest in offering a burnt offering to the Lord. His unfaithfulness was expressed in his recklessness. In his second crisis of faithfulness, Saul failed to follow the Lord's command by destroying the Amalekites and their possessions. The fact that Saul partially obeyed the Lord was tantamount to disobedience.

In this musing, we will consider Saul's third crisis of faithfulness, expressed in his remorselessness. Often, we, too, in this way, show our unfaithfulness toward God. Saul's third crisis of faithfulness happened during his final battle with the Philistines, recorded in 1 Samuel 28. When Saul saw the armies of the Philistines, he was afraid, and his heart trembled. He asked the Lord, but the Lord did not answer him (1 Sam. 28:6). So, Saul consulted a medium for guidance.

Interestingly, in 1 Chronicles 10:14, the Bible says that Saul did not inquire of the Lord. Is there a contradiction here? I think not. The chronicler seems to imply that Saul did not ask of the Lord with remorse and earnestness. There was no sign of genuine repentance in Saul. God will not hear our prayers if there is iniquity in our hearts (Ps. 66:18).

When Samuel exposed Saul's disobedience to God's command to destroy the Amalekites, the Bible says that Saul admitted his sin, but there was no indication of genuine remorse or repentance. He was more concerned about his honor before the elders of Israel; therefore, he pleaded with Samuel to uphold his reputation by a show of public support. The Bible says, "For godly sorrow produces repentance leading to salvation, not to be regretted; but the sorrow of the world produces death" (2 Cor. 7:10). The Bible says, "The LORD is near to all who call upon Him, to all who call upon Him in truth" (Ps. 145:18).

One of the evilest kings to rule Judah was Manasseh. He made his sons pass through the fire, practiced soothsaying and witchcraft, and consulted spirits and mediums. He shed innocent blood, till he had filled Jerusalem from one end to the other with it. (2 Kings 21:16). God was so angered that He empowered the Assyrian king to take Manasseh with hooks to Babylon. When he was in affliction, he cried out to God. The Bible says that he humbled himself greatly before God and prayed to Him. God heard his cry and brought him back to his kingdom in Jerusalem. Then Manasseh knew that the Lord was God. The Bible says, "The sacrifices of God *are* a broken spirit, a broken and a contrite heart—these, O God, You will not despise" (Ps. 51:17). God is always quick to respond when we cry out to Him in repentance and brokenness.

God places a high premium on a legacy of faithfulness. God is looking for people who will follow Him faithfully to the end. Saul did not leave for us a legacy of faithfulness. In fact, most kings of Israel and Judah failed to follow the Lord completely. With rare exceptions, the whole history of Israel was tainted by the rule of unfaithful kings. Even David, about whom God said, "He is a man after my own heart," was not perfect. So, if the earthly monarchs of Israel could not model for us the virtue of faithfulness, who can? Only God can. And He did exactly that when He sent His beloved Son, Jesus Christ. Jesus entered our world and the human experience as David's spiritual son to rule all those who put their trust in Him.

The kings of Israel, imperfect as they were, foreshadowed the coming of the perfect King, Jesus Christ, who would perfectly fulfill the role of king, priest, and prophet. God promised through Isaiah that "of the increase of His government and peace there will be no end" (Isa. 9:7). Jesus, the Son of God, was obedient and faithful to His Father in heaven. In Philippians 2:5–8, we read:

> Let this mind be in you which was also in Christ Jesus, who being in the form of God, did not consider it robbery to be equal with God, but made Himself of no reputation, taking the form of a bondservant, and coming in the likeness of men. And being found in appearance as a man, He humbled Himself and became obedient to the point of death, even the death of the cross.

As a result, God exalted Christ and gave Him the name above every name that every knee should bow at the name of Jesus, and every tongue should confess that Jesus Christ is Lord, to the glory of God the Father. The Bible teaches that Jesus remains faithful to us even when we are faithless (2 Tim. 2:13).

Jesus is the paragon of faithfulness. But most importantly, He is the one who empowers us to be faithful to the end. Jesus is the pioneer and perfecter of our faith (Heb. 12:1). He said, "Without me you can do nothing" (John 15). In 1 Corinthians 1:30, we read, "Of Him [God the Father], you are in Christ Jesus, who became for us wisdom from God—and righteousness and sanctification and redemption." It is by Christ, and through Christ, that we leave a legacy of faithfulness. Not in our strength!

Saul had a great beginning, but his end was tragic. He left behind a legacy of unfaithfulness marked by recklessness, rebelliousness, and remorselessness. If Christ were to write your epitaph, what would He write? Would you want Him to write that you were a great preacher, a great doctor, a great father, a great mother, or a great philanthropist? Or would you want Him to write: "Here lies a good and faithful servant who was faithful over a few things and has entered into the joy of his Lord"? The choice is yours!

# Use All Your Arrows

Then he said, "Take the arrows;" so he took *them*. And he said to the king of Israel, "Strike the ground;" so he struck three times, and stopped. And the man of God was angry with him, and said, "You should have struck five or six times; then you would have struck Syria till you had destroyed *it*. But now you will strike Syria *only* three times."

—2 Kings 13:18–20

In 2 Kings 13, we read the story of King Joash of Israel, who went to see the prophet Elisha lying in bed, deathly ill. The king was distressed and troubled by the impending attack of the Syrians. He wept and said, "My father, my father! The chariots of Israel and its horsemen." Joash repeated what Elisha had said earlier when his mentor, Elijah, was taken up into heaven. So, Joash may have expressed his regret of losing Elisha, the last hope of Israel. Or, more likely, Joash may have been saying, as Moffatt's translation puts it, "My father, my father, you are worth chariots and horsemen to Israel," meaning that Israel's true strength was not its army but the Lord.

Elisha told Joash to take up his bow and arrows and instructed him to shoot an arrow through the window toward the region of Gilead in the east that the Syrians invaded. Elisha held Joash's hand when he shot the arrow and said that it was the Lord's arrow of victory of the Israelites over the Syrians. Then Elisha told Joash to take the bow and arrows and strike them into the ground. Joash struck three arrows to the ground and stopped. Elisha was visibly angry and rebuked him, saying, "You should have struck five or six times; then you would have struck down Syria until you had made an end of it, but now you will strike down Syria only three times." Joash failed to realize the promise of God of a total victory over Syria for lack of faith and trust. This obscure and enigmatic story powerfully demonstrates how we often show our lack of faith.

First, we show a lack of faith by our unwillingness to use all the resources God has given us. God promised Joash total victory over Syria and affirmed His promise symbolically by having him shoot an arrow through the window eastward. When he was told to strike the ground with his arrows, he only struck three arrows. He didn't use all the arrows in his quiver for fear of running out of them.

Often, we forfeit God's full measure of blessings when we refuse to expend all that God has already deposited in us. Like the unfaithful servants in the parable of talents (Matt. 25:14–30), we don't use all God has given us because we don't think these things matter much. We refuse to use them for the glory of God. Jesus fed five thousand men because a boy was willing to give up his lunch of five loaves of bread and two fish. He was ready to use all that he had. Ask yourself this question: Are you willing to use all the arrows in your quiver? Are you willing to put into the hands of God all the talents and gifts He has deposited in you?

Second, we show a lack of faith by our uncertainty of what God can do for us. God promised total victory over Syria, but Joash had his doubts. He was willing to settle for a few victories. He was uncertain about what Yahweh could do for His people if they turned to Him and followed Him. Joash's uncertainty about God's power limited his capacity to expect a total victory over Syria.

The Bible says, "Behold, the LORD's hand is not shortened, that it cannot save; nor His ear heavy, that it cannot hear" (Isa. 59:1). Remember, we can only rise to the level of what we expect of God. Often, when Jesus healed the sick, He said, "Your faith has made you well." Do you trust God enough to expect great things from Him? Don't be uncertain of what God can do for you, and don't resist doing great things for God.

Third, we show a lack of faith by our unpreparedness to persevere until we receive what God has purposed for us. When Joash shot the first arrow, Elisha said, "The arrow of the LORD'S deliverance and arrow of deliverance from Syria; for you must strike the Syrians at Aphek till you have destroyed *them*" (2 Kings 13:17). This meant that Joash needed to persevere until the destruction of Syria was achieved. But Joash showed his unpreparedness to persevere by stopping after striking the ground with three arrows (2 Kings 13:18). He gave up too soon. Perhaps he was discouraged by what the Syrians had done to Israel during his father and grandfather's reign and didn't think he had any chance of destroying them.

Strong faith is persistent. Calvin Coolidge said, "Nothing in this world can take the place of persistence. Talent will not: nothing is more common than unsuccessful men with talent. Genius will not: unrewarded genius is almost a proverb. Education will not: the world is full of educated derelicts. Persistence and determination alone are omnipotent."[97] Jesus said, "Men always ought to pray and not lose heart" (Luke 18:1).

Joash was not a godly man. He did evil in the sight of God and engaged in idolatry and Baal worship. So, the prophet Elisha could have condemned him for his sin of idolatry. No! Instead, Elisha was compassionate toward Joash and gave him a message of hope and deliverance. In so doing, Elisha prefigured the redemptive ministry of Jesus. The Bible says, "For God did not send His Son into the world to condemn the

---

97. "Calvin Coolidge Quotes," BrainyQuote, accessed June 7, 2022, https://www.brainyquote.com/quotes/calvin_coolidge_414555.

world, but that the world through Him might be saved" (John 3:17).

We can be victorious over our enemies through Christ. But to avail of His power, we must be willing to use all the resources God has given us; we must be sure of what God can do for us, and we must be prepared to persevere until we receive what God has purposed for us. Go now and use all the arrows in your quiver.

# Responding to Nasty People

Do not keep silent, O God of my praise! For the mouth of the wicked and the mouth of the deceitful have opened against me; they have spoken against me with a lying tongue. They have also surrounded me with words of hatred, and fought against me without a cause. In return for my love they are my accusers, but I *give myself* to prayer. Thus they have rewarded me evil for good, and hatred for my love.

—Psalm 109:1–5

What will be your response when people deal deceptively with you? Or when those around you slander you with lies, hate you, and fight you for no cause? When someone reciprocates your love with unfounded accusations, or the good you do is rewarded with evil, will you respond with rejection, retribution, revenge, or retaliation?

In Psalm 109:1-5, David lamented before God about these very same treatments he received from people around him. But, interestingly, amidst his lamentation, he expressed a profound resolve. He said, "But I give myself to prayer." What kind of prayer do you think David had in mind? The rest of Psalm 109 gives us a clue. He was praying an imprecatory prayer, calling on God to judge his enemies and pour out His anger on them.

David, who lived under the Mosaic covenant, could legitimately pray such a prayer because the standard of justice was "eye for an eye, tooth for tooth, hand for hand, foot for foot, burn for burn, wound for wound, stripe for stripe" (Ex. 21:24). David himself prayed such an imprecatory prayer aimed at himself. He prayed, "If I repaid evil to him who was at peace with me, or have plundered my enemy without cause, let the enemy pursue me and overtake me; yes, let him trample my life to the earth, and lay my honor in the dust" (Ps. 7:4–5).

Is there a place for offering an imprecatory prayer by us who live under the new covenant? The answer is not a straightforward one. Didn't Jesus say, "Love your enemies, bless those who curse you, do good to those who hate you, and pray for those who spitefully use you and persecute you, that you may be the sons of your Father in heaven" (Matt. 5:44–4)? Jesus reminded His disciples about the old covenant standard—an eye for an eye and tooth for a tooth—but said, "I tell you not to resist an evil person. But whoever slaps you on your right cheek, turn the other to him also" (Matt. 5:38–39).

Jesus commanded us to love, bless, and pray for our enemies, which we must do. That said, we can legitimately pray to God, who is the judge of all, that He may deal with our enemies according to their works. Paul prayed: "Alexander the coppersmith did me much harm. May the Lord repay him according to his works" (2 Tim. 4:14). In praying, we acknowledge that taking vengeance is the Lord's prerogative, not ours (Rom. 12:19). We defer to the judge of all to do that which is right (Gen. 18:25). In the next breath, Paul petitioned God: "At my first defense no one stood with me, but all forsook me. May it not be charged against them" (2 Tim. 4:16). In praying thus, the apostle Paul followed the pattern of Christ (Luke 23:34) and showed love for his enemies.

It is worth noting that every time we say, "Thy kingdom come," we are, in essence, making an imprecatory statement, asking Christ to execute His judgment on the wicked when He returns, which is one of the things God in Christ will do when He comes back.

Nasty people can be an instrument of God for refining us and testing our spiritual maturity and mettle. David understood this truth—the beneficial effects of the afflictions he suffered at the hands of the ungodly people around him (Ps.119:69, 78, 85-87). He wrote, "Before I was afflicted I went astray, but now I keep Your word" (Ps. 119:67). He said, "It is good for me that I have been afflicted, that I may learn Your statutes" (Ps. 119:71). Afflictions brought David closer to God. They made him appreciate the richness and consolation of His word (Ps. 119: 50, 72).

Yes, God's people will suffer afflictions of various sorts from many directions and for many reasons because afflictions are a part of our life's journey in this fallen world. However, they are not without a divine purpose (Rom. 8:28). The poem "When God Wants To Drill A Man" (attributed to Anonymous), eloquently captures how the hand of God is at work behind our trials. When God wants to drill, thrill, and mold a person to play the noblest part so that the world may be amazed, watch His methods. Watch how God ruthlessly perfects and hammers with mighty blows converting the person into trial shapes of clay without breaking, to display His splendor. Only God knows what He is about.[98]

So, when we face afflictions, let us not be shaken, for we are destined for them (1 Thess. 3:3). The take-home message for us is, no matter what situation we may be in, let us give ourselves to prayer and let God work out His plan and glorify Himself in our trial.

---

98. "When God Wants To Drill A Man," Truth Renaissance, accessed August 1, 2022, https://thetruthrenaissance.wordpress.com /2010/09/14/poetry-when-god-wants-to-drill-a-man/.

# Making a Difference

For we are His workmanship, created in Christ Jesus for good works, which God prepared beforehand that we should walk in them.

—Ephesians 2:10

The American anthropologist Loren Eiseley told the story of a man who saw a boy picking something and throwing it into the ocean while walking along the beach. He became curious, so he approached the lad and asked what he was doing? The youth replied: "I am throwing starfish back into the ocean. The surf is up, and the tide is going out. If I don't throw them back, they'll die." "Son," the man said, "Don't you see there are thousands of starfishes and miles and miles of the beach? You can't make a difference." After listening politely, the boy bent down, picked up another starfish, and, throwing it into the ocean, said with a smile on his face, "I made a difference for that one."[99]

We live in a time where we find the needs and challenges surrounding us daunting and overwhelming. We wonder if we can make a difference in anyone. We conclude that the needs around us far outweigh our meager resources and retreat into our private enclaves with a sense of resignation and defeatism. But there is a better way. Within each of us is the God-given capacity to make a difference in someone's existence

---

99. Loren Eiseley, "The Star Thrower," Touch Point Connection, accessed May 2, 2022, https://touchpointconnection.org/starfish-story/.

irrespective of our station in life. The Bible teaches that "we are God's workmanship, created in Christ Jesus for good works, which God prepared beforehand that we should walk in them" (Eph. 2:10). Christine Todd Whitman said it well: "Anyone who thinks that they are too small to make a difference has never tried to fall asleep with a mosquito in the room."[100]

To make a difference in someone's life, we must be ready and willing to give out of love, and not out of coercion and self-interest. Such giving is bound to make the receiver feel better and joyful. It may be a word of encouragement, a smile, a positive affirmation, timely assistance, sharing our food, or other tangible help. The list is endless. No act of kindness, however great or small, is ever wasted. No task is too tiny or trifling, for each one is an opportunity to make a difference in one life at a time. Winston Churchill understood the incredible power and nobility of one's giving of self when he said, "We make a living by what we get, but we make a life by what we give."[101] What defines us is our giving, not our getting. The world is full of getters, but finding a selfless giver is a rarity.

"Fruitfulness" is the biblical term used to describe our impact on others through good works or making a difference. The apostle Paul wrote: "Walk worthy of the Lord, fully pleasing *Him*, being fruitful in every good work" (Col. 1:10). Jesus said, "Let your light shine before men, that they may see your good works, and glorify your Father which is in heaven" (Matt. 5:16). Fruitfulness is also seen as the outworking of our salvation for God's glory. The Bible says, "Work out your own salvation with fear and trembling, for it is God who works in you both to will and to do for His good pleasure" (Phil. 2:12).

100. "Christine Todd Whitman Quotes," BrainyQuote, accessed May 2. 2022, https://www.brainyquote.com/authors/christine-todd-whitman-quotes.

101. "Winston Churchill Quotes," BrainyQuote, accessed May 2, 2022, https://www.brainyquote.com/quotes/winston_churchill_131192.

Martin Luther and Calvin preached that we are justified by faith alone but by faith that justifies is never alone. In other words, justifying faith must necessarily and inevitably be validated by our actions. This is what the apostle James had in mind when he said, "I will show you my faith by my works." Our good works are not the root of our salvation but the fruit. Fruitfulness is the most definitive evidence of a Spirit-filled life (Gal. 5:22).

So, what is holding you back from making a difference in someone's life? An old African proverb says that the best time to plant a tree was twenty years ago; the next best time is now. So, begin now to make a difference. Yesterday is dead and gone; tomorrow may never be yours. Seize the day (Latin: *carpe diem*) and its opportunities. Live in the moment. Remember, charity begins at home; therefore, take the first step of that adventurous journey in your own home with your family and friends, and expand your sphere of influence into the community where you live. Don't be surprised if your daring venture lights up the dark canyons of your life and of those around you in ways you never imagined.

---

# Being a Neighbor in an Unneighborly World

But he, wanting to justify himself, said to Jesus, "And who is my neighbor?"

—Luke 10:29

Most of us are familiar with Jesus' parable of the good Samaritan. It's about a man whom thieves attacked during his journey from Jerusalem to Jericho. They beat him up, stripped him of his clothes, and left him on the roadside, half dead. As he lay on the roadside bleeding, a priest happened to go by that road. He saw the dying man but did nothing. He just passed him by. Then a Levite came by and saw the wounded man on the roadside. But he, too, passed him by and did nothing to help him. The priest and Levite were officials of the Jewish temple and held very respectful positions. One would expect that they would have readily helped the man in need. They were too concerned about their own needs and safety.

Then along came a Samaritan, at that time the most hated and marginalized member of Jewish society. When this Samaritan saw the injured man, he had compassion. He got down from his donkey, disinfected the man's wounds with oil and wine, and bandaged them. Then he set the man on his donkey and took him to an inn so he could rest. The following day, before the Samaritan checked out of the inn, he gave the innkeeper two denarii (two days' wages) and said to him, "Take care of him, and whatever more you spend, when I come again,

I will repay you." The Samaritan, from whom very little was expected, saw one man in need and made a difference in his life.

Interestingly, Jesus told this parable because a lawyer had approached Jesus, saying, "Teacher, what shall I do to inherit eternal life?" The question he asked was, indeed, the most critical and consequential question one can ask. The person to whom he asked it was the right person to give him a definitive answer. Jesus said, "What is written in the law?" The lawyer answered: "You shall love the LORD your God with all your heart, with all your soul, with all your strength, and with all your mind, and your neighbor as yourself." Jesus said, "Young man, you said it right. Do this and you will live." But the lawyer, desiring to justify himself, said to Jesus, "And who is my neighbor?"

In response, Jesus told this parable of the good Samaritan. Afterwards, Jesus asked, "Which of these three—the priest, Levite, and the Samaritan—do you think was a neighbor to him who fell among the thieves?" The lawyer said, "He who showed mercy on the dying man." Jesus said to him, "Go and do likewise." Notice that the lawyer wanted Jesus to tell him who his neighbor was. But Jesus reversed the question and challenged him to be a neighbor. To be a neighbor is to see the need of a person the Lord has brought to your attention, whose need you are able to meet. The challenge before us is not finding who our neighbor is; it is being willing to be a neighbor to one in need. To be a neighbor to one who is in need requires three critical traits.

First, we must have a willing heart. The Samaritan could have produced a thousand reasons to justify leaving the injured man on the roadside. But he didn't. Instead, when he saw a need, he was willing to set aside his discomforts and overcome cultural, social, and societal barriers to help the man. The Bible says, "Do not withhold good from those to whom it is due when it is in the power of your hand to do so" (Prov. 3:27).

Second, we must have a caring heart. The Samaritan had compassion for the man. Compassion is not sympathy, empathy, or feeling sorry for a person. The Greek word for compassion is *splanchnizomai,* which refers to intestines, entrails, or bowels. Compassion is a deep-seated visceral response that leads one to action. The Samaritan got down from his mule, bandaged the man's wounds, and poured oil and wine to help heal them. He then took the man to an inn for his care. What he did was an act of compassion.

Third, we must have a giving heart. The Samaritan took the dying man to an inn and gave sufficient money to the innkeeper for his care. He assured the innkeeper that he would repay whatever additional cost he incurred to care for the man who fell among the thieves. The Samaritan gave his treasure for taking care of the man.

The parable of the good Samaritan was, in fact, an autobiographical sketch of Christ's willing, caring, and giving mission to rescue us from our own "road to Jericho." Like the Good Samaritan, Jesus came to our rescue lovingly while we were fallen in our trespasses and sins. He came to give us life. And now, Jesus wants to transform and empower us to be a neighbor to others who lay on the side of the Jericho Road of life.

The ability to love the one in need, as we love ourselves, is not possible in our own strength. Jesus said, "What is impossible with man is possible with God" (Luke 18:27 ESV). Paul wrote, "Therefore, my beloved, as you have always obeyed, not as in my presence only, but now much more in my absence, work out your salvation with fear and trembling; for it is God who works in you both to will and to do for His good pleasure" (Phil. 2:12).

Unless God transforms our hearts, we cannot be a neighbor to others in the way that pleases God. Once God in Christ gives us a new heart, we begin to love others as we love ourselves and become a neighbor to them. Be on the lookout for that man on the road to Jericho who needs your help. It may be a family member, a coworker, a relative, or a person in your neighborhood. This journey of becoming a neighbor to those in need is a Spirit-empowered ministry where we grow day by day. I pray that you will become a neighbor by God's empowerment and make a difference to the one whom the Lord brings into your path.

# Believe in Yourself. Really?

Let not your heart be troubled; you believe in God, believe also in Me.

—John 14:1

Satya Nadella is the CEO of Microsoft and one of the top ten highest-paid executives in America. His sterling accomplishments should make every East Indian proud. Without question, he is a luminous role model for youngsters who aspire to a brilliant career in the corporate world.

In a recent interview, when asked what's the best professional advice he ever was given, he replied, "Believe in yourself, more so than you think you do."[102] "Believe in yourself" is the revered mantra of the world's most successful people. But from a divine perspective, it's a sure prescription for everlasting loss. The prophet Jeremiah wrote, "Cursed *is* the man who trusts in man and makes flesh his strength, whose heart departs from the LORD" (Jer. 17:5). The apostle Paul wrote, "For we are the circumcision, who worship God in the Spirit, rejoice in Christ Jesus, and have no confidence in the flesh" (Phil. 3:3).

From a biblical perspective, the mess we are in today can be traced to one man, Adam, who believed in himself for His success. Presently, we are going through a terrible crisis in our nation because people in general and leadership in particular

---

102. Twitter, accessed April 25, 2022, https://twitter.com/producthunt/status/1101845365614133248?lang=en.

are acting out of self-confidence. If we trust in ourselves instead of in God, we will continue to grope in darkness and chaos.

At a moment when Jesus' disciples were distraught and discouraged, Jesus comforted them, saying, "Let not your heart be troubled; you believe in God, believe also in Me" (John 14:1). Notice, Jesus didn't say, "believe in yourself." The answer to our present predicament is not believing in ourselves; it is trusting in God. Let us turn to God as a nation and seek Him for our deliverance.

# In Search of Success

The thief does not come except to steal, and to kill, and to destroy. I have come that they may have life, and that they may have *it* more abundantly.

—John 10:10

If someone were to ask you what success in life means to you, what would you say? I recently searched on Amazon for publications on "Success in life." To my astonishment, more than 40,000 volumes came up to deal with this topic in some fashion. It is fair to say that almost all people desire to be successful in life in one way or another, and they spend considerable time, treasure, and talent to achieve it. If you are a Freudian psychology student, you might consider experiencing pleasure to be the supreme goal of life. If you follow Adlerian psychology, you might regard yourself as very successful if you ride on the crest of power. Suppose you are a student of psychologist Carl Rogers (1902–1987). In that case, you are likely to be driven by the notion that you have within you all the resources necessary for maximizing your potential and achieving success as you define it.

Human experience affirms the familiar adage: "Victory has many fathers; failure is an orphan." The historian Tacitus once quipped, "This is an unfair thing about war: victory is claimed by all, failure to one alone."[103] While we all seek to experience success, the idea itself is elusive to most people. In my view, one person who had understood what it means to be successful was the famous Holocaust survivor, Victor Frankl. In 1945, he wrote a book titled *Man's Search for Meaning* in nine days in the German language, with a "firm determination that the book should be published anonymously." The first printing of this book did not have his name on the cover. Victor Frankl wanted to write it anonymously so that he would not get any literary fame; he simply wanted to share his experiences of the concentration camp at Auschwitz to help those prone to despair. Later, at his friends' insistence, he agreed to have his name on the cover of subsequent editions.

The remarkable thing about his book, which he wanted to publish anonymously, was that it became the most successful of all the books he had written. It was published in twenty-one languages besides English. It went through a hundred printings in English and sold more than three million copies. Success came to him when he was not looking for it. He wrote:

> Again and again, I, therefore, admonish my students both in Europe and in America: Don't aim at success— the more you aim at it and make it a target, the more you are going to miss it. For success, like happiness, cannot be pursued; it must ensue, and it only does so as the unintended side-effect of one's dedication to a cause greater than oneself or as the by-product of one's surrender to a person other than oneself. You have to let it happen by not caring about it.[104]

Frankl, the pioneer of logotherapy in psychiatry, learned that success ensues when one sees beyond oneself and

---

103. Daily Stoic, "Success Has Many Friends, Failure is an Orphan," accessed June 3, 2021, https://dailystoic.com/success-many-friends-failure-orphan/.

104. Victor E. Frankl, *Man's Search For Meaning*, xiv.

"surrenders to a person other than oneself." Whether he realized it or not, what Frankl said about success essentially echoed the biblical prescription for fulfillment in life— surrendering to God in Christ in whom alone one finds meaning, purpose, and fulfillment in life. In Jesus alone, one finds the highest quality of life—eternal life. Jesus said, "The thief comes only to steal and kill and destroy; I have come so that they may have life, and may have it abundantly" (John 10:10 NET) The life (*zoe*) that Jesus gives (God's life) has no parallel on the earth.

In God's eyes, successful people are those who have the life that God alone gives. God said to Abraham, "Do not be afraid, Abram, I *am* your shield, your exceedingly great reward" (Gen. 15:1). The Bible says that Joseph was a successful man even though he served as a slave servant of Potiphar because "the LORD was with Joseph" (Gen. 39:2). When the apostle Paul met Jesus, and his life was transformed, he said, "I count all things loss for the excellence of the knowledge of Christ Jesus my Lord, for whom I suffered the loss of all things, and count them rubbish, that I may gain Christ" (Phil. 3:8).

The Lord is the fountain of living waters that will satisfy our deepest thirst, hunger, and longings (John 4:10; 6:35; 7:38). To seek fulfillment in any other source is like using broken cisterns that can hold no water (Jer. 2:13). So don't search for success, but come to Christ, the fountain of all blessings. Let Him define your success. Martin Luther King, Jr. put it well:

> So I say to you, seek God and discover him and make him a power in your life. Without him, all our efforts turn to ashes and our sunrises into darkest nights. Without him, life is a meaningless drama with the decisive scenes missing. But with him, we can rise from the fatigue of despair to the buoyancy of hope. With him, we can rise from the midnight of desperation to the daybreak of joy. St. Augustine was right—we are made

for God, and we will be restless until we find rest in him.[105]

If you do not know Jesus Christ and possess the life He gives, you are the most unsuccessful person on earth, all pleasures, power, and possessions notwithstanding (Matt. 16:26). You are fundamentally lost. I pray that you will surrender your life to Jesus Christ and experience a new dimension of "successful" living.

---

105. Martin Luther King, Jr., *The Measure Of A Man* (Auckland, New Zealand: Papamoa Press, 2017), chap. 2, Kindle.

# Lot Chose for Himself

Then Lot chose for himself all the plain of Jordan, and Lot journeyed east. And they separated from each other.

—Genesis 13:11

If we are honest, we must agree that we are the sum of our choices made throughout our lives. Choices have consequences. In Genesis 13:5–18, we read about Abram and Lot journeying toward the land God had promised Abram and his descendants. Lot, Abram's nephew, had been tagging along with Abram, enjoying God's blessings on account of Abram. Just like Abram, Lot became wealthy with flocks, herds, and tents. As one might expect, conflict developed over time between the herders of Abram and Lot because the land was not sufficient to support both flocks. Abram sought to end the fight between their herdsmen by making a generous offer: Abram said, "Please let there be no strife between you and me...for we are brethren. Please separate from me. If you take the left, then I will go to the right; or, if you go the right, then I will go to the left" (Gen. 13:9).

Lot "lifted his eyes" and looked at the plain of Jordan that was well watered and "chose for himself" all the plain of Jordan, and he journeyed east. Thus, Lot separated himself from Abram and chose for himself what appeared good to his eyes. There is no indication in the biblical narrative that Lot had asked the Lord for His direction. If he had, the Lord might have told Lot that Jordan means "death," and that He was going to destroy Sodom and Gomorrah. Lot went by what appealed to his eyes. The Bible says, "There is a way that seems right to a man, but its end is the way of death" (Prov. 14:12).

On the other hand, Abram let God choose for him. Abram, too, "lifted his eyes" and looked northward, southward, eastward, and westward at the direction of God. And God said, "For all the land which you see I give to you and your descendants." The German philosopher Immanuel Kant said that when we look at an object, we only see what it appears to be (phenomenon) and not what it is in and of itself (noumena). I say God alone knows what a thing is in and of itself. Thus, it behooves us to let God choose for us because He knows the end from the beginning. Both Lot and Abram had no idea what would happen to Sodom and Gomorrah and the plain of Jordan. Only God knew what would happen to what appeared to be a well-watered plain. So, when Abram let God choose for him, he escaped the destruction looming over Sodom.

Paul Anka wrote a song for Frank Sinatra titled "My Way," which became a big hit. A line in that song goes: "I planned each charted course, each careful step along the byway. And more, much more than this, I did it my way." Many people chart the course of their lives and live their way, winding up in places where they don't want to be. Like Lot, they are oppressed and tormented by the consequences of their choices (2 Peter 2:7). Someone rightly said hell would be populated with people who lived their lives singing, "I did it my way."

The Bible says, "In all your ways acknowledge Him [God], and He shall direct your paths" (Prov. 3:6). I pray that you will let God choose for you. Let go of "your way" and embrace "God's way" for your life. When Abram let God choose for him, he found his way to the "oaks of Mamre." Mamre means "fatness." When we let God choose for us, we will reach our Mamre, where God's best will fatten our soul.

A sure way of allowing God to choose for us is to pray, read His Word [Bible] daily, and do what He says. God's word is a lamp to our feet and a light to our path (Ps. 119:105). Perhaps, you may be wondering about the mess you are in because of all the wrong choices you made. There is hope for you. Just as God rescued Lot from the destruction of Sodom, He can spare your life from ruin if you let Him and restore to you the years that the "locust has eaten" (Joel 2:25).

# A Letter of Recommendation

> Do we begin again to commend ourselves? Or do we need, as some *others,* epistles of commendation to you or *letters* of commendation from you? You are our epistle written in our hearts, known and read by all men; clearly you are an epistle of Christ, ministered by us, written not with ink but by the Spirit of the living God, not on tablets of stone but on tablets of flesh, *that is,* of the heart.

—2 Corinthians 3:1–3

We will be required to produce a letter of recommendation for authenticating our credentials at some point in our lives. Usually, it is a letter from a previous employer or someone we worked with or served in some capacity.

The apostle Paul found himself in a position where the false teachers of his day, especially those distracting the church at Corinth, demanded that he produce a letter of recommendation affirming his apostolic authority. These false teachers or Judaizers penetrated the early church, often using letters of recommendation, allegedly written by some prominent church members at Jerusalem. For Paul, any human attestation was an insult to the testimony of God concerning his apostleship. He described his apostleship as an assignment, not from men nor through man, but from and through Jesus Christ (Gal. 1:1).

In 2 Corinthians 3:1–3, Paul reminded the Christians at Corinth that the best letter of recommendation he could produce was the letter written by Christ—their transformed lives under his ministry. In other words, the disciples of Christ at Corinth were his letter of recommendation in flesh and blood, written upon his heart and read by all people. They were his attestation, far superior to any letter of attestation human hand could ever write on stones or perishable parchments.

The best and irrefutable witness of our lives is God Himself (Rom. 1:9; Phil. 1:8). He testifies to our legacy through people who have crossed our path or were positively influenced by us. One beautiful morning, I heard of the passing of a saintly eighty-five-year-old woman. The person who informed me of her homegoing said, "Nancy was such a role model for my children and me. She was an excellent example of self-sacrifice and unconditional love. Her passing is like losing a member of my family." I dare to say one of Nancy's letters of recommendation was my friend whom she positively influenced by her life and conduct.

One day all the applause we receive will subside, awards tarnish, achievements be forgotten, and letters of recommendation written on our behalf on perishable paper return to dust. The only lasting witnesses of our lives and legacy are the people we touch through our words and actions.

# Being a Good Person Behind a Great Person

> And Joses, who was also named Barnabas by the apostles (which is translated Son of Encouragement), a Levite of the country of Cyprus, having land, sold *it*, and brought the money and laid *it* at the apostles' feet.
>
> —Acts 4:36–37

> For he was a good man, full of the Holy Spirit and of faith. And a great many people were added to the Lord.
>
> —Acts 11:24

In his picturesque biographical sketch of Barnabas, Clarence Macartney, the nineteenth-century Presbyterian preacher, called him "the good man behind a great man."[106] His original name was Joseph, but the apostles gave him the name "Barnabas," which means "son of consolation," for he was an encourager of people. He was also a generous giver. He sold a field that he owned and gave the apostles the proceeds to advance the gospel (Acts 4:36).

True to his name, Barnabas befriended the newly converted Paul (formerly Saul of Tarsus) when he was a "nobody" in the apostles' eyes and the church in Jerusalem. In Paul, Barnabas saw a "stalwart of faith," so he took it upon himself to

---

106. Clarence E. Macartney, *The Wisest Fool And Other Men of the Bible* (New York: Abingdon-Cokesbury Press), 44.

introduce Paul to the church in Jerusalem. If it were not for Barnabas, Paul would have been lost to the church of Christ. Barnabas was the only one who gave Paul a welcome. From Barnabas's life, we learn three guiding principles for organizing our lives.

**The Principle of Doing**: Barnabas did what God enabled him to do rather than regret the good he could not do. He knew that he did not have Paul's eloquence, theological knowledge, or intellectual abilities. But he was content being the person God wanted him to be—an encourager of people. Encouraging others is good work that we all can do. It does not cost anything to promote and lift a person who is sad or discouraged with life.

It is interesting to note that the encouragement of Barnabas rubbed off on Paul. The Bible says that Paul went on his missionary tours with the sole purpose of encouraging believers (Acts 20:2). He wrote to the church at Thessalonica that he sent Timothy to encourage and build them up in the faith. Jesus, our Savior, encouraged Peter when he said, "Simon, Simon! Indeed, Satan has asked for you, that he may sift you as wheat. But I prayed for you, that your faith should not fail; and when you have returned to Me, strengthen your brethren" (Luke 22:31). Christ had in mind Peter's denial of the Lord and his subsequent recovery from backsliding to strengthen the brethren.

Let us resolve to be quick to encourage those who need a word of comfort to press on with life. One of the recipients of our encouragement may turn out to be a great man or woman to grace the landscape of human history. Only God knows! Let us meet the challenge of being an encourager and let God write the history of the impact of our encouragement on others.

**The Principle of Being**: Barnabas did not try to be Paul. He knew his limitations and strengths. When the church at Antioch was growing exponentially, Barnabas went to Tarsus looking for Paul. He brought Paul out of obscurity. Why?

Because he knew that Paul was a great man with the right qualifications for strengthening the body of Christ at Antioch. Barnabas did not think twice about playing second fiddle to Paul. He chose just to be a "good man behind a great man," for the Bible says that Barnabas was "a good man, full of the Holy Spirit and of faith" (Acts 11:24). Ironically, we can never learn anything about Paul without reading about the life and ministry of Barnabas. Strangely, he who sought to be just a "good man" became a "great man" in the annals of church history.

Few of us are called to be a Moses, Paul, Peter, John, Martin Luther, or John Calvin, but by the grace of God, we all can do what God called us to do. If we know Christ as Lord and Savior, we are called. If we are called, we have a ministry to do. In fact, we may be the only ones uniquely suited for the task assigned to us. Martin Buber, the famous Jewish philosopher, said:

> Man's earthly task is to realize his created uniqueness. As a Hasidic rabbi called Zusya put it on his deathbed: "In the world to come, they will not ask me, 'why were you not Moses?' They will ask me, 'Why were you not Zusya?'"[107]

World-renowned Cellist Yo-Yo Ma said it well: "The worst thing you can do is say to yourself, 'I want to be just like somebody else.' You have to absorb knowledge from someone else, but ultimately you have to find your own voice."[108]

The apostle Paul encouraged Timothy to stir up the gift of God, which was in him. In his case, the gift was that of preaching and being an elder in the church. I challenge you to stir up the gift God has given you for Christian service. It may

---

107. Quoted in Stephen R. Covey, *Everyday Greatness* (Nashville: Rutledge Hill Press, 2006), 21.

108. "Yo-Yo Ma Quotes," Quotefancy, accessed March 31, 2022, https://quotefancy.com/yo-yo-ma-quotes.

be the gift to preach, teach, show mercy, give liberally, or provide leadership. Whatever that gift may be, use it as the Lord gives you grace. Don't try to be someone that you are not! Find your voice and use it for the glory of God.

**The Principle of Possessing**: The Bible says that Barnabas was a good man, full of the Holy Spirit and of faith. This is especially important to note! He was an encourager because he was possessed, controlled, and directed by the Holy Spirit. The Bible calls the Holy Spirit "the Comforter" or *paracletos*, one who comes by our side and encourages us. Barnabas was also a man of deep faith. That is, he trusted God without reservation.

We must trust God to direct us to the work He has ordained for us (Eph. 2:10). Victor Frankl, the famous Jewish psychiatrist, maintained that life's supreme purpose is achieved when we look beyond ourselves. He wrote:

> Don't aim at success. The more you aim at it and make it a target, the more you are going to miss it. For success, like happiness, cannot be pursued; it must ensue, and it only does so as the unintended side effect of one's personal dedication to a cause greater than oneself or as the by-product of one's surrender to a person other than oneself.[109]

Our purpose in life is not us; it is other than us. If we focus only on ourselves, we will miss life's true purpose. The Bible teaches that life's true purpose is to glorify God and be conformed to the image of Christ (Isa. 43:7; Rom. 8:29). When we seek to fulfill our calling in dependence on the Holy Spirit, we are propelled to look beyond ourselves and become God-centered. We willingly and delightedly direct all our gifts and talents toward God for His glory.

---

109. Victor Frankl, *Man's Search For Meaning*, xiv.

Barnabas was a "good man behind a great man" by being an encourager. Barnabas did the good that he could do rather than regret the good that he could not do. He sought to be what God wanted him to be, not someone else. He fulfilled his calling by entirely depending on the Holy Spirit. I pray that God will empower you by His Spirit to exercise the gifts He has given you for His glory.

# Giving Up Too Soon

And let us not grow weary while doing good, for in due season we shall reap if we do not lose heart.

—Galatians 6:9

Bishop Ernest Fitzgerald tells a fascinating story about a Baptist preacher named Russell H. Conwell, who started a small night school for children, eventually becoming the famous Temple University in Philadelphia. Besides being the founder of this distinguished university, he was also known for a lecture entitled "Acres of Diamonds," which he gave more than six thousand times across the United States. Out of this one lecture, he earned more than eight million dollars in honorariums, and he gave most of it for the development of Temple University.[110]

In "Acres of Diamonds," Conwell told the story of a man who had discovered gold in western Nevada. The man mined the gold for a while and thought it was running out, so he sold the land for eleven thousand dollars. The purchasers of that property later made a mind-staggering discovery called the "Comstock lode," which turned out to be the richest gold and silver deposits anywhere in the world. Thirty years later, said Bishop Fitzgerald, the property owners, made nearly three hundred million dollars on their investment.

---

110. Ernest A. Fitzgerald, *Keeping Pace: Inspirations In The Air* (Greensboro, North Carolina: Pace Communications, 1988), 23.

This story, which captured the imagination of the American people, teaches us two powerful lessons. First, never give up too soon. God has invested in each of us enough resources and talents to make our lives worthwhile if we are determined to use them to the fullest with endurance. The apostle Paul wrote, "And let us not grow weary while doing good, for in due season we shall reap if we do not lose heart" (Gal. 6:9). Jesus reinforced this principle when He said, "Men always ought to pray and not lose heart" (Luke 18:1). The key is not to lose heart!

Second, there is a lesson for preachers in this story. Often, people ask how many times a preacher should preach the same sermon. In the words of my mentor, Dr. Stephen Olford, "If a sermon was not good enough to preach the second time, it was not good enough the first time."[111]

Many Bible scholars estimate that Jesus Christ, the greatest preacher who ever graced the landscape of human history, repeated His message in different ways more than five hundred times. As preachers of the gospel, we must never neglect to repeat a message for the glory of God if the occasion and audience call for it and the Holy Spirit leads us.

---

111. Personal communication.

# The Christian Work Ethic

Bondservants, be obedient to those who are your masters according to the flesh, with fear and trembling, in sincerity of heart, as to Christ; not with eyeservice, as men-pleasers, but as bondservants of Christ, doing the will of God from the heart, with goodwill doing service, as to the Lord, and not to men, knowing that whatever good anyone does, he will receive the same from the Lord, whether he is a slave or free.

—Ephesians 6:5–8

One of the things that impressed me most about the United States when I arrived here in 1967 was the dignity of labor displayed by Americans, which was unheard of when I was growing up in India. Certain jobs in India were relegated to people belonging to society's lower strata (low caste). But in America, my first job was as a dishwasher in our university cafeteria, a job I proudly did for $1.25 an hour side-by-side with a student who came from a wealthy family. Unfortunately, that dignity of labor is eclipsed in our present-day society, where not working has increasingly become more profitable than working.

But we are created to work. Soon after God created man (Adam), He put him in a garden to tend and keep it. In other words, God gave Adam work to do. God, Himself, was busy working for six days and rested on the seventh day. In no other belief system is work dignified to the level it is in Christianity. The apostle Paul wrote, "If anyone will not work, neither shall he eat" (2 Thess. 3:10). He also wrote that those who choose not to work are worse than unbelievers (1 Tim. 5:8). Ancient Greeks thought that work was a curse on humanity. Aristotle believed that not having to work was a mark of a worthwhile life.

If you are a Christian, I challenge you to make a paradigm shift in your work ethic and attitude toward your work. The Christian work ethic calls for excellence in everything we do, whether our work is duly recognized or rewarded. Ephesians 6:5–8 beautifully summarizes the Christian work ethic. We learn three things:

First, our work ethic is rooted in our being. Our work reflects who we are in Christ—we are the bondslaves of Jesus Christ. We don't like the term "slave" in our culture nor consider ourselves slaves to anyone. The Greek word *dulos,* translated as "bondservant," literally means a bondslave. If you are a Christian, you were formerly a slave of sin, but now you are a slave of righteousness (Rom. 6:18). Our work is an expression of our belonging to Christ. As slaves of Christ, we do our work "from the heart" as an act of submission to God's will. Our dedication to work reflects our allegiance to Christ. What we do follows who we are. We are defined not by what we do, but by to whom we belong.

Second, our work ethic is displayed in our doing. How we do our work should reflect the motivation behind our work. What is our motivation? Our motivation is pleasing God. We do our job "with goodwill as to the Lord." We work not "with eyeservice, as men-pleasers, but as the servants of Christ" to please Him. Once when President Franklin Roosevelt was in the office, a visitor named Wendell Wilkie went to see him. He asked the president why he kept a frail-looking, sickly man, Harry Hopkins, at his side. The president replied, "Mr. Wilkie, see that door there. Through that door come in many to see me every day, and invariably every one of them wants something from me. But Harry Hopkins only wants to serve me. That's why he is near me."[112] Christian workers ought to be the best in what they do. Employers should be eager to hire Christian workers because of their excellence, integrity, competence, and faithfulness.

Third, our work ethic is anchored in our knowing. Even if the people around us do not acknowledge or appreciate our work, we should know that we have a God in heaven who keeps score of our good works. Whatever good we do, we will receive a reward from the Lord without partiality. Our consolation is that the record of our good works is written in God's book. Paul wrote, "And let us not grow weary while doing good, for in due season we shall reap if we do not lose heart" (Gal. 6:9).

The Bible teaches that we are God's workmanship, created in Christ for good works that God has prepared for us before the foundation of the world. John Calvin put it this way: "The good works we do are ours by God's gift, but they are God's by His prompting."[113] Augustine said, "To will is of nature, but to will aright is of grace."[114] We need God's grace and the empowerment of the Holy Spirit to do the work God has given us in a way pleasing to the Lord. I pray that you will resolve on that you will do your work, whatever legitimate work that may be, for the Lord and let it shine as a witness to the power of God working in you.

---

112. "Willingness to Serve," Bible.org, accessed April 1, 2022, https://bible.org/illustration/willingness-serve.

113. John Calvin, *Institutes of the Christian Religion*, ed. John T. McNeil, trans. Ford Lewis Battles (Louisville: Westminster John Knox, 2006) 1:335.

114. Ibid.

# Are You Weary and Tired?

God has told his people, "Here is a place of rest; let the weary rest here. This is a place of quiet rest." But they would not listen.

—Isaiah 28:12 NLT

Are you weary and tired? Do you feel overwhelmed? Are you longing for peace and rest? If you are, God is inviting you to enter His rest: "Here is a place of rest; let the weary rest here. This is a place of quiet rest" (Isa. 28:12 NLT). Many centuries ago, God extended this invitation to rebellious Judah, but it would not listen. The people of Judah said, "Who does the LORD think we are? Why does he speak to us like this? Are we little children, just recently weaned?" (Isa. 28:9 NLT).

In simple and understandable language, Isaiah instructed Judah that true rest and peace could be found only in Yahweh. But the proud and drunken people of Judah viewed his instructions as the condescending repetitions a parent might use on a young child (Isa. 28:9–10). They rejected God's prescription for rest and chose instead to listen to the language of Assyria and come under its yoke.

Isn't this the course of action pursued by many today? Jesus invites all who are longing for repose: "Come to me, all of you who are weary and carry heavy burdens, and I will give you rest. Take my yoke upon you. Let me teach you, because I am humble and gentle at heart, and you will find rest for your souls" (Matt. 11:28, 29 NLT). Yet, many reject His invitation just as ancient Judah did long ago. The tragic outcome of continued rejection is that His invitation, which is meant to be understood and obeyed for peace and rest, will become to them an unintelligible noise of a foreign language leading to their judgment (Isa. 28:9–10). It behooves us, therefore, to run to Christ, the living Word, and find our rest in Him. St. Augustine said it well: "You [God] stir us up to take delight in your praise; for you have made us for yourself, and our heart is restless till it finds its rest in you."[115]

---

115. Augustine, *Confessions*, 5.

# Live Circumspectly

See then that you walk circumspectly, not as fools but as wise [wise people], redeeming the time, because the days are evil. Therefore do not be unwise, but understand what the will of the Lord is.

—Ephesians 5:15–17

The arrow of time moves ever forward with relentless speed. Some mark the passing of time with anguish and pain; others with renewed optimism, urgency, and passion. Herbert Rappaport, a psychologist at Temple University, observes:

> Somehow, New Year's Eve is not just like any other holiday—the passing of the old year and the birth of the new one carry enormous meaning and bring forth a whole array of emotions. Some people are happy, while others sink into intoxicated melancholy. Some revel at having accomplished what they set out to do for the year, while others are depressed about failing yet again to live up to expectations and resolutions. As the calendar changes, everyone experiences the anxiety inherent in examining one's life and asking difficult questions. What have I done with my life? Why isn't my life happy? Where is my life going? Each of these questions addresses a different element of time—the past, the present, and the future. It is no wonder that we associate New Year's Eve with an elaborate consumption of alcohol. Coping with the reality of time passing is an arduous affair. Looking at New Year's Eve we can see

how people feel about the momentum of their lives and how modern society struggles with the concept of time passing.[116]

Can you identify with the anxiety described by this psychologist? I certainly can. Each year that has passed by in my life, I have had my share of missed opportunities, unrealized goals, and unmet expectations. If I dwell on them, I could quickly plunge into a mood of depression. Instead, I must move on "forgetting the past and looking forward to what lies ahead" (Phil. 3:13). As children of God, we ought to see our past, present, and future in the light of God's redemptive plan for us. God is preparing for us a glorious future, which should give us hope and reason to "strain to reach the end of the race and receive the prize for which God, through Christ Jesus, is calling us up to heaven" (Phil. 3:14).

Our lives are inextricably linked to how we mark the movement of time. Thus, it is essential to know how we ought to use the time God has given us. The Bible says, "See then that you walk circumspectly, not as fools but as wise [wise people], redeeming the time, because the days are evil. Therefore do not be unwise, but understand what the will of the Lord is" (Eph. 5:15–17). The apostle Paul reminds us how to behave in a morally and spiritually bankrupt era. Today, we see an intense proliferation of evil everywhere—debauchery, wars, famine, natural disasters, and breaking of the family. The list goes on. We don't have to look far to find evil. As the famous American Thomas Payne once said, "These are the times that try men's souls."

What should we do in a time such as this? Paul gives us a threefold prescription.

---

116. Herbert Rappaport, *Marking Time: How our personalities, our problems, and their treatment are shaped by our anxiety about time* (New York: Simon & Schuster, 1990), 11–12.

First, we must scrutinize the time in which we live. We cannot afford to bury our heads in the sand and pretend that all is well. We are to act wisely. The word "wise" in the Greek text has the idea of a watchman surveying his surroundings to determine what is happening and what needs to be done. We must respond to our times appropriately, both individually and as a society. The Bible says the sons of Issachar understood the times they lived in and knew what Israel should do (1 Chron. 12:32).

To be sure, one thing that God is actively doing in our time is preparing the people's hearts to receive the gospel as never before. Let us be ready to meet this challenge and do what we can to reach the world's people for Christ. Let us actively engage in "hastening" the consummation of God's redemptive plan (2 Peter 3:12).

Second, we must seize our opportunities. Paul said we must redeem the time, which means making use of every opportunity to advance the kingdom of God. God's ultimate goal is to establish His kingdom. All of history is moving towards that end. The time of our life is the most valuable asset God has given us. Therefore, let us seize every opportunity to herald the glorious truth that all our hopes and dreams are met in Christ alone.

Third, we must seek to do the will of God. Paul encourages us to understand the will of the Lord and do it. God seeks from us not our offerings and sacrifices but our obedience to His revealed will. There is nothing we can do for Him to meet His need, for He has none. God is self-sufficient. God is looking for people through whom He can display His power and glory (2 Chron. 16:9). We delude ourselves if we think we can somehow "do things" for God and meet some intrinsic need He has. This is wishful thinking! The only service we can do is make ourselves available to Him, so He is glorified in us, for God is in the business of glorifying Himself in everything He does. Paul reminds us that submitting to the Holy Spirit is essential to do His will. We must continually be filled with the Holy Spirit and possessed by Him.

Friend, I challenge you to take these truths to heart and act. Scrutinize your setting and know what you must do to advance the cause of Christ. Seize every opportunity to promote the gospel. Seek to do God's will by being controlled by the Holy Spirit and allowing the Lord to magnify Himself in you.

# Man Gives up His Life to Save Others

For when we were still without strength, in due time Christ died for the ungodly. For scarcely for a righteous man will one die; yet perhaps for a good man someone would even dare to die. But God demonstrates His own love toward us, in that while we were still sinners, Christ died for us.

—Romans 5:6–8

"Jasim Issa Mohammed Hassan gave up his own life to save 300 others," said a report from *The Inquirer*.[117] The Boeing 777 flight from Trivandrum, India, carried 282 passengers and eighteen crew members when it crash-landed at Dubai National Airport on Wednesday, August 3, 2016. Mr. Hassan, a brave firefighter, put out the raging flames during the rescue operation, enabling everyone aboard to escape from the burning jet alive. Once everyone evacuated, the aircraft exploded, and the ensuing blaze killed Mr. Hassan. Mr. Saif Al Suwaidi, director of General Civil Aviation Authority (GCAA), paid tribute to the fallen hero saying, "I salute his ultimate sacrifice that kept many from harm's way. Our thoughts and prayers are with his family."

---

117. "Hero firefighter dies saving passengers in Emirates plane crash," Inquirer.Net, accessed April 5, 2022,
https://newsinfo.inquirer.net/803035/hero-firefighter-dies-after-saving-282-passengers-in-emirates-plane-crash.

Mr. Hassan sacrificed his life so others could live. Despite the life-threatening danger at the site, he bravely continued to extinguish the fire, and in the process, he lost his life. Jesus said, "Greater love has no one than this, than to lay down one's life for his friends" (John 15:13). In a way, Mr. Hassan was a true friend of the passengers of Flight EK521 even though he did not know them personally. The rescued passengers will certainly have a special place in their hearts for Mr. Hassan.

As I reflected on Mr. Hassan's untimely death, I could not help but think that his death was an imperfect picture of the perfect sacrifice that Jesus Christ made for us two thousand years ago. First, Jesus willingly died so that we may have everlasting life. He said, "I am the good shepherd. The good shepherd lays down his life for the sheep" (John 10:11 ESV). Jesus came down to the earth for the express purpose of dying so that we may live forever. Second, Jesus died while we were still sinners and in enmity with God. The Bible says, "For when we were still without strength, in due time Christ died for the ungodly. For scarcely for a righteous man will one die; yet perhaps for a good man someone would even dare to die. But God demonstrates His own love toward us, in that while we were still sinners, Christ died for us" (Rom. 5:6–8). Third, Jesus died and rose again from the grave. He said, "This is why the Father loves me—because I lay down my life, so that I may take it back again" (John 10:17 MNT). He died and rose from the grave to make our salvation effectual.

Many passengers of Flight EK521 expressed their gratitude for what Mr. Hassan had done to save their lives. How should one respond to what Christ has done for humankind? You believe in the Lord Jesus Christ and escape the fire of divine judgment. The Bible says, "If you confess with your mouth the Lord Jesus and believe in your heart that God has raised Him from the dead, you shall be saved" (Rom. 10:9). The apostle John wrote, "He who believes in the Son [Jesus] has everlasting life; and he who does not believe the Son shall not see life, but the wrath of God abides on him" (John 3:36). Interestingly, some passengers interfered with the evacuation because they were more concerned about taking their baggage. Jesus said, "For what profit is it to a man if he gains the whole world, and loses his own soul? Or what will a man give in exchange for his soul?" (Matt. 16:26).

If you believe in Jesus Christ, you respond by sharing the gospel with others and "snatching them out of the fire" (Jude 1:23). Indeed, Christianity is a rescue religion, for God in Christ stooped down to rescue us from the sinking sand when we could not help ourselves. Jesus said, "For the Son of Man has come to seek and to save that which was lost" (Luke 19:10).

# Judge Spends the Night with the Offender

For scarcely for a righteous man will one die; yet perhaps for a good man someone would even dare die.

—Romans 5:7

A few years ago, I read a story on Facebook that touched my heart deeply. It was the story of Green Beret veteran Joe Serna, a recipient of three Purple Hearts for his heroism in Afghanistan, who was sentenced to spend a night in jail in Fayetteville, North Carolina, for probation violation. Lou Olivera, a veteran of the Gulf War, was the presiding judge.

When Joe returned home after his duty in Afghanistan, life was hard for him, as memories of war haunted him relentlessly. While on tour in Afghanistan, he and three other soldiers rode along a creek when the road suddenly gave way, and their vehicle plunged into the water. They were trapped in their car and could not move. The water slowly rose until it reached Joe's chin and suddenly stopped. He was the only survivor of that horrible accident.

Joe was tormented by this experience and other memories of the war. He eventually turned to alcohol to relieve his post-traumatic stress disorder (PSD) and emotional pain. Joe was arrested on several occasions for alcohol-related infractions and was put on probation. When he violated his probation, he was arrested and brought to the Veterans Treatment Court, which helped struggling veterans get back on track. Judge

Olivera sentenced Joe to spend the night in the Cumberland County jail. Olivera felt that he had to hold Joe accountable for his actions.

When Joe entered the jail, he was gripped with fear, anxiety, and memories of the war in Afghanistan. He began to panic as the door of his cell was shut behind him. But a few minutes later, something unexpected happened. His cell door was opened, and Judge Olivera walked in. He had come to spend the night with Joe. Olivera said that he knew that Joe was a "good soldier and a good man...I wanted him to know that I had his back...I didn't want him to do this alone." The moment Joe saw the judge, he knew that everything was going to be alright. The judge spent the night with Joe in jail because he knew that Joe needed help to get through the night. At the same time, the judge wanted Joe to face the consequences of his actions. "He is a judge, but that night, he was my buddy," said Joe.

When I read this story, my heart was strangely warmed, and I could not help but think of what Christ has done for us sinners. In some ways, this story parallels what Christ did for us. Just as Olivera put aside his judicial robe and entered the jail cell of the offender, Jesus set aside his robe of glory in heaven and entered our experience to suffer pain and alienation. He did so because He knew that we were under divine condemnation and needed help to rise from our despair and helplessness. The writer of Hebrews reminds us that in Christ, "we do not have a high priest who is unable to sympathize with our weaknesses, but one who in every respect has been tempted as we are, yet without sin" (Heb. 4:15, ESV).

On the other hand, what Christ did for us was profoundly different and unique. Olivera chose to spend the night with Joe because he thought Joe was a "good soldier and a good man." Joe's service for our country elicited compassion in Olivera. But Jesus suffered for us while we were still sinners and ungodly (Rom. 5:6–8). Moreover, in contrast to Judge Olivera,

Jesus "died for us" or "in our place." Though Olivera spent the night with Joe in jail, Joe still had to pay the penalty of violating his probation. But Jesus died in our place so that we don't have to pay the penalty of our sin. This is called the doctrine of penal substitution. Philosopher William Craig defines it as "Christ voluntarily took upon himself the suffering that we deserved as the punishment for our sins, thereby removing our liability to punishment."[118] In other words, God sent His Son for the express purpose of paying the penalty of our sin and freeing us from divine condemnation and resultant punishment.

What does this mean to us? It means that "there is therefore now no condemnation for those who are in Christ Jesus" (Rom. 8:1). In Christ, we have a more compassionate judge than Olivera or any other human being, however noble or virtuous. In Christ, we have a loving Redeemer and Savior. Because of His death on the cross, we have been reconciled to God, so we are no longer in enmity with Him. Do you know Christ as your Savior? If not, will you surrender your life to Him and receive His offer of salvation?

118. William L. Craig, "The Atonement," Biola University, accessed Aprill 5, 2022, https://www.biola.edu/blogs/think-biblically/2019/the-atonement.

# If the Foundations Are Destroyed, What Can the Righteous Do?

> If the foundations are destroyed, what can the righteous do? The LORD *is* in His holy temple, The LORD'S throne *is* in heaven; His eyes behold, His eyelids test the sons of men.
>
> —Psalm 11:3–4

One morning, the Lord drew my attention to Psalm 11 for my meditation. King David, who was deeply troubled by the moral condition of Israel and the dangers within and without, lamented, saying, "If the foundations are destroyed, what can the righteous do?" (Ps. 11:3). He then answered his own question: "The LORD is in his holy temple; the LORD's throne is in heaven; his eyes see, his eyelids test the children of man" (Ps. 11:4 ESV). From this psalm, we learn three powerful truths about God and His governance of human affairs.

First, we learn that the Lord reigns. "The LORD is in His temple; the LORD's throne is in heaven." The throne represents the reign of a sovereign king. The Bible teaches that God "changes the times and the seasons; He removes kings and raises up kings" (Dan. 2:21). Because God is ruler over all that He has created, including our political systems, we can rest assured that God is in control of our affairs and guides the movement of history toward His intended purpose. We may not always understand what God is doing, but we can be confident that His ways and judgments are always right (Pss. 105:7; 119:75).

Second, we learn that the Lord hears. "The LORD is in His holy temple." At the time David penned these words, the temple was not yet built in Jerusalem. However, like the tabernacle before it, the temple represented God's meeting place with His people. The expression, "The LORD is in His holy temple," means that the Lord dwells with His people and hears their petitions.

"If the foundations are destroyed, what can the righteous do?" (Ps. 11:3). What the righteous can do is to turn to the One who rules the earth and hears our prayers. The Bible says that the Lord is in His holy temple. His eyes behold the wicked and their devices (Ps. 11:4). Our ultimate vindication comes from the Lord. When Herod Agrippa (A.D. 37–44), grandson of Herod the Great, imprisoned the apostle Peter to please the Jewish rulers of his day, the church prayed for him earnestly. And God answered their prayer and miraculously delivered Peter from the prison (Acts 12). We must pray for the leaders in authority that "we [might] lead a quiet and peaceable life in all godliness and reverence" (1 Tim. 2:1).

Third, we learn that the Lord sees. "His eyes behold, His eyelids test the sons of men." Nothing is hidden from the view of an omniscient God. He sees our coming and going and is a "discerner of the thoughts and intents of the heart" (Heb. 4:12). Disclosures of secret sins of many political leaders in recent years have brought to the fore the divine truth: "Be sure your sin will find you out" (Num. 32:33). No one can hide from the searchlights of God. He knows our thoughts even before we think. "Do not be deceived, God is not mocked; for whatever a man sows, that he will also reap" (Gal. 6:8).

I pray that these truths will comfort you in times of difficulty and guide you to live a life pleasing to God.

# The Gift of Giving

> Having then gifts differing according to the grace that is
> given to us, *let us use them*: if prophecy, *let us prophesy* in
> proportion to our faith; or ministry, *let us use*
> it in *our* ministering; he who teaches, in teaching; he who
> exhorts, in exhortation; he who gives, with liberality; he
> who leads, with diligence; he who shows mercy, with
> cheerfulness.
>
> —Romans 12:6–8

Christmas is the most beautiful time of the year because, in this
season, we celebrate the birth of Christ and prepare to enter a
brand-new year with anticipation. Christmas is all about God's
greatest gift to the world, for God so loved the world that He
gave His only begotten Son. Christmas is a vivid reminder that
we are never more like God than when we give.

In his letter to the church in Rome, the apostle Paul wrote
that "giving liberally" is a spiritual gift (Rom. 12:8). We all give
to others at one time or another, but to give generously at a
personal cost is a spiritual endowment. A case in point was the
church in Philippi, Thessalonica, and Berea, collectively known
as Macedonia's churches (2 Cor. 8:1). When these churches
heard of the Jerusalem church's poverty, they willingly, eagerly,
and gladly made a financial contribution even though they were
poor and experienced great afflictions. These churches
compelled Paul to take their monetary gift to help the saints in
Jerusalem. Despite their poverty, they could give liberally
because they first gave themselves to the Lord (2 Cor. 8:5).

Paul uses the example of Macedonia's churches to motivate and encourage the church at Corinth to fulfill a commitment they had made a year earlier to help the poor in Jerusalem (2 Cor. 9:2). From his letter to the church at Corinth, we learn three powerful truths about the gift of giving.

First, when we give, we attest to the grace of God in Christ. Giving is an act of grace. The apostle Paul encouraged the saints of God at Corinth to excel in the grace of giving just as they were abounding in faith, doctrine, knowledge of God, and love (2 Cor. 8:7). The sole motivator of grace-giving is one's love for God. Such giving is always God-centered and never self-centered. So, every time we give sacrificially and liberally, we testify to the grace of God.

Second, when we give, we acclaim the riches of God in Christ. The apostle Paul wrote, "For you know the grace of our Lord Jesus Christ, that though He was rich, yet for your sakes, He became poor that you through His poverty might become rich" (2 Cor. 8:9). The second person of the Trinity, equal with the Father, became poor by taking the form of a bond slave. He set aside the independent use of His divine prerogatives, died on the cross, and rose from the grave so that we might rise from our spiritual impoverishment and become rich in Him. When we give, we acclaim the riches of God, of which we are partakers through Christ (Rom. 8:17; Eph. 1:3).

Third, when we give, we affirm the supply of God in Christ. Paul informed the Christians at Corinth that their giving would motivate the church in Jerusalem to supply their own needs and that there would be equality in giving. God uses people to meet each other's needs. To bear one another's burdens is the law of Christ that governs us all (Gal. 6:2).

I pray that God will empower you in the days ahead to give liberally of your time, treasure, and talents for the glory of God.

# The Grace of Forgiveness

Take heed to yourselves. If your brother sins against you, rebuke him; and if he repents, forgive him. And if he sins against you seven times in a day, and seven times in a day returns to you, saying, "I repent," you shall forgive him.

—Luke 17:3–4

Then Jesus said, "Father, forgive them, for they do not know what they do."

—Luke 23:34

Some time ago, I read the story of a Christian mother in Mosul, Iraq, who answered the doorbell and opened to see a group of ISIS militants. They barged into her house and demanded that she flee the town immediately or pay the Jizya tax required of non-Muslims. The woman begged them to give her a few minutes to bring the payment, but they refused to wait. Instead, they torched her house while her daughter was taking a shower. The raging fire soon engulfed her daughter, and before she could be rescued, she died in the arms of her mother. According to the *Catholic News World* that reported this story, her final words before she breathed her last breath were, "Forgive them."[119]

119. "Christian Girl Burned to Death by ISIS," Catholic News World, accessed April 7, 2022, http://www.catholicnewsworld.com/2016/05/breakingnews-christian-girl-burned-to.html.

We are never more like God than when we forgive. In fact, to receive forgiveness from God and to extend forgiveness to others is at the heart of the Christian faith. Many years ago, in a moment of surprising candor on television, Marghanita Laski, a well-known secular humanist, said: "What I envy most about you Christians is your forgiveness; I have nobody to forgive me."[120] When the Roman and Jewish leaders crucified Jesus, He prayed, "Father, forgive them, for they know not what they do" (Luke 23:34). Jesus asked the Father in heaven not to hold this sin of crucifying Him against these "lawless men" because they were ignorant of the significance of what they were doing. He was not absolving either the Jews or the Romans of their responsibility in crucifying Him. What Jesus was doing was to forgive their specific sin of nailing Him to the cross, not all their sins for their salvation.

Stephen, the first martyr in the history of the Christian church, also prayed a similar prayer when he was being stoned to death. He said, "Lord, do not hold this sin against them" (Acts 7:60). Jesus did not grant His offenders salvation, forgiveness for all their sins, or entrance into the kingdom of God, because the requirements for salvation are repentance and believing in Jesus as Lord (Acts 3:13–20; 13:3–5; Rom. 10:10–13; 1 John 1:9). It is crucial to keep in view this distinction for rightly understanding the grace of forgiveness.

**Meaning:** In the New Testament, four Greek words— *charizomai, aphiemi, apoluo,* and *aphesis*—are commonly translated as "forgive" or "forgiven." *Charizomai* refers to the act of freely bestowing favor on someone. *Aphiemi* means to let go or send away. *Apoluo* denotes acquitting one accused of a crime and setting him free. *Aphesis* conveys the idea of releasing an offender from personal retaliation. Based on the meaning of these words, we may define biblical forgiveness as

---

120. Quoted in John Stott, *Contemporary Christian: Applying God's Word To Today's World* (Downers Grov: InterVarsity Press, 1992), 48.

a volitional act in which we freely bestow favor upon an offender, let go of the offense, and release the offender from any form of personal retaliation. Total forgiveness involves not only forgiving but also praying for the offender. This is what Jesus meant when He said, "Pray for those who persecute you" (Matt. 5:44).

There is a cost to extending forgiveness. If I forgive a debt, I lose the amount of money owed to me. If I forgive one who hurt me, I still bear the pain of the injury inflicted on me. If I pardon one who insulted me, I endure the humiliation caused to me. As one eminent legal scholar noted, "The germ of all forgiveness, and therefore a latent principle of all atonement, lies in the fact that whosoever forgives deliberately sustains the consequences of the wrong done so that the forgiven may be exempt. Every act of forgiveness is an act of substitution, whereby he who is sinned against, being innocent, substitutes himself as a bearer of the consequences of the sin, from which, by doing so, he relieves the guilty person."[121] Indeed, this is the ethical and judicial basis of God forgiving our sins.

**Method:** Jesus said, "If your brother sins against you, rebuke him; and if he repents, forgive him. And if he sins against you seven times in a day, and seven times in a day returns to you, saying, 'I repent,' you shall forgive him" (Luke 17:3, 4). The Scripture says that repentance is required of the offender to receive forgiveness, especially when seeking divine forgiveness. However, in the case of interpersonal forgiveness, what if the offender does not repent or seek forgiveness? In such a case, we can take our cue from Jesus Christ and extend grace to the offender (*charizomai*), let go of the offense (*aphiemi*), and release the offender from personal retribution (*aphesis, apoluo*).

---

121. D. M. Panton, "Note on the Ethics of Atonement" in P. V. George, *The Unique Christ And The Mystic Gandhi* (Tiruvalla: The Malabar Christian Office, 1934), 118–119. This book is out of print.

We hear and read a lot about forgiveness offered to us by God, but little is said about forgiving fellow human beings for the wrong done to us. For years, this topic of person-to-person forgiveness was ignored by secular psychologists and even biblical scholars. The late Dr. Lewes Smedes of Fuller Seminary made this observation as he reflected on the gospel: "Forgiving fellow human beings for wrongs done to them was close to the quintessence of Christian experience. And, more, that the inability to forgive other people was a cause of added misery to the one who was wronged in the first place."[122]

**Mandate:** We have a divine order to forgive. When Jesus told His disciples to forgive their offenders when they repent, it was an imperative or a command (Luke 17:3). We who have received the forgiveness of Christ must be quick to forgive others unconditionally in obedience to Christ's mandate, recognizing that to forgive and receive forgiveness can be one of the most liberating experiences of our lives.

Perhaps you may have been hurt by someone close to you: a spouse, father, mother, sibling, son, daughter, an employee, or an employer. You've been struggling with bitterness, and it is eating you up inside. You are emotionally wounded and desperately in need of healing and freedom. Jesus said, "For if you forgive men their trespasses, your heavenly Father will also forgive you" (Matt. 6:14). The key to forgiving others is to receive first the forgiveness of Christ, so you can be empowered by His Spirit to do that which you cannot do in your strength (Eph. 4:32).

I pray that you will repent of your sins, receive Christ's forgiveness, and experience the freedom He gives you to live a victorious life of total forgiveness.

---

122. Lewis Smedes, *Forgive and Forget: Healing the Hurts We Don't Deserve* (New York: Harper Collins, 1987), quoted in Gary Thomas, "The Forgiveness Factor," *Christianity Today* (January 2000):42.

# The Last of Human Freedoms

They do not consider in their hearts *that* I remember all their wickedness; Now their own deeds have surrounded them; They are before My face.

—Hosea 7:2

They return, *but* not to the Most High; They are like a treacherous bow. Their princes shall fall by the sword for the cursings of their tongue. This *shall* be their derision in the land of Egypt.

—Hosea 7:16

Viktor Frankl, the famous psychiatrist who survived the Holocaust, wrote, "Our greatest freedom is the freedom to choose our attitude... The last of the human freedoms [is]—to choose one's attitude in any given set of circumstances, to choose one's own way."[123] I will argue that how we exercise this "last of one's freedom" toward God leads to more consequences with eternal significance than any attitude we might have toward another human being, thing, or circumstance.

In Hosea 7, we read how Israel (northern kingdom) responded to God when He leveled a series of charges against Israel, the chief being its spiritual and moral harlotry. Israel's

---

123. Victor Frankl, *In Search of Meaning*, 66.

"spirit of whoredom" and its evil deeds were continually before God's face. God was so disgusted with Israel that He turned to Judah (the southern kingdom) and said, "Ephraim [Israel] is joined to idols, leave him alone" (Hos. 4:17). Yet God continued to wait on Israel to return to Him. Despite God's relentless plea for Israel to repent, Israel's impudence reflects our own attitude toward God in different life situations. Israel responded to God in three ways that proved to be fatal. We must guard against these destructive ways at any cost.

First, we must guard against an unruly attitude toward God. "The pride of Israel testifies to his face, yet they do not return to the LORD their God" (Hos. 7:10). Israel openly rebelled against God and refused to return to Him in repentance. Sometimes, we also show such open rebellion toward God when He confronts us with our sin. Instead of begging God for His forgiveness, we react with hostility and seek to justify and rationalize our offense. When the prophet Nathan confronted David about his sin of adultery, David quickly confessed his transgression and sought God's forgiveness (Ps. 51:3–4). When the Holy Spirit convicts us of sin, let us be quick to pray as David prayed: "Against You, You only, have I sinned and done this evil in Your sight" (Ps. 51:4). When we confess our sins, God is ready to forgive us our sins and cleanse us from all unrighteousness (1 John 1:9). Our God's willingness to forgive and restore us far outweighs our capacity to fail Him.

Second, we must guard against an unrepentant attitude toward God. "They [Israel] do not cry to me from the heart" (Hos. 7:14 ESV). God sees our heart, for we are an open book before Him. We can't hide anything from Him. He knows when we are sincere and when we are duplicitous. The Bible says, "For the LORD does not see as man sees; for man looks at the outward appearance, but the LORD looks at the heart" (1 Sam. 16:7). God is looking for a contrite spirit in us (Ps. 34:18) and godly sorrow born from the heart (2 Cor. 7:10).

Third, we must guard against an unreliable attitude toward God. "They return, but not upward; they are like a treacherous bow" (Hos. 7:16). Israel returned but not to God. The people of Israel were foolish, impulsive, and rash in their response. Instead of turning to God, they turned to Assyria for help (Hos. 8:9). They were unreliable, like a treacherous bow. God knows when we are truthful. He also knows when we turn to all the wrong places for help and refuge. The Bible says, "God is our refuge and strength, a very present help in trouble" (Ps. 46:1; Isa. 31:1). He alone can make way for us where there is no way and make the "crooked places straight" (Isa. 45:2).

Israel refused to turn to God in obedience, repentance, and faith. As a result, it reaped the judgment of God and was taken into captivity by the very nation to which it turned for help. Our attitude toward God determines our destiny.

How are you exercising the last of all human freedoms, the freedom to choose your attitude toward what is happening to you right now? May the following prayer always be on your lips: "Search me, O God, and know my heart! Try me and know my thoughts! And see if there be any grievous way in me, and lead me in the way everlasting" (Ps. 139:23-24 ESV).

# The Splendor of the Queen
# of the Night

Bondservants, be obedient to those who are your masters according to the flesh, with fear and trembling, in sincerity of heart, as to Christ; not with eyeservice, as men-pleasers, but as bondservants of Christ, doing the will of God from the heart, with goodwill doing service, as to the Lord, and not to men, knowing that whatever good anyone does, he will receive the same from the Lord, whether he is a slave or free.

—Ephesians 6:5–8

One evening, my wife and I had the opportunity to visit a dear friend of ours to observe the blooming of the Queen of the Night (*Ephyphyllum oxypetalum*), also known as orchid cactus. For most of the year, it remains obscure and resembles a dead bush. But once a year, usually between July and October, it blooms in the middle of the night, exuding an exquisite fragrance, and wilts by early dawn. This flower is native to the dry regions of Mexico and South America. In North America, it can be grown indoors as a houseplant.

As I watched the Queen of the Night bloom, with its bright white petals welcoming the beholder, I couldn't help but think of the beauty and splendor of those who do the Lord's bidding in obscurity. The Queen of the Night normally grows hidden from people and blooms for a short time. Though it remains hidden, it blooms to bring pleasure to the Lord who created it.

Like this orchid cactus, many Christians live and serve the Lord in obscurity. They may not be in the limelight or on stage to talk about their Christian service, but they bring delight to their Master, who appointed the time and place of their blooming.

The apostle Paul wrote, "Work with enthusiasm, as though you were working for the Lord rather than for people. Remember that the Lord will reward each one of us for the good we do, whether we are slaves or free" (Eph. 6:7–8 NLT). Paul should know what he was talking about. Following his conversion on the road to Damascus, Paul spent nearly fourteen years in obscurity serving the Lord. He was not on anyone's invite list until Barnabas brought this "orchid cactus" from the desert to Antioch's church for people to see him bloom. If you ever feel as if you are serving the Lord in obscurity, don't lose heart. Bloom where you are planted to the delight of your Master. He is all that counts!

I also noticed the Queen of the Night's intense fragrance that lingered long after the flower withered. One nature enthusiast wrote: "She blooms in full and her beauty is only witnessed by the night sky and, by dawn, she wilts ever before the sun's first kiss; with only her fragrant scent left as the ghost of her evening arrival."[124] The Queen of the Night's fragrant scent was the unforgettable signal of its beauty and splendor, though it bloomed only for a short time.

Just as with the Queen of the Night, what matters is the "fragrance" we give out. The apostle Paul wrote, "Now thanks be to God who always leads us in triumph in Christ, and through us diffuses the fragrance of His knowledge in every place" (2 Cor. 2:14). Philip, the evangelist, had four unnamed daughters. But we know them by the "fragrance" of prophesy that they gave out. The Holy Spirit made this memorable statement about them: "Now this man [Philip] had four virgin

---

124. "Queen of the Night Flower Facts," accessed April 8, 2022, https://eastandsunset.com/site/queen-of-the-night-flower-facts-7f7062.

daughters who prophesied" (Acts 21:9). That's all we read about them; that's all we need to know about them. They are remembered for their "fragrance."

Do those who meet you smell the fragrance of the knowledge of the Lord in you? When they walk by where you have been, do they smell the aroma of your devotion to the Lord? Though your service for Christ is short-lived, you are most remembered by the fragrance you emit. Go and bloom fragrantly for the Lord where He planted you.

# What Is Your Ministry?

But we all, with unveiled face, beholding as in a mirror the glory of the Lord, are being transformed into the same image from glory to glory, just as by the Spirit of the Lord. Therefore, since we have this ministry, as we have received mercy, we do not lose heart.

—2 Corinthians 3:18–4:1

Today, many Christians scurry around looking for some "ministry" to do. They think that if they don't have a ministry, they are not serving the Lord. Or they feel that they are floating like driftwood in the kingdom of God's stream. Sadly, this frantic search for "ministry" has thrust many into what the Quaker theologian Thomas Kelly describes as "an intolerable scramble of panting feverishness."[125]

There is one preeminent ministry that God has given to all of us in the body of Christ, which is often neglected at our peril in our desire to serve Him. This all-important ministry is to behold the glory of the Lord and be transformed into His image from glory to glory. The apostle Paul wrote, "And we all, with unveiled face, beholding the glory of the Lord, are being transformed into the same image from one degree of glory to another…Therefore, having this ministry by the mercy of God, we do not lose heart" (2 Cor. 3:18–4:1 ESV). In the final analysis, the only ministry that counts is the one in which

---

125. Thomas R. Kelly, *A Testament Of Devotion* (New York: HarperCollins Publishers, 1969), 100.

you are progressively being transformed into the image of Jesus Christ.

Service to God is essential, but it is always secondary to the serious call to a devout life. The apostle Paul wrote, "It pleased God… to reveal His Son in me, that I might preach" (Gal. 1:15–16). Paul's preaching ministry was secondary to the higher ministry of revealing Christ in him. Oswald Chambers understood this indubitable truth: "Beware of anything that competes with loyalty to Jesus Christ. The greatest competitor of devotion to Jesus is service for Him."[126] Jesus rebuked Satan, saying, "You shall worship the LORD your God and Him only shall you serve" (Matt. 4:10). Service is secondary to worship or devotion to God.

It is conceivable that a person could gallivant around the globe "serving Christ" while being impoverished in their soul. I pray that you will make "beholding the glory of the Lord and being transformed into His image" your supreme ministry. When His nature is expressed in you, you will find the "ministry" that is exactly right for you as an outflow of your devotion to God.

---

126. Oswald Chambers, *My Utmost For His Highest* (Westwood, New Jersey: Barbour and Company, 1935), 13.

# SOCIETAL

Righteousness exalts a nation, but sin is a reproach
to any people.

—Proverbs 14:34

We do not want, as the newspapers say, a church that will
move with the world. We want a church that will move the
world.

—G. K. Chesterton

# Lessons from National Events

O LORD, how long shall I cry, and You will not hear?
Why do you show me iniquity and cause me to see
trouble?

—Habakkuk 1:2–3

There is a familiar saying: every event has the potential to make us bitter or better. A national event such as a presidential election is no different; it makes us bitter or better. The gyrations and repercussions of a national event are bound to leave their effects on us for years to come. As Christians, we must turn to Scripture to gain a perspective on the national events we face. The book of Habakkuk is an excellent place to achieve such a view.

Habakkuk was a sixth-century B.C. prophet who ministered to Judah's people (southern kingdom of Israel). During his time, Judah had morally, politically, and socially disintegrated beyond repair. Violence, murder, strife, contention, debauchery, and profligacy were rampant. The moral compass of the land was spinning out of control. The judicial system in Judah had utterly broken down. There was no justice in the land. The rich got away with crime, but the poor paid the price for any violations with their lives. If justice ever was administered, it was perverted justice. Habakkuk was confused, angry, and frustrated with God and others, which led him to a state of despair and hopelessness. He cried: "How long shall I cry, and You will not hear? Why do you show me iniquity and cause me to see trouble?" (Hab. 1:2–3).

I am sure many God-fearing Christians feel the same way Habakkuk felt when they see, for example, what is going on in America. I dare say that Habakkuk 1 is an accurate description of America today and the ills plaguing our nation, which once was called the beacon of hope and a light to other nations. So, what can we learn from the challenges we face as a nation?

First, we learn about the sovereignty of God. God said to Habakkuk, "Look among the nations and watch—be utterly astounded! For *I will* work a work in your days *which* you would not believe, though it were told you" (Hab. 1:5). As a Christian, I know that God is sovereign, and He is always at work, even when I am snoring in the middle of the night. God will not always reveal what He is planning to do in advance, all the modern-day prophets of Baal notwithstanding. For instance, if a political leader of our choice is defeated, we can rest assured that God is in control. The Bible says, "For exaltation comes neither from the east nor from the west nor from the south. But God is the Judge: He puts down one and exalts another" (Ps. 75:6–7). If God allowed a particular evil to enter our experience, we must believe that God sovereignly ordained it to be so. The late theologian R. C. Sproul said it well: "Evil is not good, but it is good that there is evil; otherwise, it wouldn't be in a universe governed by a perfect God."[127] Sproul's point is that God always has a purpose for all that He does, even if we do not understand what it is (Rom. 8:28).

Second, we learn about the responsibility of Christians. Habakkuk was wise to recognize that he needed to wait to hear what God had to say to him and not try on his own to make sense of what was going on around him. Habakkuk said, "I will climb my watchtower now, and wait to see what answer God

---

127. From a speech by R. C. Sproul published on YouTube. Accessed March 22, 2022, https://www.youtube.com/watch?v=cUrZz__12fM.

will give to my complaint." I wish we could all learn to do what Habakkuk did—wait for God to speak to us through His Word (Bible) rather than scurrying around from place to place or person to person for insight and direction. God told Habakkuk what He would do and that it would undoubtedly happen; it would not tarry. Then God gave him a piece of life-changing insight: the wicked trust in themselves; but the righteous trust in God and live by faith (Hab. 2:4; Rom. 1:17; Gal. 3:11; Heb. 10:38). This means that, as a Christian, I must live my life trusting that God has a purpose in all that I am going through, even if I do not see or know the outcome of my life situation.

Third, we learn about the accountability of nations. God assured Habakkuk that Judah was not going to get away scot-free for its atrocities. God said that He was preparing the brutal, violent, and ungodly Chaldeans to be His instrument for punishing Judah. America is accountable to God. God is keeping a score of America's sins: lawlessness, indiscriminate abortions, the desecration of marriage and human sexuality, injustices, unrestrained hedonism, the emasculation of truth, oppression of Christians, and unbridled greed, to name a few. In His forbearance, God patiently waits for America to repent of her sins and turn to God.

America's hope is not in any political leader or system of government. Her hope is found in God alone. When God's patience runs its course and America remains unrepentant, God will unleash His judgment on this nation. Let us turn to God in faith for His salvation and direction.

# America's Cup of Iniquity Rapidly Filling Up

But in the fourth generation they shall return here, for the iniquity of the Amorites *is* not yet complete.

—Genesis 15:16

Millions of Americans, both religious and non-religious, received with horror and profound sadness the recent news of the passage of a law by New York that allows a mother to abort a baby at any point during pregnancy. The state in which I live (Delaware) has passed a similar law. I cannot even begin to imagine how much this act of savagery and moral depravity breaks the heart of God.

In Fyodor Dostoevsky's novel *The Brothers Karamazov*, Ivan Karamazov voices a riveting truth: "If there is no God, then everything is permitted."[128] For the followers of Christ, what New York has done should not be surprising because it is the inevitable result of jettisoning God from our society. Professing to be wise, many people in our country have become fools and have exchanged God's truth for Satan's lie.

---

128. Some argue that this line is not found in Dostoevsky's novel. Andrei I. Volkov, a Russian writer, refutes the nay-sayers and gives detailed evidence, including the translation of the original Russian text, to show that this line does exist in the novel. See "Dostoevsky Did Say It: A Response to David E. Cortesi (2011)," accessed May 23, 2021, https://infidels.org/library/modern/andrei_volkov/dostoevsky.html.

Therefore, God has given them up to "uncleanness, in the lusts of their hearts, to dishonor their bodies" (Rom. 1:24).

Just as the blood of Abel cried out to God from the earth for justice, the blood of millions of babies sacrificed on the altar of expediency in America's abortion clinics cries out for divine vengeance. God's forbearance of America's unrestrained wickedness should not be taken lightly. God patiently waits for America to turn to Him in repentance instead of filling up its cup of destruction with iniquity. When the sin of America reaches its full measure, God will unleash His judgment on her. This is precisely what happened to the Amorites of Canaan three thousand years ago. God waited patiently for 430 years until the iniquity of the Amorites— bestiality, sodomy, child sacrifice, and other vices—reached full measure. And when God's patience ran out, He judged the Amorites, obliterating them from the face of the earth (Gen. 15:12–16). During the time of God's patient waiting, the Amorites could have heeded the witness of Abram and turned to God in repentance, but they did not.

America has a choice to make: either repent and experience the mercies of God or face His wrath. King David wrote: "For You *are* not a God who takes pleasure in wickedness, nor shall evil dwell with You. The boastful shall not stand in Your sight; You hate all workers of iniquity. You shall destroy those who speak falsehood; the LORD abhors the bloodthirsty and deceitful man" (Ps. 5:4–6). The Bible also says, "God demonstrates His own love toward us, in that while we were still sinners, Christ died for us" (Rom. 5:8). God's justice and mercy met together on the cross (Ps. 85:10). God could not have shown His love at the expense of His justice or vice versa. Therefore, by letting His Son, Jesus Christ, die on the cross in our place for the remission of our sins, God demonstrated that He is both just and the justifier of the one who has faith in Jesus (Rom. 3:26).

The divine verdict is unmistakable: "He who believes in the Son has everlasting life; and he who does not believe the Son shall not see life, but the wrath of God abides on him" (John 3:36). Will America choose to be under God's canopy of mercy or be swept away by His withering wind of judgment?

# God's Answer to the Evil of Natural Disasters

For I consider that the sufferings of this present time are not worthy to be compared with the glory which shall be revealed in us. For the earnest expectation of the creation eagerly waits for the revealing of the sons of God. For the creation was subjected to futility, not willingly, but because of Him who subjected it in hope; because the creation itself also will be delivered from the bondage of corruption into the glorious liberty of the children of God.

—Romans 8:18–21

Many of us who have witnessed hurricanes, such as Harvey and Irma, have been troubled by them. I was deeply saddened and distressed by the loss of property of thousands of people who had to be relocated to various shelters. Millions of Floridians were without electricity and access to clean water. In moments like these, it is natural for us to experience a whole gamut of emotions—anger, despair, rejection, sorrow, sadness, hatred, hopelessness.

During natural disasters, feel-good sermons no longer cut the mustard. We want credible answers to the question of pain and suffering. The destruction caused by hurricanes is an excellent example of what is commonly called natural or physical evil. How could such evil happen in a world that is under the watchful eye of a good and an all-powerful God?

What is the answer to the problem of evil? Our search for a biblical perspective takes us to creation when God created a perfect world—a world without death and decay— and put Adam in a pristine environment to tend and care for God's creation. He was to live under God's rule and authority. But Adam chose to become autonomous and free himself from God's control by eating the forbidden tree's fruit, the tree of the knowledge of good and evil.

As a result of Adam's sin, the whole earth came under the curse of God, and natural disasters, death, and decay have become a part of the earth's fallen estate (Gen. 3:17–19). It is crucial to keep in mind that when God created the universe out of nothing (*ex nihilo*), all the cosmic constants such as gravity, the mass of the electron, speed of light, electromagnetic forces, rate of expansion of the universe, and electric charge were fine-tuned precisely for producing life as we know it on earth (the anthropic principle). Even the slightest change in any one of these constants would have led to a universe unlike our own, and a life-producing planet such as the earth would not have been possible. Unfortunately, because of sin, the forces of nature that are supposed to work in perfect harmony became disrupted under God's curse. Consequently, all the geological, meteorological, climatological, tectonic, and atmospheric factors that make life possible on earth and give us rain and seasons also produce earthquakes and other natural disasters.

Though the earth came under the curse of God, He has not abandoned it. God is in control of His creation (Hab. 2:20). In God's plan for humanity, the present fallen earth is only a temporary state. The Bible says, "Yet what we suffer now is nothing compared to the glory He will reveal to us later. For all creation is waiting eagerly for that future day when God will reveal who his children are. Against its will, all creation was subject to God's curse. But with eager hope, the creation looks forward to the day when it will join God's children in glorious freedom from death and decay" (Romans 8:18–21 NLT).

A day is coming when Christ shall usher us into a new earth with no suffering, pain, hurricanes, earthquakes, disasters, or death. We will inhabit a world that is free of all moral, physical, and metaphysical evil. Most importantly, we will be free from the presence of sin.

In the meantime, those who put their trust in God stand to experience comfort and strength even in their suffering on this fallen earth. For Christians, suffering is not meaningless. When we suffer, we are partners with Christ in His suffering so that we will have the incredible joy of seeing His glory when it is revealed to the entire world (1 Peter 4:13). Furthermore, in times of suffering, it helps to remind ourselves of what Jesus said to those who told Him about the death of eighteen on whom the tower in Siloam fell. He asked, "Do you think that they were worse offenders than all the others who live in Jerusalem? No, I tell you; but unless you repent, you will likewise perish" (Luke 13:4–5 ESV). The victims of hurricanes are no worse sinners than those who escaped them. Irrespective of who we are, we all are subject to calamities of one kind or another simply because we live in a sin-tainted world. It is important to know that we will suffer eternal punishment far worse than anything we experience on this earth unless we repent.

When we go through suffering, it is easy for us to get bogged down by "why" questions. Ancient Job did precisely that—he bombarded God with many questions as to why he suffered. God never answered any of his questions directly. Instead, God opened Job's eyes to have a glimpse of His majesty, glory, and power by posing a series of questions. Job's response to God was, "I know that you can do all things, and no purpose of yours can be thwarted...I have uttered what I did not understand, things too wonderful for me, which I did not know...but now my eye sees you; therefore, I despise myself, and repent in dust and ashes" (Job 42:2–6 ESV). Seeing

God's glory evaporated all of Job's questions, and answers to them were no longer necessary.

A Christian may take consolation because even when natural disasters fall on us, God works out His purpose, which we may not (or be meant to) understand. Philosopher and theologian R. C. Sproul puts the matter into perspective: "Evil is not good, but it is good that there is evil; otherwise, it wouldn't be in a universe ruled by a perfect God."[129] Evil has no power to enter human experience unless a Sovereign God ordains it for His purpose!

---

129. From a speech given by R. C. Sproul published on YouTube. See https://www.youtube.com/watch?v=cUrZz__12fM.

# Peering into the Mystery of the Coronavirus Crisis

For My thoughts *are* not your thoughts, nor *are* your ways
My ways.

—Isaiah 55:8

In an insightful article titled "The Most Mysterious Word," Clarence Macartney asked: "What is the word that if we knew the answer, we would know as much as God?"[130] That word is "why," said Macartney, "a word that sums up the inscrutable mystery of human life." In the closing chapter of Steven Hawking's *A Brief History of Time*, he states, "If we know the answer to the question of 'why,' we will understand the mind of God."[131]

In the face of the present (2020–2022) Coronavirus pandemic, when we ask why God would allow this plague to afflict the nations of the world at this time, we are probing the mind of God. And that's a tall order for finite beings such as us. God says, "For My thoughts are not your thoughts, nor are your ways My ways" (Isa. 55:8). God makes no apology because His plans are not like our plans, and His works are not like our works. That said, when we encounter a crisis like the

---

130. Clarence Macartney, *The Greatest Words in The Bible And in Human Speech* (London: Whitmore & Smith, 1938), 91.

131. Stephen Hawking, *A Brief History Of Time* (New York: Bantam Books, 1990), 175.

one we are in right now, the proper question is not "why?" but "what?" We must seek to understand what God might be doing for His glory and our transformation. On the day of Pentecost, when the people who gathered from different parts of the then-known world saw the mighty move of the Holy Spirit and the disciples of Christ speaking in other languages, they asked, "Whatever could this mean?" (Acts 2:12).

The question we should be asking is, what is the meaning of the Coronavirus pandemic? Victor Frankl, the famous psychiatrist who survived the Holocaust, wrote, "Man's concern is not to gain pleasure or to avoid pain but rather to see a meaning in his life. That is why man is even ready to suffer, on the condition, to be sure, that his suffering has a meaning." He continues: "In some way, suffering ceases to be suffering at the moment it finds a meaning, such as the meaning of a sacrifice."[132] These profound words should provoke us to explore the mystery of our present suffering from a biblical perspective and find meaning and purpose. If we don't, we will grope in darkness and frustration.

In 2 Corinthians 12, we read about Paul's "thorn in the flesh,"[133] which God permitted as a "messenger of Satan to buffet" him. The primary purpose of this "thorn in the flesh" was to keep Paul humble lest he boast about his experience of having been to paradise and hearing "inexpressible words." Through that experience, the apostle Paul discovered three essential purposes of suffering.

First, suffering can be a means of divine revelation. Through his pain, Paul learned the sufficiency of God's grace and the adequacy of God's power. God said to Paul, "My grace is sufficient for you, for My strength is made perfect in weakness" (2 Cor. 12:9). God revealed to Paul that he was not in control of his life situations, but God was. We all want to be

132. Victor Frankl, *Man's Search For Meaning*, 113.

133. See footnote 45 (page 116).

in control of all that happens to us. And when we aren't, we think the world is falling apart. When we feel the world is out of our control, it indicates that we don't rule the world, but God does. The psalmist lamented, saying, "If the foundations are destroyed, what can the righteous do?" (Ps. 11:3). The next verse says, "The LORD is in His holy temple, the LORD's throne is in heaven."

The Coronavirus pandemic has shown that we are not in control of the world. We think we are, but we aren't—God is. He is on His throne, and He rules the world and all the events that occur in this world. Therefore, the proper response in this crisis is to trust God to see us through. In Paul's case, he recognized that his helplessness was God's opportunity to show His power. As America deals with the present crisis and its effects, it must realize that God is the Sovereign King of this world and turn to Him to resolve the Coronavirus crisis. On our coin is inscribed, "In God We Trust." It's time for America to trust in God. David said, "Whenever I am afraid, I will trust in You [LORD]" (Ps. 56:3). Every human-made and human-oriented system will crumble. Only God will prevail.

Second, suffering can be a means of divine transformation. Paul experienced a mighty change in his life due to the "thorn in the flesh." He learned that God's strength was manifested fully when he was weak. His attitude toward suffering and pain was no longer one of avoidance; rather, he welcomed them as an opportunity to experience the power of God and grow in the faith. He gladly accepted his "thorn in the flesh" so that He might know God more intimately.

As we go through the pandemic, we should ask what God is doing in us through this crisis. Perhaps, it may be to make us more dependent on Him in our lives. It may be to cause us to repent of our sins and seek His face. In *The Problem of Pain*, C. S. Lewis notes: "We can ignore even pleasure. But pain insists upon being attended to. God whispers to us in our pleasures, speaks in our conscience, but shouts in our pains; it is His megaphone to rouse a deaf world."[134] Perhaps, God is using the megaphone of the pandemic to rouse America to turn to God for healing and restoration. Sometimes, pain can draw us to God's word for comfort and repose. The psalmist affirmed: "It is good for me that I have been afflicted, that I may learn Your statutes" (Ps. 119:71).

Third, suffering can be a means of divine glorification. God's goal is to glorify Himself in our pain and prosperity. In life and death, God seeks to glorify Himself. The apostle Paul said, "Therefore most gladly I will rather boast in my infirmities, that the power of Christ may rest upon me" (2 Cor. 12:9). He understood that when the power of Christ rested on him, God received the glory.

How is God glorified through the Coronavirus crisis in America? God is glorified when people will know that He is God and there is none other. God is glorified when America turns to Him for refuge. Let America cease from glorying in its might and riches. Instead, let it glory in understanding and knowing God who exercises lovingkindness, judgment, and righteousness in the earth (Jer. 9:23–24). The Bible says that the sons of Issachar understood the times they were living in and knew what Israel ought to do. If we realize the times we live in, we will pay close attention to what God is doing in us and around us, respond to Him in faith, and prepare for our redemption (Luke 21:28).

---

134. C. S. Lewis, *The Problem of Pain*, 91.

# Preparing for the Siege

Get ready for the siege! Store up water! Strengthen the defenses! Go into the pits to trample clay, and pack it into molds, making bricks to repair the walls.

—Nahum 3:14 NLT

The prophet Nahum prophesied the destruction of Assyria during its zenith of power and prosperity. He saw the impending devastation of Assyria and taunted it, saying, "Get ready for the siege! Store up water! Strengthen the defenses!" (Nah. 3:14, NLT). Nineveh was the Assyrian Empire's proud capital, with impenetrable walls that rose to one hundred feet and towers that stretched an additional one hundred feet above the walls. Assyrians thought they were invincible.

But God told them that they would be destroyed by fire and consumed by the enemy despite all the water they could store and their fortified walls. This is what precisely happened when the Medes and the Babylonians invaded Assyria in 612 B.C.

Today, we are facing a political, economic, and moral siege. While we take pride in our military and economic power, moral decay has set in to destroy our nation's foundation from within. In the words of the prophet Nahum, all our material strongholds are being "devoured like the ripe figs that fall into the mouths of those who shake the trees" (Nah. 3:12 NLT).

Where do we turn for our refuge? The answer: "The LORD is good, a stronghold in the day of trouble; And He knows those who trust in Him" (Nah. 1:7). During the Civil War, a pastor said to Abraham Lincoln, "I surely hope the Lord is on our side." To which President Lincoln replied, "I am not at all concerned about that, for I know that the Lord is always on the side of the right; but it is my constant anxiety and prayer that I and this nation should be on the Lord's side."[135] Are you on the Lord's side? If you are, trust in Him and make Him your stronghold. Do not seek what theologian William Barclay called "rival salvation" in money, power, or other material things.[136]

Nahum said, "Draw your water for the siege!" Resolve to trust the Lord and store up water. Water is an essential provision for sustaining life. Those who trust in the Lord find that He is their provider (Gen. 22:14; Phil. 4:19). If you are oppressed and in need of relief, cast your cares upon the Lord, for He cares for you (Ps. 55:22; Phil. 4:19; 1 Peter 5:7). He will come to your rescue with healing in His wings (Mal. 4:2). Christ is the fountain of the living water, and when you drink the water He offers, you'll never thirst again (John 4: 14). In Him, you find the provisions for life, both physical and spiritual.

In a time of siege, we also need a wall of protection around us. Nahum said, "Fortify your strongholds." The fortification of Nineveh did not protect the city because the Assyrians did not trust the Lord. But those who trust the Lord will find that His salvation is a mighty fortress around them (Isa. 26:1). They will discover that the Lord will be a wall of fire around them and fight their battles (Zech. 2: 5). If you are on the Lord's side, you are safe within a never-failing bulwark.

God bestows justice on all who are oppressed. His love requires it. He told Judah to celebrate its freedom from Assyria. Unfortunately, Judah's independence was short-lived because

135. William J. Johnstone, *Abraham Lincoln: the Christian* (New York: Eaton & Mains, 1913), 89.

136. William Barclay, *Growing in Christian Faith: A Book of Daily Readings* (Louisville: Westminster John Knox Press, 2000), 3.

it strayed away from God, and it eventually went into Babylonian captivity.

The chief adversary of our soul is Satan. He wants to keep us under oppression. But Jesus, the great warrior, won a decisive victory over Satan on the cross. He disarmed Satan of his power. Satan may seek to oppress us, but we have the victory. Let us celebrate the victory we have in Christ.

# What to Do When You Don't Know What to Do

Hezekiah went up to the house of the LORD, and spread it before the LORD. Then Hezekiah prayed before the LORD, and said: "O LORD God of Israel, *the One who dwells* between the cherubim, You are God, You alone, of all the kingdoms of the earth. You have made heaven and earth. Incline Your ear, O LORD, and hear; open Your eyes, O LORD, and see; and hear the words of Sennacherib, which he has sent to reproach the living God."

—2 Kings 19:14–16

In the fourteenth year of King Hezekiah's reign over Judah, King Sennacherib of Assyria attacked Judah's fortified towns and conquered them. Hezekiah sent a message to Sennacherib, offering him whatever tribute money he wanted if he withdrew from Judah's captured cities. Sennacherib demanded a vast amount of silver and gold, which caused Hezekiah to take the silver stored in the temple and the palace treasury and strip the gold from the temple's doorposts. But Sennacherib was not satisfied. Driven by unbridled lust for power, he sent his field commander with a vast army to confront King Hezekiah in Jerusalem. The Assyrian military commander demanded that Hezekiah surrender to the Assyrian king and open the gates of Jerusalem. He said to Hezekiah that the God of Hezekiah could not rescue him from the Assyrian army, and failure to surrender meant annihilation. What did Hezekiah do in such a dire situation? He tore his clothes, put on burlap, and went to the temple to pray. He prayed:

> O LORD God of Israel, you are enthroned between the mighty cherubim! You alone are God of all the kingdoms of the earth. You alone created the heavens and the earth. Bend down, O LORD, and listen! Open your eyes, O LORD, and see! Listen to Sennacherib's words of defiance against the living God. 2 Kings 19:15–16 NLT

God answered Hezekiah's prayer and fought the battle for him. That night the angel of the Lord went out to the Assyrian camp and killed 185,000 Assyrian soldiers and rescued Hezekiah and the holy city of Jerusalem from the hands of Sennacherib.

In 1812, the mighty army of Napoleon surrounded Moscow and torched its spires and domes. The Russian army was no match for the 600,000 soldiers of Napoleon. Tsar Alexander went to church in St. Petersburg during this critical time and was on his face before God. He was not a religious man and lived a dissolute life, but at that moment, he realized that his only hope was in God's intervention. God heard Tsar Alexander's prayer and came to his rescue. Despite freezing temperatures, the Russians resisted Napoleon's army fiercely and caused them to retreat. Thus, Napoleon's army, which was disorganized, exhausted, and in short supply of food, suffered a devastating military defeat in that Russian campaign of 1812.

When Confederate Commander General Robert E. Lee led his 76,000 men into Pennsylvania during the American Civil War, President Abraham Lincoln remained firm in his faith in God. He said to a wounded general at Gettysburg: "When everyone seemed panic-stricken, I went to my room and got down on my knees before Almighty God and prayed. Soon, a sweet comfort crept into my soul that God Almighty had taken the whole business into His own hands."[137]

At present, our nation is going through a significant crisis of law and order. The death of Mr. George Floyd at the hands of a police officer ignited a blazing fire of lawlessness, leading to the destruction of properties and businesses of hard-working Black and White Americans, hospitalization of over three hundred police officers, and death of several innocent people. Our First Amendment right for conducting peaceful protests had been hijacked by thugs, mercenaries, and hooligans who used Mr. Floyd's death as a reason for embarking on a campaign of violence.

Rioting and destroying public property is not the way to solve racism, which is fundamentally a problem of the human heart. While legislative reforms and laws are necessary to curb the practice of discrimination in the public square and our institutions, in the final analysis, the definitive remedy for this evil is found only in a change of heart through Jesus Christ and the power of the Holy Spirit. Jesus Christ alone can give us the ability to love our neighbors with an eye for their wellbeing irrespective of race, color, or culture.

As people of faith, how should we respond to crises such as this, especially as America is becoming dangerously perilous? If the foundations are destroyed, what can the righteous do? The answer is to turn to God in prayer, believing that "God Almighty had taken the whole business into His own hands." Now is the time to acknowledge our inability to solve the problems of the human heart, which God in Christ alone can do. It is time not to panic, but rather do what President Lincoln did in a time of crisis—get down on our knees before the almighty God and pray.

---

137. William J. Federer, *America's God And Country Encyclopedia of Quotations* (St. Louis: Amerisearch, Inc., 2000), 385.

As people of faith, we need to pray for our nation. We must pray as the apostle Paul urged us to pray in 1 Timothy 2:1–2. He wrote, "Therefore I exhort first of all that supplications, prayers, intercessions, and giving of thanks be made for all men, for kings and all who are in authority, that we may lead a quiet and peaceable life in all godliness and reverence" (1 Tim. 2:1–2). We must pray for those who rule over us to facilitate and promote an atmosphere to live securely.

In the ancient Greco-Roman culture, people worshipped different gods, including the emperor. Christians and Jews, on the other hand, were committed to worshipping only one true God to the exclusion of all other gods. So, Paul encouraged Christians to offer prayers to God on behalf of those in authority so that they would create an environment in which Christians could worship the one true God in tranquility. You may have come across this quote from the early nineteenth century:

> I sought for the greatness and genius of America in her commodious harbors and her ample rivers, and it was not there. I sought for the greatness and genius of America in her fertile fields and boundless forests, and it was not there. I sought for the greatness and genius of America in her rich mines and her vast world commerce, and it was not there. I sought for the greatness and genius of America in her public school system and her institutions of learning, and it was not there. I sought for the greatness and genius of America in her democratic Congress and her matchless Constitution, and it was not there. Not until I went into the churches of America and heard her pulpits flame with righteousness did I understand the secret of her genius and power. America

is great because America is good, and if America ever ceases to be good America will cease to be great.[138]

Presumably, the person who penned that quote toured America and sought for its greatness. He did not find it in her commodious harbors, ample rivers, fertile fields, boundless forests, rich mines, vast commerce, public school system, her institutions of learning, democratic congress, or in her matchless Constitution. He said, "Not until I went into the churches of America and heard her pulpits flame with righteousness did I understand the secret of her greatness and power."

I believe that America will be great again if we turn to God in contrition and repentance and when our pulpits begin to roar with the thunderous and masterful "Thus saith the Lord."

---

138. Barry Popik, "America is great because she is good," accessed July 30, 2021, https://www.barrypopik.com/index.php/new_york_city/entry/america_is_great_because_she_is_good/.
This quote has been erroneously attributed to Alexis de Tocqueville (1805-1859) and his book, *Democracy in America*. The actual author of this quote is unknown.

# Lessons from the Coronavirus Pandemic

The LORD is my shepherd; I shall not want.... He restores my soul; He leads me in the paths of righteousness for His name's sake. Yea, though I walk through the valley of the shadow of death, I will fear no evil; for You *are* with me; Your rod and Your staff, they comfort me.

—Psalm 23:1, 3–4

The Coronavirus pandemic has thrust our nation into a crisis the likes of which we have not seen in a long time. Economically, we are on the verge of a recession, and people everywhere are in a state of panic, not knowing when this storm will subside. Emotionally, the nation is overwhelmed by the weight of this virus invasion. As a result, a sense of helplessness abounds in every segment of our society. The concept of a shut-in is no longer restricted to the physically disabled; it has become our national *modus operandi*. Truly, as Thomas Paine said during the American Revolution War, "these are the times that try men's souls."

As Christ-followers, when we face a crisis such as the one we are in, we can gain a perspective on the matter by asking the right question. We ought to ask God's grand purpose in allowing this pandemic to afflict the world. This pandemic did not occur outside the knowledge and the will of God. God says, "Now see that I, *even* I, *am* He, and *there* is no God besides

Me; I kill and make alive; I wound and I heal; nor *is there any* who can deliver from My hand" (Deut. 32:39). The God of the Bible is not an absentee God. He is very much in control of His creation and guides all events for His ultimate glory.

Sometimes, God allows events such as the Coronavirus pandemic to show who is in charge lest we forget. Moses said to Pharaoh, "Thus says the LORD: 'By this you will know that I am the LORD: behold, with the staff that is in my hand I will strike the water that is in the Nile, and it shall turn into blood'" (Ex. 7:17 ESV). God's preeminent aim in all that He does is His glory. God is reminding America that He is God and there is none besides Him. In a time of national crisis, it behooves us to call upon the Lord for our deliverance. Unless God intervenes, all our efforts to subdue this calamity are futile. Mathew Henry, the renowned Bible commentator, wrote: "God sometimes raises difficulties in the way of His people that He may have the glory of subduing them, and helping His people over them."[139]

Psalm 23:3–4 instructs us to respond to our present (2020–2022) crisis with confidence because the Lord is our shepherd and we are His sheep. We who have a shepherd-sheep relationship with God can confidently say, "The Lord is my shepherd, I lack nothing…He leads me down the right path for the sake of his reputation. Even when I must walk through the darkest valley, I fear no danger, for you are with me; your rod and your staff reassure me" (Ps. 23:1, 4 NET). What this means is that we can face this crisis without fear.

A follower of Jesus Christ should not be afraid of walking through the Coronavirus pandemic's dark valley. Why? Because we have in Christ the promise of His direction. He will lead us down the right paths. When we are thrust into great

---

139. "Mathew Henry's Commentary, Verses 1–9," BibleGateway, accessed April 27, 2022,
https://www.biblegateway.com/resources/matthew-henry/Exod.14.1-Exod.14.9.

adversity, we need the most divine wisdom to know what course of action to take. The Bible says, "If any of you lacks wisdom, let him ask of God, who gives to all liberally and without reproach, and it will be given to him" (James 1:5). We need wisdom in handling our finances, health, relationships, and a host of other personal matters during this crisis. We can count on the Lord to lead us down the right path through His written word, godly counsel, and spiritual discernment to wade through voluminous information thrown at us and act on the most relevant.

Second, as we live under the rule of the Good Shepherd Jesus Christ, we can claim the promise of His protection. The psalmist says, "Even when I must walk through the darkest valley, I fear no danger, for you are with me." As we traverse the dark valley of the Coronavirus pandemic, we can trust the Lord to protect us because He is with us. When God commissioned Joshua to enter Canaan, He promised Joshua, saying, "As I was with Moses, so I will be with you. I will not leave you nor forsake you" (Josh. 1:5). We need not face the Coronavirus crisis alone. The Lord, our healer, is with us and leads us through this valley.

This does not mean we should ignore the precautions we need to take to ward off the Coronavirus infection. In Acts 27, we read about Paul's voyage to Rome. He and his fellow sailors suffered shipwreck, but God had promised Paul that there would be no loss of life. As the storm intensified, they had to let down the anchors to keep the ship from running aground on the rocky coast. When they did that, the prisoners tried to escape. So, Paul said to the centurion and the sailors that the prisoners had to remain on the ship to be saved. God's promise of no loss of life was contingent on everyone remaining in the boat. We must do what is required of us to keep the infection from spreading, keeping in mind that God is with us to see us through this crisis triumphantly.

Finally, we can face the present crisis with confidence because we can claim the promise of His consolation. The psalmist says, "Your rod and your staff reassure me." In other words, the Lord is near us to comfort us. He does it through His Spirit, who dwells in us. The Holy Spirit is rightly called the Comforter. He brings comfort and peace during our storm. When others are torn apart by fear and anxiety, He keeps us in the safety of His wings. So, let us take our concerns to the Lord in prayer, knowing that He will guard our hearts and minds with His peace. Let us seek the comfort of the Holy Spirit when we go through a crisis individually or nationally.

# A Nation in Shock

The heart *is* deceitful above all *things*, and desperately wicked; who can know it?

—Jeremiah 17:9

In 2020, the killing of George Floyd by a police officer shocked us. The police apprehended Mr. Floyd for using a counterfeit twenty-dollar bill. As the bystanders watched, the police officer thrust the man to the ground and knelt on his neck even though Floyd was handcuffed and posed no threat to the police officer. The victim's desperate cry for a breath of air fell on deaf ears as the policeman continued to kneel on the man's neck. Finally, Mr. Floyd collapsed and died on the way to the hospital.

As you probably were, I was deeply saddened and troubled by this blood-curdling murder of an unarmed and helpless man. As I watched the video on television, I was sick to my stomach. I experienced a whole gamut of emotions—anger, despair, rejection, sorrow, sadness, hatred, hopelessness, revenge.

As we reflect on those events, it will help us to pause for a moment and realize that what we witnessed was fundamentally a symptom of the human heart, which is "deceitful above all things and desperately wicked" (Jer. 17:9). Unless we are given a new heart, the pathology of the old unregenerate heart inevitably finds its vicious expression in every aspect of our lives, both personal and national. We can raise many questions and wallow in a philosophical mire, but what we need the most at such a time is a healing of our lacerated psyche.

The presence of evil in this world is not an illusion. The scepter of suffering and pain looms over us with every breath we take. We don't have to look far to find it. A former professor of mine used to say, "If you don't think you have problems, just wait. It's in the mail." It comes to us in many ways and in many proportions: sickness, natural catastrophes, war, racism, murder, stealing, starvation, ethnic cleansing, rape, the pandemic of COVID—the list goes on. Indeed, the presence of evil is as old as humanity. We experience suffering and pain in our own way as we go about our lives: a sudden diagnosis of a terminal disease, the rape of a loved one, an unexpected layoff from work, depression, or the anxiety of an uncertain future. Mildly put, suffering is a "problem that won't go away." If there is one truth most religions agree on, it is the universality of suffering.

You will agree that what the police officer did was an evil act. That said, it's so easy for us to justify demonizing and caricaturing him as the "face of evil." We all can point to other faces of evil that have indelibly tarnished the landscape of history. Some of these "faces" still haunt us from their graves. When we point a finger of accusation at these personages of evil, it behooves us to remember that we too have the potential of turning into a face of evil because "the heart is deceitful above all things and desperately wicked; who can know it?" (Jer. 17:9).

We may lull ourselves into thinking that we are ethical and moral and that extraneous influences trigger our evil acts. But when a holy God weighs us in His balance, He finds us wanting. Every unregenerate soul has the potential to turn into a "face of evil" such as Hitler, Mussolini, or Osama bin Laden. Notice how the prophets of old saw their hearts in the light of God's revealed holiness. Job cried out, saying, "I have heard of you by the hearing of the ear, but now my eye sees you.

Therefore, I abhor myself, and repent in dust and ashes" (Job 42:5-6). Isaiah confessed his depravity, saying, "Woe is me, for I am undone! Because I am a man of unclean lips" (Isa. 6:5). Peter fell before Christ and muttered, "Depart from me, for I am a sinful man, O Lord!" (Luke 5:8).

How can we find deliverance from this ugly face of sin? We see it in the forgiveness of Christ and the ministrations of His grace. The Bible says, "Therefore, if anyone is in Christ, he is a new creation; old things have passed away; behold, all things have become new" (2 Cor. 5:17). Friend, Christ can lift you from the depths of sin into the buoyancy of hope and give you a new heart, a heart on which He writes His law. That new law of Christ is the law of love and bearing one another's burdens. Therefore, the most scriptural response at an hour of national pain is for us to return to God in repentance, enter into a relationship with Him, and live the law of Christ.

It is comforting to know that evil in this world is not forever. It has neither an eternal past nor an eternal future. It is finite. The Bible says, "In the beginning was the Word." It does not say, "In the beginning was the Word and Evil." For a Christian, then, evil has a point of origin and a point of termination. The anticipated point of termination is when Christ returns in all His glory and removes us from the very presence of sin.

In the final analysis, our strength to cope with evil comes from the assurance that this same Jesus, who ascended into heaven, will soon come in like manner as His disciples saw Him go into heaven. When He returns, He will remove us from the presence of evil (Rev. 21:34; 22:4-5). Therefore, let us take comfort amid our pain and look for the return of the Lord Jesus Christ. May the longing of our hearts be, "Even so, come, Lord Jesus!" (Rev. 22:20).

# Our Greatest Need: Mercy, Not Justice

Righteousness and justice *are* the foundation of Your throne; mercy and truth go before Your face.

—Psalm 89:14

When the District Court of Minnesota rendered the guilty verdict on Derek Chauvin for the death of George Floyd, Americans of all stripes aired a flurry of opinions, comments, and sentiments on various social media regarding the death of George Floyd and the guilty verdict rendered by the jury on Chauvin. Speaker of the House Nancy Pelosi tweeted her thanks to George Floyd "for sacrificing your life for justice." President Biden called the verdict "a step forward" and tweeted, "And while nothing can ever bring George Floyd back, this can be a giant step forward on the march towards justice in America." Senator Raphael Warnock termed the verdict "right outcome in this trial but is not justice." In his press conference, Minnesota Attorney General Keith said that the verdict "isn't justice, it's just one step towards it." Appearing on Tucker Carlson's show, Candice Owen called the verdict "mob justice."

Admittedly, the mood of Americans surrounding this verdict was varied, and the temperature measurably hot. While we may spend days and months analyzing the political, social, judicial, and racial nuances and ramifications of this case, let us not overlook a simple act—mercy—that could have avoided this stain on the landscape of American history. When Mr. Floyd cried out that he could not breathe, all Mr. Chauvin had to do was ease the pressure of his knee on Mr. Floyd's neck and let him live. Mr. Floyd posed no threat to the police because he was handcuffed. Instead, Mr. Chauvin decided to "go by the manual of police procedures" and not take the high road of showing mercy. What George Floyd most needed at that moment was not justice, but mercy, which Mr. Chauvin could have given to him, but he did not.

Now Mr. Chauvin got justice, but what he needed the most was mercy, which the court could not give. In 1951, Julius and Ethel Rosenberg were tried and sentenced to death for espionage and providing atomic bomb secrets to the Russians. The lawyer who defended the Rosenbergs pleaded passionately before Judge Kaufman, saying, "Your honor, what my clients ask for is justice." Judge Kaufman calmly replied: "The court has given what you ask for—justice! What you really want is mercy. But that is something this court has no right to give."

As I reflected on this unfortunate incident in our history, I could not help but think that what we need most desperately is His mercy, not justice, as we stand before a holy God. As sinners by birth, choice, and divine verdict, we all stand before God guilty and deserving the just punishment of death and destruction. But thank God for the judgment throne of God, which is unlike any human judgment seat. From His judgment throne flow both justice and mercy. The Bible says, "Righteousness and justice are the foundation of Your throne. Mercy and truth go before Your face" (Ps. 89:14).

If it were not for the mercy of God, we would not be at peace with God and enjoy His fellowship. The song "Mercy Rewrote My Life," penned by Mike Murdock, beautifully captures the wonder of God's mercy.

> For years I've traveled this road all wrong,
> My heart had lost its joy and its song.
> Till grace placed me, right where I belonged,

When mercy rewrote my life.

Mercy rewrote my life; mercy rewrote my life.
I could have fallen, my soul cast down,
But mercy rewrote my life.

My mistakes God turned into miracles,
And all my tears, he turned into joy.
My past forgiven, my new name was written,
When mercy rewrote my life.[140]

God is presently showing mercy toward us in His forbearance by not swiftly dispensing the just punishment we deserve. Instead, He is showing His goodness and longsuffering toward us so that we may repent and escape His coming wrath and judgment.

The apostle James wrote: "For judgment is without mercy to the one who has shown no mercy. Mercy triumphs over judgment" (James 2:13). So, for all the crying we do for "imperfect justice in this imperfect world," let us not lose sight of showing mercy toward those in distress. God said, "For I desire mercy and not sacrifice" (Hosea 6:6). The only sure way of showing genuine mercy is by being in Christ, the fountain of mercy (Matt. 9:35–36; 2 Tim. 1:2), and having a love for God and people birthed in our hearts by the Holy Spirit.

140. Mike Murdock, "Mercy Rewrote My Life," Spirit Filled: Worship and Praise Songs, accessed August 16, 2022, http://sanfordremy.blogspot.com/2015/01/mercy-rewrote-my-life.html.

# A Biblical Response When Disaster Strikes

For this cause everyone who is godly shall pray to You in a time when You may be found; surely in a flood of great waters they shall not come near him. You *are* my hiding place; You shall preserve me from trouble; You shall surround me with songs of deliverance.

—Psalm 32:6–7

Some years ago, hurricane Laura hit Texas, Louisiana, and Arkansas, destroying property and life. Government officials had warned nearly 500,000 people to leave their homes and go to a higher and safer area to weather the wind and the rain. As I heard the reports on the news, a Scripture passage came to my mind: "For this reason, every one of your faithful followers should pray to you while there is a window of opportunity. Certainly, when the surging water rises, it will not reach them. You are my hiding place; you protect me from distress. You surround me with shouts of joy from those celebrating deliverance" (Ps. 32:6–7 NET).

King David wrote psalm 32 after he experienced God's forgiveness of the sin of adultery he committed with Bathsheba, wife of his trusted and loyal soldier Uriah. When he tried to conceal his sin, guilt, physical ailment, and emotional distress haunted him. He spent many sleepless nights as his body ached with pain. His vitality turned into the drought of summer. But when he finally confessed his sin with contrition, he received God's forgiveness, and with that, he found relief and freedom from guilt. Having received God's forgiveness, he penned verses 6 and 7.

I want to draw your attention to three truths from these two verses, which help us biblically respond when disaster strikes our lives.

First, when disaster strikes, we must respond by making our petition to the Lord. As David says, everyone who is godly should pray. He meant that every person who has received God's forgiveness and is a member of the family of God must pray. Prayer is a privilege of believers granted to them by their relationship to God as His children. As the children of God, we have access to His throne room and make our petition to obtain mercy and find grace and help in time of need (Heb. 4:16). Dick Eastman put it well: "Prayer is the divine enigma— that marvelous mystery hidden behind the cloud of God's omnipotence. Nothing is beyond the reach of Prayer because God Himself is the focus of Prayer."[141]

Second, when disaster strikes, we must respond by seeking the protection of the Lord. David wrote, "Surely in a flood of great waters they shall not come near him. You are my hiding place; You shall preserve me from trouble." In times of impending disasters, our protection is in God alone. He is the king of the universe and controls all the forces of nature. He can calm the raging sea and still the storm.

Third, when disaster strikes, we must respond by expressing our exultation in the Lord. David wrote, "You surround me with shouts of joy from those celebrating deliverance." A believer's exultation flows from the deliverance they received from the Lord. Our joy is rooted in the Lord. Before Jesus went to the cross, He said to His disciples, "Until now you have asked nothing in My name. Ask, and you will receive, that

---

141. Dick Eastman, *The Hour That Changes the World*, E-book edition (Grand Rapids: Chosen, 2011), Loc. 130.

your joy may be full" (John 16:24). Jesus was encouraging His disciples to pray in His name and experience the joy of answered prayers.

Perhaps you may be going through a severe trial in your life. It may be a health crisis, a financial disaster, the breakdown of your family, or the unexpected destruction of your property. Whatever the nature of your problem, petition the Lord to deliver you from the "hurricane" you are facing. Seek the protection of the Lord. Trust that you will see the salvation of the Lord and rejoice in His deliverance. Jesus Christ, who stilled the storm, can calm the storm in your life.

# ABOUT THE AUTHOR

Abraham Philip is a Stephen Olford Fellow of Expository Preaching and president of Proclamation Ministries. Formerly, he worked for the DuPont Company for twenty-one years in microbiology research, marketing, and product management. An Assembly of God ordained minister, Abraham has held evangelistic meetings and spoken at leadership conferences in Nigeria, Kenya, Guyana, India, the Philippines, and Myanmar. He holds a B.S. in biology, an M.S. in microbiology, an M.A. in religion, and a Ph.D. in expository preaching. He is the author of *Thrown Overboard: A Reluctant Prophet's Encounter with a Gracious God; Strength to Strength: Christ-Centered Devotionals for Growing in Faith; Basic Statistics in Quantitative Research: A Primer for Seminary Students;* and *Divorce and Remarriage: A Biblical Perspective.*

Made in USA - Kendallville, IN
88501_9798839764040
09.02.2022 1541